TO

R. H. W.

YOU promised me once that, if ever the 'Chronicles of Dustypore' shaped themselves into being, they might be dedicated to you. While writing them my thoughts have often turned to happy hours passed in your society, and pleasant scenes witnessed beneath your roof. If the story has profited thereby, and Felicia has borrowed whatever charms she may possess from those remembered scenes and hours, forgive me, and let me lay the portrait, with all its imperfections, at your feet.

H. S. C.

Chronicles of Dustypore; a tale of modern Anglo-Indian society

H S. Cunningham

DUSTYPORE.

Ballantyne Press,
BALLANTYNE, HANSON AND CO.
EDINBURGH AND LONDON

CHRONICLES OF DUSTYPORE

A TALE OF

MODERN ANGLO-INDIAN SOCIETY

BY

H. S. CUNNINGHAM

AUTHOR OF "WHEAT AND TARES," "LATE LAURELS," ETC

A New Edition

LONDON

SMITH, ELDER, & CO., 15 WATERLOO PLACE

1877

CONTENTS.

CHRONICLES OF DUSTYPORE.[1]

CHAPTER I.

THE SANDY TRACTS.

He seems like one whose footsteps halt,
Toiling in immeasurable sand;
And o'er a weary, sultry land,
Far beneath a blazing vault,
Sown in a wrinkle of the monstrous hill,
The city sparkles like a grain of salt.

Any one who knows or cares anything about India—that is, say, one Englishman in a hundred thousand—is familiar with the train of events which resulted in the conquest of the Sandy Tracts, the incorporation of that unattractive region in the British Indian Empire, and the establishment of an Agency at Dustypore. The ninety-nine thousand nine hundred and ninety-nine, who neither know nor wish to know, would not be grateful

[1] For the sake of readers who might mispronounce the name of the fam[illegible] spelling [illegible]ned, the name [illegible]

for an account of battles fought at places of which they never heard, of victories gained by generals whose fame is already forgotten, or of negotiations which nobody but the negotiators understood at the time, and which a few years have effectually relegated to the oblivion that awaits all that is at once dull, profitless, and unintelligible.

Suffice it to say that the generally admired air of 'Rule Britannia,' which has been performed on so many occasions for the benefit of admiring audiences in different parts of the Indian continent, was once again piped and drummed and cannonaded into the ears of a prostrate population. The resistless 'red line,' historical on a hundred battle-fields, once again stood firm against the onset of despairing fanaticism, and once again in its advance moved forward the boundaries of the conquering race. The solid tramp of British soldiers' feet sounded the death-knell of a rule whose hour of doom had struck, and one more little tyranny—its cup of crime, perfidy, and folly full—was blotted for ever from the page of the world's story. The sun set into a horizon lurid with the dust of a flying rabble, and the victorious cavalry, as it returned, covered with sweat and dirt, from the pursuit, found all the fighting done, an English guard on duty at the city gates, a troop of English artillery drawn up in front of the principal mosque, and a couple of English sentinels plodding up and down with all the stolidity of true Britons in front of the Officers' Quarters. The Sandy Tracts were ours.

The next morning at sunrise the British flag was flying on the Fort of Dustypore, and a British General and his staff were busy with maps, orders, and despatches in quarters from which the ladies of a royal seraglio had fled in post-haste the afternoon before. Thenceforward everything went on like clockwork. Before the week was out order, such as had not been dreamed of for many a long year, prevailed in every nook and corner of the captured city. One morning an elderly gentleman, in plain clothes, attended by two or three uniformed lads and a tiny cavalry escort, rode in, and a roar of cannon from the Fort announced that the 'Agent' had arrived. Then set in the full tide of civil administration. Courts began to sit, pickpockets and brawlers were tried; sanitary regulations were issued; returns were called for, appointments were made. The 'Dustypore Gazette,' in its first issue, announced with the greatest calmness, and in the curt language appropriate to an everyday occurrence, the annexation of the Sandy Tracts; and a gun fired from the Fort every morning, as near as might be to mid-day, announced to the good people of Dustypore that, by order of Queen Victoria, it was twelve o'clock, and twelve o'clock in a British cantonment.

The new addition to Her Majesty's possessions resembled the Miltonic hell in one particular at any rate—in being a region of fierce extremes. On winter mornings a biting wind, fresh from its icy home in the distant snow-clad range, cut one to the core; and people clustered, with chattering teeth and blue fingers, round blazing hearths, where great logs worthy of an English Christmas tempered the cruel atmosphere to a genial glow. When the 'Rains' came it poured a little deluge. During the eight months of summer the state of things resembled that prevailing in the interior of a well-constructed and well-supplied Arnott's stove. Then it was that the Sandy Tracts were seen in the complete development of their resources and in the fullest glory. Vast plains, a dead level but for an occasional clump of palms or the dome of some despoiled and crumbling tomb, stretched away on every side, and ended in a hazy quivering horizon that spoke of infinite heat. Over these ranged herds of cattle and goats, browsing on no one could see what, or bewildered buffaloes would lie, panting and contented, in some muddy pool, with little but horns, eyes, and nostrils exposed above the surface. Little ill-begotten stunted plants worked hard to live and grow and to weather the roaring fierce winds. The crows sat gasping, open-beaked, as if protesting against having been born into so sulphurous an existence. Here and there a well, with its huge lumbering wheel and patient bullocks, went creaking and groaning night and day, as if earth grudged the tiny rivulet, coming so toilfully from her dry breast, and gave it up with sighs of pain. The sky was cloudless, pitiless, brazen. The sun rose into it without a single fleck of vapour to mitigate its fierceness, and pierced, like a red-hot sword, the rash mortal who dared, unprotected, to meet its ray. All day it shone and glistened and blazed, until the very earth seemed to crack with heat, and the mere thought of it was pain. 'Ægypt,' to use the poet's phrase, 'ached in the sun's eye.' The natives tied their heads up in bags, covered their mouths, and carried their clothes between the sun and themselves. Europeans entrenched themselves behind barriers of moistened grass, lay outstretched under monster fans and consoled themselves with what cool drinks their means allowed, and with the conviction, which seemed to spring perennial in each sufferer's breast, that the present was by far the hottest summer ever known.

Dew there was none. You stepped from your door in the morning into a bed of sand, which no amount of watering could reduce to the proper solidity of a garden-path. As you came in at night you shook off the dust that had gathered on you in your evening stroll. Miles away the galloping horseman might be tracked by the little cloud that he stirred up as he went. The weary cattle trudged homeward from their day's work in a sandstorm of their own manufacture. There was sand in the air one breathed, in the food one tried to eat, in the water that pretended to assuage one's thirst: sand in heaven and sand on earth—and a great deal of sand in the heads of many of the officials.

This getting of sand into the head, and getting it in in a degree compatible neither with health, comfort, or efficiency, was a recognised malady in the Sandy Tracts. It cost the Government a great deal of money and the services of many a useful brain. Officers, when they felt themselves becoming unendurably sandy and their ideas proportionately confused, used to take furlough, and go home and try to get washed clear again at Malvern or Wiesbaden: and there was a famous physician in Mayfair, renowned for his skill in ridding the heads of those poor gentlemen of the unwelcome deposit, who made a reputation and a fortune by, so to speak, dredging them.

There was one official head, however, at Dustypore in which no particle of sand was to be found, and that was Mr. Strutt's. It was for this reason, probably, amongst others, that he was made Chief Secretary to the Salt Board, a post which, at the time when this history commences, was one of the most important, responsible, and lucrative in the entire service. For the Salt Board, as will hereafter be seen, was an institution whose dignity and powers had grown and grown until they almost overtopped those of the Agency itself. If the Salt Board was the embodiment of what was dignified and powerful in Dustypore, Mr. Strutt had concentrated in his own person the functions and attributes of the Board. He was prompt, indefatigable, self-satisfied, and, what his superiors valued him for especially, lucky.

A long career had taught him and the world that those who attacked him came off second-best. His answers were unanswerable, his reports effective, his explanations convincing. His nervous hand it was that depicted the early triumphs of the Dustypore Administration and in sonorous periods set forth the glories of the British rule—the roads, the canals, the hospitals and schools—the suppression of crime, the decreased mortality, the general passion of the inhabitants for female education. His figures were constantly quoted by people who wished to talk about India to English audiences, and his very name was a pillar of strength to the champions of the English rule. Even his enemies were constrained to admit that he possessed the art of 'putting it' to a degree of fearful and wonderful perfection.

The maxim, 'like master like man,' was as far as possible from being verified in the case of Mr. Strutt and his superiors. Of these Mr. Fortheringham, the Chairman, was lymphatic in temperament, inordinately vain, and the victim of an inveterate habit of enunciating platitudes. Cockshaw, who came next, was off-hand, superficial, and positive, with the positiveness of a man who hates deliberation and despises every form of uncertainty. Blunt, the third member, was a non-civilian, and had been brought out from England on account of his practical acquaintance with salt-mines, and of his having been a secretary in the Board of Trade. He was business-like, straightforward, and unconciliating; generally thought differently from his colleagues, and had the roughest possible manner of saying what he thought.

Such a trio had sometimes, as may well be imagined, no little trouble in preserving toward the outer world the aspect of serene, benevolent, and consistent infallibility, the maintenance of which Fotheringham regarded as the first of duties. Cockshaw did not in the least mind a row, so long as he was not kept too long at office for the purpose of making it. Blunt would have stayed at office till midnight, arguing doggedly, sooner than abandon his point. Happily Fotheringham had a great sense of propriety, concealed the dissensions of his colleagues from the public eye, and preserved the Board's dignity from ignominious collapse.

Under Strutt came a hierarchy of less important subordinates, who paved the long descent, so to speak, from the official altitudes in which the Salt Board had its being to the vulgar public who consumed the salt. Chief of these was Vernon, with whom the reader will speedily become better acquainted. Under him, again, came Mr. Whisp, the Assistant-Secretary, a young gentleman whose task it was to draw up minutes of the Board's proceedings, to draft its circulars and to collect the statistics out of which Strutt concocted his reports. He had thus, it will be seen, an opportunity of acquiring much useful information and a highly ornamental style, and Whisp was generally regarded in the service as a rising man.

CHAPTER II.

MAUD.

Nature said, 'A lovelier flower
On earth was never sown:
This child I to myself will take;
She shall be mine, and I will make
A lady of my own.'

When Vernon was appointed Under-Secretary to the Salt Board, he no doubt imagined that it was in connection with that august body that he would be known to fame and (as Strutt would grandiloquently have put it) leave his mark on his epoch. He was destined, however, as the reader of these pages will presently perceive, to become remarkable on the less unusual ground of relationship to an extremely pretty girl. His cousin Maud, of whom years before, in a rash moment of benevolence, he had consented to become guardian and trustee, had been suddenly thrown upon his hands. She was no longer a remote anxiety which could be disposed of by cheques, letters to governesses, and instructions to solicitors, but an immediate, living reality, with a highly effective pair of eyes, good looks—as to which women might cavil, but every man would be a firm believer—the manner of an eager child, and a joyousness which Vernon was obliged to admit was at once deliciously infectious to the world at large, and a very agreeable alterative to the state of mind produced by Indian summers, salt statistics, letters polished by Whisp or commonplaces enunciated by Fotheringham. With the timidity of indolence he shuddered to think of the social entanglements and disturbances which so new an element in his household was calculated to produce.

Maud, on the other hand, had come out to India with a very low opinion of herself and of her claims upon the good-will of society. At Miss Goodenough's establishment for young ladies, where her education had been completed, her shortcomings had been impressed upon her in a manner wholesome, perhaps, and necessary, but decidedly depressing. She had been haunted by the awful consciousness that she was a 'Tomboy.' Her general demeanour, her mode of expressing herself, her ignorance of many things with which no one ought to be unfamiliar, had been the object of the most unflattering comment. The elder Miss Goodenough—between whom and Maud there existed a real though somewhat fitful attachment—used to have her into a solemn little chamber and administer the most awful lectures on her sins of commission and omission, and the disgrace and suffering which they would justly entail. These interviews were generally tearful and tender; for Miss Goodenough, to whom Maud had been consigned as a child on her first arrival from India, loved her with a sort of rapture which made itself felt amid all the vehement fault-finding which Maud's delinquencies necessitated. Maud had always regarded the old lady in something of a maternal light, and never could be brought to abandon the familiar abbreviation of 'Goody,' by which she had been allowed, as a child, to address her instructress. She accepted her instructress's sentences accordingly with unquestioning faith and submission. The two used to weep together over Maud's shortcomings. She looked upon Miss Goodenough as a friend whose heart it was her unlucky fate to lacerate. Miss Goodenough regarded Maud as a creature whose alarming impulses and irregularities justified the darkest forebodings as to her future, and succeeded in infecting her pupil with some of her own apprehensions. Some judgment must, so both agreed, sooner or later overtake one whose shoulders seemed guided by a hidden law to unequal altitudes, whose toes defied every endeavour to keep them pointed in the conventional direction, and whose impetuous behaviour was constantly producing a scandal of more or less gravity.

'Dearest child,' Miss Goodenough would say, with an air of profound commiseration, 'if you could see how you look, with one shoulder up to your ears and the other near to what should be your waist!'

This taunt particularly grieved Maud, for she felt bitterly that her form was unromantically plump, and not at all of the refined tenuity of several of her companions.

'My shoulders!' she would exclaim, with the tears in her eyes; 'I wish they were both at Jericho. I am sure I am made wrong, dearest Goody, indeed I am.'

'Then, my dear,' Miss Goodenough would say, not encouragingly, 'we should try all the more to remedy natural defects; at any rate, you might know your Bible. Now, dear Maud, your ignorance is, you know, simply shocking.'

'Yes I know,' said Maud, 'but I can't help it. Those horrid kings of Israel and Judah! They made Israel to sin, they make me to sin, indeed they do. Jehoshaphat, Jehoiakim, Jonadab, Jehu—all wicked—all beginning with J—how can any one remember them?'

'Then, my dear,' her inexorable monitress would reply, 'you can never know what every well-educated young lady, what every mere school-child, is acquainted with. How can you be fit to go into the world?'

'I wish,' said Maud, passionately, in despair at the difficulties of existence, 'that when the tribes got lost they had taken their histories with them, and lost them too. Darling Goody, let me learn texts, hymns, all the Sermon on the Mount, as much poetry as you please, only not those dreadful Chronicles!' Maud used on these occasions to throw her arms round Goody's neck in an outbreak of affectionate repentance, in a way that the elder lady, who was absurdly impressionable, found it difficult to resist.

But Miss Goodenough's kindness made Maud's conscience all the less at ease. Calmness, self-restraint, composure, a well-stocked mind, and sensible judgment were, Miss Goodenough told her, the great excellencies of character to be aimed at. Maud looked into herself, and felt, with agonies of self-reproach, that in every particular she fell miserably short; that she was the very reverse of calm; the least thing roused her into passion, or sent her spinning from the summit of serene high spirits to the lowest depths of despair; as for self-restraint, Maud felt she was just as capable of it as of flying to the moon.

From time to time she made violent efforts to

be diligent, and set to work with sudden zeal upon books which her instructress assured her were most interesting and improving. These attempts, for the most part, collapsed in grievous failure. Improvement, Maud felt ruefully, there might be, though unbeknown to herself; interest, she was certain, there was none. On the other hand, a chance novel, which had somehow or other passed scatheless through the rigid blockade which Miss Goodenough established around her young ladies, had filled her with a sort of ecstacy of excitement; and no amount of poetry—no such amount, at any rate, as came within the narrow limits of her mistress's literary horizon—seemed capable of fatiguing or even of satisfying her. Displaying the most complete inaptitude for every other form of diligence, she was ready enough to learn any amount that any one liked to give her. She even signalised her zeal by the spasmodic transcription of her favourite passages into a precious volume marked with a solemn 'Private,' protected from profane eyes by a golden padlock and destined by its proprietress to be the depository of all her intellectual treasures.

Miss Goodenough, however, though admitting perforce the merits of the great masters of English song, regarded the claims of poetry as generally subordinate to those of history, geography, arithmetic, and various other branches of useful and ornamental learning, and treated Maud's passion for Sir Walter Scott as but another alarming symptom of an excitable disposition and ill-regulated mind.

A crisis came at last. It happened at church, where Miss Goodenough's young ladies used to sit just under the gallery, while the boys of 'The Crescent House Academy' performed their devotions overhead. One fatal Sunday in February, just as the Service was over, and the two Misses Goodenough had already turned their backs to lead the way out, and the young ladies were preparing to follow, a little missive came fluttering down and fell almost into Maud's hands; at any rate, she slipped it into her Prayer-book; and all would have gone well but for that horrid Mademoiselle de Vert, who, turning sharply round, detected the occurrence, and the moment Maud was outside the church demanded her Prayer-book.

Maud turned fiery red in an instant, and surrendered her book.

'And the note,' said Mademoiselle de Vert.

'What note?' said Maud. But alas! her telltale cheeks rendered the question useless, and made all evasion impossible. Maud was speedily driven to open resistance.

'No, thank you,' she said, with an air that told

Mademoiselle de Vert that further attempts at coercion would be labour thrown away; 'it was not intended for you; it was a valentine.'

After this appalling disclosure there was, of course, when they got home, an explanation to be had with Miss Goodenough, who professed herself, and probably really was, terrified at so new a phase of human depravity.

Maud was presently in floods of tears, and was obliged to confess that she and the offending culprit had on more than one occasion let each other's eyes meet, had in fact exchanged looks, and even smiles; so that, perhaps, she was the real occasion for this unhallowed act of temerity.

'Forgive me, forgive me!' she cried; 'it was nothing wrong; it was only a heart with an arrow and a Cupid!'

'A Cupid!' cried Miss Goodenough, in horror at each new revelation, 'and some writing too, I suppose?'

'Yes,' said Maud, whose pleasure in the valentine was rapidly surmounting the disgrace into which it had got her; 'really pretty verses. Here it is!' And thereupon she produced the offending billet, and proceeded to read with effusion:—

I would thou wert a summer rose,
And I a bird to hover o'er thee;
And from the dawn to evening's close
To warble only, 'I adore thee!'

'Stop!' cried Miss Goodenough, with great decision, and white with indignation; 'do you know what you are reading? Do you know that that vulgar rubbish is the sort of odious impertinence that shop-boys send to their sweethearts, but which it is an insult to let a lady even see, and which, transmitted in a church, is little less than sacrilege?'

So saying, Miss Goodenough took the offending letter and consigned it to the flames, and poor Maud stood ruefully by, watching the conflagration of the silver Cupid, mourning over Miss Goodenough's hard-heartedness, and consoling herself with the reflection that at any rate she remembered the verses.

'I must write to your aunt Felicia to remove you. What an example for other girls!'

'Well,' said Maud resignedly, and blushing in anticipation at the thought of such an exposure; 'do not, at any rate, tell her about the valentine. Dear Goody, did you never have one sent to you when you were my age?'

Miss Goodenough quite declined to gratify this audacious inquiry, and made up her mind that it was high time for Maud to be under more masterful guidance than her own. The result was that in the following November Maud was a passenger on the P. & O. steamship 'Cockatrice,' from Southampton to Calcutta, where her cousin Vernon was to meet her and escort her to her new home in Dustypore.

She had been, it must be acknowledged, to a certain degree reassured by the experience of her voyage. She found that the kings of Israel and Judah did not occupy a prominent place in general conversation; that a precise acquaintance with the queens of England was not expected of her; and that nobody resented the impetuosity of her movements or her want of self-restraint. On the contrary, several of her fellow-voyagers had evinced the liveliest sympathy and interest in her, and had devoted themselves successfully to keeping her amused. Maud, in fact, had gone down to her cabin on more occasions than one during the voyage and shed some tears at the approaching separation from friends, whom even those few weeks of chance companionship had carried close to her heart. It had been in truth a happy time. The captain, to whose special care she was committed, had watched over her with a more than paternal interest. The doctor insisted on her having champagne. The purser set all his occult influences at work to increase her comfort. The stewards conspired to spoil her. Maud felt that nothing she could do would at all adequately express her feelings to all these good people who had ministered to her wants and tried, with so much success, to please her. There are people, no doubt, to whom a voyage to India is the height of boredom; but there are other happier natures to whom it presents a continuous series of excitements, interests, and joys. Maud, at any rate, enjoyed it with a sort of rapture, and trembled to think how faintly Miss Goodenough's admonitions even now began to fall upon her conscience's ear.

Then there had been some very charming fellow-passengers on board, with whom she had formed the warmest friendship. There was a certain Mr. Mowbray, for instance—a comely, curly-headed, beardless boy, on his way to join his regiment—whom she found extremely interesting, and who lost no time in becoming confidential. It was very pleasant to sit on deck through long lazy mornings and play bésique with Mr. Mowbray; and pleasant too, when the day was done, to sit with him in the moonlight and watch the Southern Cross slowly wheeling up and the waves all ablaze with phosphoric splendour, and to talk about home and Mr. Mowbray's sisters, and the stations to which each of them were bound, never, probably, to meet again. There was something mysterious about it, Maud felt, and impressive, and very, very charming.

And then, on some evenings, the stewardess would declare that Maud looked pale, or had a headache, and that she should have a little dinner on deck; 'Just a bit of chicken, miss,' this benevolent being would say, 'and a slice of ham, and the doctor will give you a glass of champagne. The cabin is a deal too hot for you.' And then, by some happy fatality, Mr. Mowbray would also have a headache that very afternoon, and nothing but dining on deck would do for him; and so there would be a very pleasant little repast going on over the heads of the hot, noisy crowd who were gobbling up their food below; and the two invalids would forget their maladies, fancied or real, in the innocent excitement of a congenial *tête-à-tête*. On the whole, Maud had arrived at Dustypore with the conviction that existence, though beset with almost innumerable difficulties and dangers, was replete with enjoyments, which made it, despite every drawback, most thoroughly well worth while to be alive.

CHAPTER III.

WAR AT THE SALT BOARD.

Hos motus animorum atque hæc certamina tanta—

The Salt Board had excessively respectable traditions. Its commencement dated far back in Indian history, long before the conquest of the Sandy Tracts, and its *prestige* had been maintained by a series of officials all of whom had been in the habit of speaking of one another with the utmost respect. The 'illustrious Jones,' 'the great administrator Brown,' the 'sagacious and statesmanlike Robinson,' all threw the lustre of their abilities over the institution, and were appealed to with unhesitating faith by their successors in the department. When one member referred to another he spoke of himself as 'sitting at his feet,' or as 'formed in his school,' or as 'guided by his principles,' in language that was perhaps a little unnecessarily grandiloquent, but which had, at any rate, the effect of investing the Board with a sort of moral grandeur with the uninitiated. Even the mistakes of the Board acquired a sort of dignity and were not to be spoken of in an off-hand or irreverential manner. They might seem mistakes, but it was not prudent to be too sure that they were so. Many other decisions of the Board had been cavilled at by rash critics, and time had shown their wisdom. The Board, moreover, had a certain grand, misty way of its own of talking, which made its proceedings somewhat hard to criticise. Indeed, all outside criticism was resented as an impertinence, and those rash critics who had the temerity to attempt it were put down with the contemptuous decisiveness appropriate to ill-judged advisers. There was a regular conventional way of crushing them: first it was contended that, being outsiders, they could not, in the nature of things, understand the matter; as if there was a sort of inner and spiritual sense, by which the affairs of the Salt Board must be apprehended. Then there were stereotyped phrases, which really meant nothing, but which were understood and accepted in the Sandy Tracts as implying that the Board considered the subject disposed of and did not want further discussion. Arguments which could not be otherwise met were smothered in an array of big names, or parried by pathetic references to the zeal of the Salt officials and the conscientious manner in which they worked in the sun. Whatever line was adopted, it was the invariable tradition that Government should express its concurrence, and so the whole thing ended comfortably to all parties concerned. All this was naturally regarded as being highly satisfactory. But the maintenance of this agreeable equilibrium depended on the persons concerned being tempered of the right metal, imbued with the right spirit, and what Strutt used to call 'loyal.' The intrusion of an alien spirit could not fail to produce deplorable disturbance, disquiet and the dissipation of all sorts of agreeable illusions. And this was what happened when Blunt—who was an outsider, the hardest, roughest, most matter-of-fact of commercial Englishmen—was appointed to the Board. Blunt violated every tradition in the most ruthless fashion, was unimpressed by all the solemnities which awed conventional beholders, and had the most inconvenient way of asking what things meant, and (as he used to say with a sort of horrid glee) 'of picking out the heart of a thing.' Now, the Board did not at all relish having its heart picked out in this unceremonious fashion, and resented it with a sort of passionate dislike. Fotheringham felt that he had indeed fallen on very evil times, and that the pleasant days of peace were numbered. Cockshaw, when he found that Blunt would neither smoke nor play whist, gave him up as a bore. The very clerks in the office became agitated and depressed. When Blunt pulled out his spectacles and produced his papers, and went ruthlessly into figures, looking rigid and tough, and implacable and indefatigable, both Fotheringham and Cockshaw knew that their places were not worth having and that they must look for comfortable quarters elsewhere. Fotheringham counted the months to the time when his pension would be due. Cockshaw, who was a man of action, applied forthwith for the Chief Commissionership of the Carraway Islands, which was just then in the market.

Blunt had not been many weeks at Dustypore before he showed to demonstration at the Board that the accounts were kept on an entirely wrong footing, and that a vast sum of money, five or six lakhs, was not traceable.

'It is the floating balance,' said Fotheringham, with an air of quiet assurance, arising from his having given the same reply frequently before, and always found it answer.

'Perhaps you will trace it, then,' said Blunt, pushing the papers across to Fotheringham in the most unfeeling way. '*I* cannot.'

'We had better send for Strutt,' said Cockshaw, who knew nothing about the accounts himself, and had a nervous distrust of Fotheringham's explanations. Thereupon Strutt appeared, radiant and self-satisfied, and cleared up everything with the easy air of a man who is and who feels himself thoroughly master of the situation.

'No,' he said, in reply to Fotheringham's inquiry, not in the floating balance, but in Suspense Account A: here it is, you see: one item, 2 lakhs —85,000 rs. 15 annas 3 pie.'

'Of course,' said Fotheringham, ignoring his blunder with an air of placid dignity, 'there, you see, it is!'

'Well,' said Blunt, insatiable of explanation, 'but you said it was in the floating balance; and pray where are the other items, and what is Suspense Account A, and how many other Suspense Accounts have you? Pray go on, Mr. Strutt.'

So Mr. Strutt had to go on, and then it was sad to see the brightness fade out of his face, and his pleasant swagger disappear, and his answers get wilder and wilder as Blunt led him from figure to figure, puzzled him by putting things in all sorts of new lights, and finally took him completely out of his depth.

This was not the sort of treatment to which

Strutt had been accustomed, or for which he was constitutionally fitted. At last, in despair, he sent down for Vernon and the Head Accountant, and these two brought up a pile of ledgers, and traced the missing sums from one account into another in a manner which baffled all Fotheringham's attempts to follow them, and proved at last to their own satisfaction that all was right.

Still the horrible Blunt was only half convinced.

'All *may* be right,' he said, 'and I will take your words that it *is* so. But the figures do not prove it; nor do they prove anything except that the system of accounts is deplorable. Any amount of fraud might be perpetrated under them. I can't understand them: Strutt does not understand them: not one of you gentlemen understands them. This may suit you; but, as for me, I hate what I cannot understand.'

So no doubt did Fotheringham, and this was one reason why he so cordially hated Blunt.

Another thing about Blunt that irritated his colleagues was his way of coughing—a loud, harsh, strident cough—whenever he was vexed.

'His coughs are quite like oaths,' Fotheringham said with a shudder; and it must be confessed that Blunt could throw an expression that sounded horribly like 'damn it' into his mode of clearing his throat; and that when Fotheringham was arguing with him he cleared his throat oftener and more vigorously than can have been necessary.

CHAPTER IV.

FELICIA.

The laws of marriage character'd in gold
Upon the blanched tablets of her heart;
A love still burning upward, giving light
To read those laws; an accent very low
In blandishment, but a most silver flow
  Of subtle-paced counsel in distress,
Right to the heart and brain, tho' undescried,
  Winning its way with extreme gentleness
Through all the outworks of suspicious pride.

THE new home in which Maud found herself might well have contented a more fastidious critic than she was at all inclined to be. The Vernons were delightful hosts. Maud had established thoroughly comfortable relations with her cousin during the long journey to Dustypore; and though he was too indolent or perhaps too much absorbed in work for anything but a sort of passive politeness, still this was, upon the whole, satisfactory and reassuring, and Maud felt very much at her ease with him. Mrs. Vernon, the 'Cousin Felicia,' whom Maud now realised in flesh and blood for the first time, inspired her with a stronger, keener feeling of admiration than any she had known before. She was beautiful, as Maud had often heard; but beauty alone would not account for the thrill of pleasure which something in Felicia's first greeting gave her. The charm lay in an unstudied, unconscious cordiality of manner that fascinated the new-comer with its sincerity and grace. Felicia coruscated with cheerfulness, courage, mirth. She was bright, and infected those about her with brightness. Transplanted from the quiet luxury of an English country-house to the rough experiences of Indian life, she bore through them all an air of calmness, joyousness, refinement, which the troubles of life seemed incapable of disturbing. When, years before, just fresh from the schoolroom and with all the dazzling possibilities of a London season before her, she had admitted her attachment to Vernon and her unalterable desire to go with him to India, her father's face had looked darker than she had ever seen it before, and a family chorus of indignation had proclaimed the unwisdom of the choice. The rector's son and the squire's daughter, however, had played about together as boy and girl, and long years of intimacy had cemented a friendship too strong to be shattered by such feeble blows as worldliness or prudence could inflict upon it. Vernon had nothing but the slender portion which a country clergyman might be expected to leave his children at his death—nothing, that is, except a long list of school and college honours and a successful candidature for the Indian Civil Service. Felicia, as her deploring aunts murmured amongst themselves, 'was a girl who might have married *any one;*' and her parents, without incurring the charge of a vulgar ambition, might naturally complain of a match which gave them so little and cost them the pang of so complete a separation. Felicia, at any rate, had never repented of her choice; she was greatly in love with her husband, and had the pleasant consciousness that his taste—fastidious, critical, and not a little sarcastic—found in her nothing that was not absolute perfection. India had developed in her a self-reliance and fortitude which never could have been born in the safe tranquillity of her home. The hot winds of Dustypore had not quite robbed her cheeks of their English bloom; but there were lines of suffering, anxiety, and fatigue which, when her face was at rest, let out the secret that her habitual brightness was not as effortless as it seemed.

The fact was that life, with all its enjoyments, had been to her full of pangs, of which, even at a safe distance, she could scarcely trust herself to think. The separation from her home was a grief that long usage made none the easier to bear. On the contrary, there was a sort of aching want which was never appeased, and which the merest trifle—a letter—a message—a word—was sufficient to light up into something like anguish. Felicia never achieved the art of reading her home letters with decent composure, and used to carry them, with a sort of nervous uneasiness, to her own room, to be dealt with in solitude. Then four children, all with an air of Indian fragility, and whose over-refined looks their mother would thankfully have bartered for a little vigour and robustness, had cost her many a heartache. On the horizon of all her married life there loomed the dreadful certainty of a day when another series of separations would begin, and the choice would lie between the companionship of her husband in India, or the care of her children at home.

From this horrid thought it was natural for such a temperament as Felicia's to seek refuge in merriment, which, if sometimes a little strained, was never wholly unnatural. Excitement was a pleasant cure for gloomy thought, and it was to Felicia never hard to find. Every sort of society amused her, and those who saw her only in public would have pronounced her a being to whom melancholy was inconceivable. Her husband, however, could have told that Felicia was often sad. There were afternoons, too, when she was quite alone, when she would order the carriage and drive away by an unfrequented road to the dreary, lonely Station Cemetery, and weep passionate tears over a grave where years before she and her husband had come one morning together and left a precious little wasted form, and Felicia had felt that happiness was over for her, and that life could never be the same again. Nor was it, for there are some griefs which travel with us to our journey's end.

Charmed as Maud had been with her newly-found relation, she was conscious of the stiffness of a perfectly unaccustomed life, and thought wistfully of the pleasures of the voyage and even of her French and geography with Miss Goodenough. Felicia, with all her kindness, just a little alarmed her; she was so brilliant, so dignified, and quite unconsciously, so much of a fine lady. Vernon was buried in his books or away at office, and very seldom available for the purposes of conversation. The days, despite the excitement of novelty, dragged heavily, and Maud began to think that if every day was to be as long as these, and there were three hundred and sixty-five of them in the year, and fifty years, perhaps, in a life-time, how terrific an affair existence was!

Before, however, she had been a week at Dustypore the ice began to melt. Felicia came in one morning from a long busy time with nurses, children, servants and housekeeping, established herself in an easy-chair, close to Maud, and was evidently bent upon a chat. Maud fcund herself presently, she knew not how, pouring out all her most sacred secrets, and giving her heart away in a most reckless fashion, to a companion whom, so far as time went, she still regarded as almost a stranger. Such a confession she had never made, even to Miss Good-enough, nor felt inclined to make it. Now, however, it seemed to come easily and as a matter of course. Felicia was sympathetic and greatly interested. Even the episode of the valentine was not forgotten.

'There,' Maud cried, with a slightly nervous dread of telling something either improper or ridiculous; 'that was my very last schoolgirl scrape. Was it very bad?'

'Very bad!' cried Felicia, with a laugh, the joyousness of which was entirely reassuring; 'it was that naughty boy who got you into trouble. Fortunately there are no galleries in our church here, and no boys, so there is nothing to fear.'

That evening Felicia was singing an old familiar favourite air, as she was fond of doing, half in the dark, and unconscious of a listener. Vernon was deep in his papers in the adjoining room. Maud, at the other end of the piano, where she had been turning over the leaves of some music, stood with her hand still resting on the page, gazing at the singer and wrapt in attention. Something, she knew not what, nor stopped to ask—the time, the place, the song or the tone of Felicia's voice—touched her as with a sudden gust of feeling. When the song was over Maud walked across, flung her arms round her companion and kissed her with a sort of rapture.

Felicia, looking up, surprised, saw that the other's eyes were full of tears.

'That is pretty, is it not?' she said, taking Maud's hand kindly in her own.

'Sing it once more,' Maud petitioned. And so, while Vernon, unconscious of the flow of sentiment so close about him, was still absorbed in the vicissitudes of Orissa, Felicia's performance was encored, and two sympathetic natures had found each other out and worked into unison.

Afterwards, when Maud had departed, Felicia, with characteristic impulsiveness, broke out into vehement panegyric:

'Come, George,' she said, 'don't be stupid, please, and uninterested; don't you think she is quite charming?'

'Felicia,' said her husband, 'you are for ever falling in love with some one or other, and now you have lost your heart to Maud. No, I don't think her charming; but I dare say a great many other people will. She will be the plague of our lives, you will see. I wish we had left her at Miss Goodenough's.'

'Of course everybody will fall in love with her,' cried Felicia, quite undaunted by her husband's gloomy forebodings; 'and I will tell you what, George—she will do delightfully for Jem.'

'Jem!' exclaimed her husband, with a tone of horror. 'Felicia, you are match-making already—and Jem too, poor fellow!'

Now, Jem Sutton was Vernon's oldest friend, and Felicia's kinsman, faithful servant and ally. Years before, the two men had boated and cricketed together at Eton, and spent pleasant weeks at each other's homes; and when they met in India, each seemed to waken up the other to a host of affectionate recollections about their golden youth. Sutton, in fact, was still a thorough schoolboy, and as delighted with finding his old chum as if he had just come back from the holidays. He had contrived to get as much marching, fighting, and adventuring into his ten years' service as a man could wish; had led several border forays with daring and success; had received several desperate wounds, of which a great scar across the forehead was the most conspicuous; had established a reputation as a rider and a swordsman, and had received from his Sovereign the brilliant distinction of the Victoria Cross, which, along with a great many other honourable badges, covered the wide expanse of his chest on state occasions.

Despite his fighting proclivities, Sutton had the softest possible pair of blue eyes, his hair was still as bright a brown as when he was a curly-headed boy at his mother's side; nor did the copious growth of his moustache quite conceal a smile that was sweetness and honesty itself. Felicia's two little girls regarded him as their especial property and made the tenderest avowals of devotion to him. Sutton treated them, as all their sex, with a kindness that was chivalrously polite, and which they were already women enough to appreciate.

Lastly, among other accomplishments, which rendered him especially welcome at the Vernons' house, he possessed a tuneful tenor voice, and sang Moore's Melodies with a pathos which was more than artistic. On the whole, it is easy to understand how natural it seemed to Felicia that two such charming people as Sutton and Maud should be destined by Heaven for each other, and that hers should be the hand to lead them to their happy fate.

CHAPTER V.

'SUTTON'S FLYERS.'

Consider this—he had been bred i' the wars
Since he could draw a sword.

'SUTTON'S FLYERS' were well known in the Sandy Tracts as the best irregular cavalry in that part of the country. Formed originally in the Mutiny, when spirits of an especial hardihood and enterprise gathered instinctively around congenial leaders, they had retained ever since the *prestigē* then acquired and a standard of chivalry which turned every man in the regiment into something of a hero. Many a stalwart lad, bred in the wild uplands of the Province, had felt his blood stirred within him at the fame of exploits which appealed directly to instincts on which the pacific British rule had for years put an unwelcome pressure. Around the fire of many an evening meal, in many a gossiping bazaar, in many a group at village well or ferry, the fame of the 'Flyers' was recounted, and 'Sutton Sahib' became a household word by which military enthusiasm could be speedily kindled to a blaze. With the lightest possible equipage, wiry country-bred horses, and a profound disregard for all baggage arrangements, Sutton had effected some marches which earned him the credit of being supernaturally ubiquitous. Again and again had Mutineer detachments, revelling in fancied security, found that the dreaded horsemen, whom they fancied a hundred miles away and marching in an opposite direction, had heard of their whereabouts and were close upon their track. Then the suddenness of the attack, the known prowess of the leader, the half-superstitious reverence which his followers paid him, invested the troop with a tradition of invincibility, and had secured them, on more than one occasion, a brilliant success against odds which less fervent temperaments than Sutton's might have felt it wrong to encounter, and which certainly made success seem almost a miracle. To his own men Sutton was hardly less than a god, and there were few of them on whom he could not safely depend to gallop with him to their doom.

More than one of his officers had saved his life in hand-to-hand fight by reckless exposure of their own; and his adjutant had dragged him, stunned, crushed and bleeding, from under a fallen horse, and carried him through a storm of bullets to a place of safety. All of them, on the other hand, had experienced on a hundred occasions the benefit of his imperturbable calmness, his inspiring confidence and unshaken will. Once Sutton had gratified their pride—and perhaps, too, his own—by a display of prowess which, if somewhat theatrical, was nevertheless extremely effective. A fight was on hand, and the regiment was just going into action, when a Mohammedan trooper, famed as a swordsman on all the country-side, had ridden out from the enemy's lines, bawled out a defiance of the English rule, couched in the filthiest and most opprobrious terms, and dared Sutton to come out and fight, and let him throw his carcase to the dogs. There are moments when instinct becomes our safest, and indeed our only, guide. Sutton, for once in his life, felt a gust of downright fury: he gave the order to halt and sheathe swords, took his challenger at his word, rode out in front of his force and had a fair hand-to-hand duel with the hostile champion. The confronted troops looked on in breathless anxiety, while the fate of either combatant depended on a turn of the sword, and each fought as knowing that one or other was to die. Sutton at last saw his opportunity for a stroke which won him the honours of the day. It cost him a sabre-cut across his forehead, which to some eyes might have marred his beauty for ever; but the foul-mouthed Mussulman lay dead on the field, smitten through the heart, and Sutton rode back among his shouting followers the acknowledged first swordsman of the day.

Such a man stood in no need of Felicia's panegyrics to seem very impressive in the eyes of a girl like Maud. Despite his gentleness of manner and the sort of domestic footing on which everybody at the Vernons', down to the baby, evidently placed him, she felt a little awed. She was inclined to be romantic; but it was rather alarming to have a large, living, incarnate romance sitting next her at luncheon, cutting slices of mutton, and asking her, with a curiosity that seemed necessarily condescending, about all the details of the voyage. There seemed something incongruous and painfully below the mark in having to tell him that they had acted 'Woodcock's Little Game,' and had played 'Bon Jour, Philippe,' on board; and Maud, when the revelation became necessary, made it with a blush. After luncheon, however, Sutton and the little girls had a game of 'Post,' and Maud begun to console herself with the reassuring conviction that, after all, he was but a man, and a very pleasant one.

After he had gone, Felicia, who was the most indiscreet of match-makers, began one of her extravagant eulogiums. 'Like him!' she cried, in reply to Maud's inquiry; 'like is not the word. He is the best, noblest, bravest, and most chivalrous of beings.'

'Not the handsomest!' interrupted Maud, tempted by Felicia's enthusiasm into feeling perversely indifferent.

'Yes, and the handsomest too,' Felicia said; 'tall, strong, with beautiful features, and eyes as soft and tender as a woman's; indeed a great deal softer than most women's.'

'Then,' objected Maud, 'why has he never'——

'Because,' answered her companion, indignantly anticipating the objection, 'there is no one half-a-quarter good enough for him.'

'Well,' said the other, by this time quite in a rebellious mood, 'all I can say is, that *I* don't think him in the least good-looking. I don't like that great scar across his forehead.'

'Don't you?' cried Felicia; and then she told her how the scar had come there, and Maud could no longer pretend not to be interested.

The next day Sutton came with them for a drive, and Maud, who had by this time shaken off her fears, began to find him decidedly interesting. There was something extremely romantic in having a soldier, whose reputation was already almost historical, the hero of a dozen brilliant episodes, coming tame about the house, only too happy to do her biddin or Felicia's, and apparently perfectly contented with their society. Felicia was in the highest spirits, for she found her pet project shaping itself with pleasant facility into a fair prospect of realisation; and when Felicia was in high spirits they infected all about her.

Sutton, innocently unconscious of the cause of her satisfaction, but realising only that she wanted Maud amused and befriended, lent himself with a ready zeal to further her wishes and let no leisure afternoon go by without suggesting some new scheme of pleasure. Maud's quick, impulsive, highly-strung temperament, her moods of joyousness or depression, hardly less transient than the shadows that flit across the fields in April, her keen appreciation of beauty and pathos, made her, child as she was in most of her thoughts and ways, an interesting companion to him. Her eagerness in enjoyment was a luxury to see; and Sutton, a good observer, knew before long, almost better than herself, what things she most enjoyed. Instead of the reluctant and unsympathetic permission which her late instructress had accorded to her poetical tastes, Sutton and Felicia completely understood what she felt, treated her taste on each occasion with a flattering consideration, and led her continually to 'fresh woods and pastures new,' where vistas of loveliness, fairer far than any she had yet discovered, seemed to break upon her.

Vernon's library, his one extravagance, was all that the most fastidious scholar could desire; any choice edition of a favourite poet was on his table almost before his English friends had got it. A beautiful book, like a beautiful woman, deserves the best attire that art can give it, and Maud felt a thrill of satisfaction at all the finery of gilt and Russian leather in which she could now behold her well-beloved poems arrayed. Sutton told her, with a decisiveness which carried conviction, what things she would like and what she might neglect; and she soon followed his directions with unquestioning faith. He used to come and read to them sometimes, in a sweet, impressive manner, Maud felt; and the passage, as he had read it, lived on in her thoughts with the precise shade of feeling which his voice had given it.

One happy week was consecrated to the 'Idylls of the King,' and this had been so especially delightful as to make a little epoch in her existence—so rich was the picture—so great a revelation of beauty—such depths of sorrow—such agonies of repentance—such calm, quiet, ethereal scenes of loveliness.

More than once Sutton, in reading, had looked up suddenly and found her eyes bent full upon him, and swimming with tears; and Maud had stooped over her work, the sudden scarlet dyeing her cheek, yet almost too much moved to care about detection.

How true, how real, how living it all seemed! Did it, in truth, belong to the far-off, misty, fabulous kingdom over which the mystic Arthur ruled, or was she herself Elaine, and Lancelot sitting close before her, and all the harrowing story playing itself out in her own little troubled world? Anyhow, it struck a chord which vibrated pleasurably, yet with a half-painful vehemence, through her mind and filled it with harmonies and discords unheard before. Certainly, she confessed to herself, there was a something about Sutton that touched one to the heart.

CHAPTER VI.

'A COMPETITION-WALLAH.'

Ainsi doit être
Un petit-maître ;
Léger, amusant,
Vif, complaisant,
        Plaisant,
Railleur aimable,
Traître adorable ;
C'est l'homme du jour,
Fait pour l'amour.

ONE of the stupid things that people do in India is to select the two hottest hours of the day for calling on each other. How such an idiotic idea first found its way into existence, by what strange fate it became part of the social law of Anglo-Indians, and how it is that no one has yet been found with courage or strength enough to break down a custom so detrimental to the health and comfort of mankind, are among the numerous mysteries which the historian of India must be content to leave unsolved. Like Chinese ladies' feet, the high heels on which fashionable Europe at present does penance, suttee of Hindu widows, and infanticide among the Rajpoot nobles, it is merely a curious instance that there is nothing so foolish and so disagreeable that human beings will not do or endure if it only becomes the fashion.

At any rate, the ladies and gentlemen of Dustypore were resolved not to be a whit less fashionable and uncomfortable than their neighbours, and religiously exchanged visits from twelve to two.

Maud's arrival was the signal for a burst of callers, and a goodly stream of soldiers and civilians arrived day by day to pay their homage to the newly-arrived beauty and her chaperon. Felicia's house was always popular, and all that was pleasantest and best in Dustypore assembled at her parties. Young London dandies fresh from home, and exploring the Sandy Tracts under the impression of having left the *Ultima Thule* of civilisation far behind them, were sometimes startled to find her drawing-room as full of taste, luxury, and refinement as if they had suddenly been transported to Eaton Square.

What is the nameless grace that some women have the art of putting into chairs and tables, which turns them from mere bits of upholstery into something hardly short of poetry? How is it that in some rooms there breathes a subtle charm, an aroma of delicacy and culture, a propriety in the behaviour of the sofas and ottomans to one another, a pleasant negligence apparent through the general order, a courageous simplicity amid elaborated comfort, which, in the absence of the mistress, tells the expectant visitor that he is about to meet a thoroughbred lady?

Some such fascination, at any rate, there lingered about the cool, carefully-shaded room in which Felicia received her guests. It was by no means smart, and not especially tidy, for it was often invaded and occupied by a victorious horde from the nursery, and bore many a sign of the common-place routine of daily life. But to Felicia's friends it was an enchanted abode, where a certain refuge might be found from whatever disagreeable things or people prevailed outside, and where Felicia, who, whatever she might feel, always looked calm and radiant and cool, presided as the *genius loci*, to forbid the possibility of profane intrusion.

One thing that made it picturesque was that at all times and seasons it abounded in flowers. Felicia was an enthusiastic gardener, and her loving skill and care could save many a tender plant which would, in a less experienced hand, have withered and sunk under the burning heat and dust that prevailed everywhere but in the confines of Felicia's kingdom. Her garden gave her a more home-like feeling than any other Indian experience. It refreshed her to go out early in the morning, while the children were yet asleep, and the sun's rays had barely surmounted the tall rows of plantains that marked the garden's boundary, and guarded her treasures from the sultry air. It soothed her to superintend ferns and roses, cuttings from some Himalayan shrub, or precious little seedlings from England. By dint of infinite care she had created a patch of turf, which, if not quite as green, fresh and dewy as the lawn at home, was at any rate a rest to eyes weary with dazzling wastes and the bright blazing air. There Felicia had a shady corner, where pots and sticks and garden-tools attested the progress of many a new gardening experiment, and where the water forced up from the well at the garden's end went rippling by with a pleasant sound, cooling and softening all the air around. Oftentimes, as she lingered here, her fancies would wander to the pleasant Manor House, where her taste for flowers had been acquired in her father's company, and she would be again fern-hunting with him through some cool mossy woodland, or roaming through a paradise of bluebells, with the well-loved beeches towering overhead, while the sweet summer evening died slowly away.

Early amongst the visitors Mr. Desvœux was announced, and Felicia, when she saw his card, told Maud that she would be sure now to be very much amused.

'He is the most brilliant of all the young civilians,' she said, 'and is to do great things. But he talks great nonsense and abuses everybody. So do not be astonished at anything you hear.'

'And is he nice?' inquired Maud.

Felicia made a little face, not altogether of approval:

'Well,' she said, 'he is more curious than nice;' and then Desvœux made his appearance, and while he was exchanging preliminary commonplaces with Felicia, Maud had an opportunity of observing the visitor's exterior claims, which were not inconsiderable, to the regard of womankind.

He was certainly, Maud felt at once, extremely handsome and, apparently, extremely anxious to be thought so. The general effect which he produced was that of a poetical dandy. He was dressed with a sort of effeminate finery, with here and there a careless touch which redeemed it all from utter fopdom. He was far too profusely set about with pretty things, lockets and rings and costly knick-knacks; on the other hand his handkerchief was tied with a more than Byronic negligence. The flower in his button-hole was exquisite, but it was stuck in with a carelessness which, if studied, was none the less artistic. On the whole he was over-dressed; but he walked into the room with the air of a man who had forgotten all about it, and who had no eyes or thoughts for anything but his present company.

Maud soon began to think him very entertaining, but, as Felicia had said, 'curious.' He was full of fun, extravagant, joyous, unconventional; he had turned, after the first few sentences, straight upon Maud and pointedly invited her into the conversation; and she soon felt her spirits rising.

'I saw you this morning,' he said, 'in the distance, riding with Sutton. I should have asked to be allowed to join you, but that I was too shy, and Sutton would have hated me for spoiling his *tête-à-tête*.'

'Three is an odious number, is it not, Mr. Desvœux?' said Felicia, 'and should be expunged from the arithmetic books. Why was it ever invented?'

'In order, I suppose,' said Desvœux, 'that we three might meet this morning, and that there might be three Graces and three witches in Macbeth, and three members of the Salt Board. Three is evidently a necessity; but when I am of the trio, and two of us are men, I confess I don't like it. It is so nice to have one's lady all to one's self. But, Miss Vernon, you are alarmed, I know, and naturally; you think that I am going to ask, what I suppose fifty people have been asking you all the week, whether you enjoyed the voyage to India, and how you like the looks of Dustypore. But I will be considerate, and spare you. Enjoyed the voyage, indeed! What a horrid mockery the question seems!'

'But I *did* enjoy it,' cried Maud; 'so you see that you might have asked me after all. It was very exciting.'

'Yes, all the excitement of wondering every day what new mysteries of horror the ship's cooks will devise for dinner; whether the sinews of Sunday's turkey can rival those of Saturday's goose; the excitement of going to bed in the dark and treading on a black-beetle; the excitement of shaving in a gale of wind and cutting one's nose off, as I very nearly did; the excitement of the young ladies who are expecting their lovers at Bombay, and of the young ladies who will not wait till Bombay but manufacture their lovers out of hand. It is too thrilling!'

'Well,' said Maud, 'we had theatricals and readings and dances, and a gentleman who played the most lovely variations on the violin, and I enjoyed it all immensely!'

'Ah,' said Desvœux, as if suddenly convinced, 'then perhaps you are even capable of liking Dustypore!'

'Poor Mr. Desvœux!' said Felicia; 'how sorry you must be to have finished your march, and be back again at stupid Dustypore!'

'No place is stupid where Mrs. Vernon is,' said

Desvœux, gallantly; 'or rather no place would be, if she were not so often "not at home."'

'That must be,' Felicia said, 'because you call on mail-days, when I am busy with my home despatches.'

The real truth was that Felicia considered Desvœux in need of frequent setting down, and closed her door inhospitably against him, whenever he showed the least inclination to be intimate.

'Well,' said Desvœux, 'the days that you are busy with your despatches and when I have written the Agent's, I do not find it lively, I admit. Come, Mrs. Vernon, the Fotheringhams, for instance—does not the very thought of them leave a sort of damp upon your mind? It makes one shudder.' Then Desvœux passed on to the other officials, upon whom he poured the most vehement contempt.

The Salt Board, he told Maud, always from time immemorial consisted of the three greatest fogies in the Service; that was the traditionary rule; it was only when you were half-idiotic that you could do the work properly. As for Mr. Fotheringham, he was a lucky fellow; his idiocy had developed early and strong.

'That is why Mrs. Vernon detests him so.'

'I don't detest him at all,' said Felicia; 'but I think him rather dull.'

'Yes,' said Desvœux, with fervour; 'as Dr.

Johnson said of some one, he was, no doubt, dull naturally, but he must have taken a great deal of pains to become as dull as he is now. Now, Miss Vernon, would you like to see what the Board is like? First, you must know that I am the Agent's private secretary, and part of my business is to knock his and their heads together and try to get a spark out. That is how I come to know about them. First I will show you how Vernon puts on his air of Under-Secretary and looks at me with a sort of serious, bored, official air, as if he were a bishop and thought I was going to say something impertinent.'

'As I dare say you generally are,' said Felicia, quite prepared to do battle for her husband.

'Well,' said Desvœux, 'this is how he sits and looks—gravity and fatigue personified.'

'Yes,' cried Maud, clapping her hands with pleasure; 'I can exactly fancy him.'

'Then,' continued Desvœux, who was really a good mimic and warming rapidly into the work, 'in comes the Board. First Fotheringham, condescending and serene and wishing us all "Good-morning," as if he were the Pope dispensing a blessing. You know his way—like this? Then here is Cockshaw, looking sagacious, but really pondering over his last night's rubber, and wishing the Board were finished.'

Felicia was forced to burst out laughing at the imitation.

'And now,' cried Maud, 'give us Mr. Blunt.'

Desvœux put on Blunt's square awkward manner and coughed an imprecatory cough.

'Gentlemen,' he said, 'your figures are wrong, your arguments false and your conclusions childish. I don't want to be offensive or personal, and I have the highest possible opinion of your service; but you must allow me to observe that you are all a pack of fools!'

'Capital,' cried Maud; 'and what do you do all the time, Mr. Desvœux?'

'Oh, Vernon and I sit still and wink at each other and hope for the time when we shall have become idiotic enough to be on the Board ourselves. We are of the new *régime*, and are supposed to have wits, and we have a great deal of intelligence to get over. But you know how the old ones were chosen. All the stupidest sons of the stupidest families in England for several generations, like the pedigree-wheat, you know, on the principle of selection; none but the blockheads of course would have anything to do with India.'

'Don't abuse the bridge that carries you over,' Felicia said: 'No treason to India—it has many advantages.'

'Innumerable,' cried Desvœux: 'first, a decent

excuse for separation between husbands and wives who happen to be uncongenial—no other society has anything to compare with it. You quarrel, you know——'

'No, we don't,' said Felicia, 'thank you. Speak for yourself.'

'Well, I quarrel with Mrs. Desvœux, we'll say—though, by the way, I could not quarrel even with my wife—but suppose a quarrel, and we become mutually insupportable: there is no trouble, no scandal, no inconvenience. Mrs. Desvœux's health has long required change of air; I secure a berth for her on the P. & Q., escort her with the utmost politeness to Bombay, have a most affectionate parting, remit once a quarter, write once a fortnight—what can be more perfect?'

'But suppose,' said Maud, 'for the sake of argument, that you don't quarrel and don't want to separate?'

'Or suppose,' said Felicia, who knew that the conversation was taking just the turn she hated, 'that we try our duet, Mr. Desvœux? You know that you are a difficult person to catch.'

'That is one of your unjust speeches,' said Desvœux, dropping his voice as they approached the piano and becoming suddenly serious: 'You know that I come quite as often as I think I have a chance of being welcome.'

Felicia ignored the remark and began playing the accompaniment with the utmost unconcern. The fact was that Desvœux, though not quite such a Don Juan as he liked to be thought, had a large amount of affection to dispose of, and had given Felicia to understand upon twenty occasions that he would like to begin a flirtation with her if he dared.

CHAPTER VII.

THE RUMBLE CHUNDER GRANT.

Monstrum horrendum—informe—ingens——

THERE were many things which a man was expected to know about in official circles at Dustypore, and first and foremost was the 'Rumble Chunder Grant.' Not to know this argued one's self not only unknown but ignorant of the first principles of society and the common basis on which thought and conversation proceeded. It was like not having read Mr. Trollope's novels or knowing nothing about the Tichborne Trial or being in any other way out of tune with the times. One of the things that gave the old civilians such a sense of immeasurable superiority over all outsiders and new-comers was the consciousness that with them rested this priceless secret, this mystery of mysteries.

One inconvenient consequence, however, of everybody being expected to know was, that everybody took for granted that everybody else did know, and that those who did not know veiled their ignorance under a decent mask of familiarity and by talking about it in a vague, shadowy sort of phraseology which conveniently concealed any little inaccuracies. It had to do with salt, moreover, and it was at the Salt Board that the unsearchable depths of the subject were best appreciated and this vagueness of language was most in vogue.

The facts were something of this sort. When the English took the country we found particular families and villages in Rumble Chunder in enjoyment of various rights in connection with salt; some had little monopolies; others might manufacture for themselves at a quit rent, others might quarry for themselves at particular times and places, and so forth.

The Gazette, which announced the annexation of the province, had declared in tones of splendid generosity that the British Government, though inexorable to its foes, would temper justice with mercy so far as to respect existing rights of property and would protect the loyal proprietor in the enjoyment of his own. The sonorous phrases of a rhetorical Viceroy had entailed on his successors a never-ending series of disputes, and had saddled the Empire with an obligation which was all the more burthensome for being undefined. Ever since that unlucky Gazette, officials had been hard at work to find out what it was that the Governor-General had promised to do and how much it would cost to do it. One diligent civilian after another went down to Rumble Chunder and made out a list of people who were or who pretended to be, entitled to interests in salt. Then these lists had been submitted and discussed, and minuted upon, and objected to, and returned for further investigation, and one set of officers had given place to another, and the chance of clearing up the matter had grown fainter every day. Meanwhile the Rumble Chunder people had gone their ways, exercising what rights they could, and happy in the possession of an interminable controversy. In course of time most of the original documents got destroyed in the Mutiny, or eaten by white ants, and a fresh element of uncertainty was introduced by the question of the authenticity of all existing copies. Then there had come a new Secretary of State at home, whose views as to the grantees were diametrically opposed to all his predecessors, and who sent peremptory orders to carry out the new policy with the least possible delay. Thus the subject had gradually got itself into a sort of hopeless tangle, for which Desvœux used to say that the only effectual remedy would be the end of the world. No one knew exactly what his rights were, and every one was afraid of endangering his position by too rigid an inquiry or too bold an assertion.

One peculiarity of this, as of most Indian controversies, was the unnatural bitterness of spirit to which it gave rise. The most amiable officials turned to gall and wormwood at its very mention, and abused each other over it with the vehemence of vexed theologians.

Whether vain attempts to understand it had engendered an artificial spitefulness, or whether discussion, like beer-drinking, is a luxury too strong for natures enfeebled by an Eastern climate, sure enough it was that, directly this wretched question came to the fore, good-nature, moderation and politeness were forgotten, and the antagonists made up for the confusion of their ideas by the violence of the language in which they expressed them.

The last phase of the story was that some of the descendants of the original grantees, thinking the plum was now about ripe for picking, took up the question in a wily, patient, vexatious sort of way, and produced a tremendous lawsuit. Then a Member of Parliament, whose ideas, by some sudden process (on which his banker's book would probably have thrown some light), had been suddenly turned Indiawards, made the most telling speech in the House, depicting in vivid colours the wrongs of the Rumble Chunder people and the satanic ruthlessness of British rule. Then pamphlets began to appear, which showed to demonstration that all the Viceroys had been either liars or thieves, except a few who had been both, and asked how long this Rumble Chunder swindle was to last. The whole subject, in fact, began to be ventilated. Now, ventilation, though a good thing in its time and place, is bad for such veteran institutions as the Salt Board, or controversies as delicate as the Rumble Chunder Grant. Every new ray of daylight let in disclosed an ugly flaw, and the fresh air nearly brought the tottering edifice about the ears of its inhabitants. It needed, as Fotheringham ruefully felt, but the rude, trenchant, uncompromising spirit of a man like Blunt to produce an imbroglio which could neither be endured, concealed, or disposed of in any of the usual methods known to Indian officialdom; and Blunt was known to be hard at work at the statistics, and already to have assumed an attitude of obtrusive hostility. Fotheringham could only fortify himself with the reflection that the Providence which had seen him through a long series of official scrapes would probably not desert him at this last stage of his career. He wished, nevertheless, that he had forestalled Cockshaw in his application for the Carraways.

CHAPTER VIII.

GOLDEN DAYS.

O lovely earth! O lovely sky!
I was in love with nature, I;
And nature was in love with me;
O lovely life—when I was free!

Felicia had been surprised, and not altogether pleased, at the unnecessary cordiality with which Maud had bade their visitor farewell. There was an excitement, an animation, an eagerness in her manner which Felicia had not before perceived, and which she felt at once might be difficult to manage. Desvœux was exactly the person whom she did *not* want Maud to like, and the very possibility of her liking him brought out in Felicia's mind a latent hostility of which, under an exterior of politeness and even familiarity, she was always dimly conscious. She did not mind talking to him herself; she was even amused by him; but then it was always with a kind of protest; she knew exactly how far she meant to go and felt no temptation to go any further. But the notion of him in any other capacity but that of a remote member of society, whose function it was to say and do absurd things in an amusing way, was strange and altogether distasteful. Anything like intimacy was not to be thought of for an instant; the merest approach to close contact would bring out some discord, the jar of which, by a sort of instinctive anticipation, Felicia seemed to feel already. So long as he moved in quite another plane and belonged to a different world, his eccentricities might be smiled at for their comicality without the application of any rigid canon of taste or morals. But a person who was at once irreligious and overdressed, who constantly had to be 'put down' for fear he should become offensive, and who was a stranger to all the little Masonic signals by which ladies and gentlemen can find each other out—the very idea of his presuming to cross the pale, and to form any other tie than those of the most indifferent acquaintance, filled Felicia with the strongest repugnance. It was provoking, therefore, that he seemed to take Maud's fancy and impress her more than any other of the many men with whom she was now becoming acquainted. It was more than provoking that she should let her impressions come so lightly to the surface, and be read in signs which Desvœux's experienced eye would, Felicia knew, have not the least trouble in interpreting.

Suppose—but this was one of the disagreeable suppositions which Felicia's mind put aside at once as too monstrous to be entertained—suppose he should come to stand in the way of the rightful, proper, destined lover? She thrust away the notion as absurd. All the same, it made her uncomfortable, and no doubt justified her to herself in pushing forward Sutton's interests with more eagerness than she might otherwise have thought it right to employ about another person's concerns. When one feels a thing to be *the* thing that ought to happen, and sees it in danger of being frustrated by some thoroughly objectionable interference, it is but natural to do something more than merely wish for a fortunate result. Felicia, at any rate, could boast of no such passivity; and, if praising Sutton would have married him, Felicia's wishes on the subject would have been speedily realised.

The course of love, however, rarely flows exactly in the channels which other people fashion for it, and Maud's inclinations required, her cousin felt, the most judicious handling. There could be no harm, however, in allowing Sutton's visits to go on with their accustomed frequency; and since Maud must forthwith learn to ride and Sutton volunteered to come in the mornings to teach her, no one could blame Felicia if, in the intervals of instruction, the pupil and teacher should become unconsciously proficient in any other art besides that of equitation. Maud used to come in from these rides with such a bright glow on her cheek and in such rapturous spirits, that her cousin might well feel reassured.

Sutton had found for her the most perfect pony, whose silky coat, lean well-chiselled head and generally aristocratic bearing, pronounced it the inheritor of Arab blood. Maud speedily discovered that riding was the most enjoyable of all human occupations. Down by the river's side, or following long woodland paths, where the busy British rule had planted many an acre with the forests of the future, or out across the wide plains of corn stretching for miles, broken only by clumps of palms or villages nestling each in a little grove under the wing of some ancestral peepul-tree, the moon still shining overhead and the sun just above the horizon, still shrouded in the mists of morning—how fresh, how picturesque, how exhilarating everything looked! How pleasant, too, to go through all these pretty scenes with a companion who seemed somehow to know her tastes and wishes, and to have no thought but how to please her! Sutton, though in public a man of few words and unsatisfactorily taciturn on the subject of his own exploits, had, Maud presently discovered, plenty to tell her when they were alone. The power of observation which made him so nice a judge of character extended itself to all the scene about him and revealed a hundred touches of interest or beauty which, to coarser or less careful vision, would have lain obscure. Maud felt that she had never known how beautiful Nature was till Sutton told her.

'There,' he would say, I brought you round this wood that we might not miss that pretty bend of the river, with Humayoun's Tomb and the palms beyond. See what a beautiful blue background the sky makes to the red dome and that nice old bit of crumbling wall. The bright Indian atmospheres have their own beauty, have they not? And see that little wreath of smoke hanging over the village. This is my pet morning landscape.'

'And those peach-groves,' cried Maud, 'all ablaze with blossom, and those delicious shady mulberries and the great stretch of green beyond. It is quite enchanting: a sort of dream of peace.'

'We had a fine gallop across here once,' Sutton said, 'when first we took the Sandy Tracts.' And then Maud learnt that they were riding over a battle-field, and that for a long summer's afternoon men had fought and fallen all along the path where now they stood, and that a battery of artillery had been posted at the very corner of the village to which her guide had brought her. 'I remember when they knocked that hole in the old wall yonder and how all the fellows behind it took to their heels. Then, afterwards we stormed the Tomb and had to finish our fighting by moonlight.'

'Was that when you got your Victoria Cross?' asked Maud, who was possessed by a spirit of insatiable curiosity about Sutton's badges, which he was slow to gratify.

'Oh no,' said Sutton, laughing; 'I got nothing then but a bullet through my shoulder and a knock on the head from a musket-stock which very nearly ended my soldiering then and there. Look now how quickly the scene changes as the sun gets up—half its beauty is gone already! Let us have a good canter over this soft ground and get home before it grows too hot.'

Maud, who had never thought of a battle except as one of the afflicting details that had to be remembered at an historical class, and if possible to be hooked on to its proper site and date, felt a delicious thrill in actually realising with her own eyes the place where one of the troublesome events took place, and in talking to a person who had actually taken part in it. 'And what became of the bullet in your shoulder?' she asked.

'It was a very troublesome bullet,' said Sutton, 'and a great deal harder to dislodge than the people from the Tomb. But I was unlucky when I was a lad and never came out of action without a *souvenir* of some sort or other.'

When Maud got home she asked Felicia about this storming of the Tomb, and learnt that Sutton's account was not as truthful as it might have been. He and half-a-dozen others had, Felicia told her, volunteered for the storming-party, had made a rush for the walls through a shower of bullets; and Sutton and two companions, getting separated from the others, had been left for some seconds to hold their own as best they could against the angry, frightened mob within. No one, perhaps scarcely Sutton himself, knew exactly what had happened. The rest of the party, however, when they made their way in, found him standing at bay over a dead comrade's body, and his antagonists too completely taken aback at his audacity to venture, at any odds, within reach of his sword. In the scuffle which ensued Sutton received the wounds of which Maud had been informed; but his exploits on that day were for ever after quoted by his followers as a proof that there is nothing which a man may not do, if only he have pluck and will enough to do it.

Maud felt all this very impressive and Sutton's society more and more delightful. Her enjoyment of it, however—by this time by no means small—began to be seriously qualified by an anxiety, increasingly present to her mind, as to her fitness for the dignified companionship thus thrust upon her. She felt passionately anxious to please Sutton, and more and more distrustful of her power to do so. He was good, noble, chivalrous, everything that Felicia had said, and how hopelessly above herself! What must he think of one who was, as Miss Goodenough had often told her, a mere congeries of defects? True, he never seemed shocked or annoyed at anything she said, and professed to like the rides as much as she did; but might not this be from mere good-nature, or the charm of novelty, or the wish to oblige Felicia, or any transitory or accidental cause? Terrifying thought, if some day he should find her wanting, and banish her from his regards! Meanwhile, happy, happy mornings, and sweet, bright world, in which such pleasure can be found, even if haunted by a doubt as to whether it is really ours or not!

CHAPTER IX.

THE FIRST BALL.

Il est aimable, car on se sent toujours en danger avec lui.

BEFORE Maud had been many weeks with the Vernons there was a Garrison Ball, and at this it was fated that she should make her first public appearance in Dustypore society. That night was certainly the most eventful and exciting one that she had ever passed. To wake and find one's self famous is no doubt an agreeable sensation; but to put on for the first time in one's life a lovely ball-dress, bright, cloudlike, ambrosial—to be suddenly elevated to a pinnacle to receive the homage of mankind—to exercise a pleasant little capricious tyranny in the selection of partners—to be seized upon by one anxious adorer after another, all striving to please, each with a little flattering tale of his own—to read in a hundred eyes that one is very pretty—to find at last a partner who, from some mysterious reason, is not like other partners, but just perfection—to know that one's views about him are entirely reciprocated—it was, as Maud, on going to bed, acknowledged to herself with a sigh, which was half fatigue and half the utterance of an over-excited temperament, too much enjoyment for a single human soul to carry!

In the first place, Sutton, all ablaze with medals, tall, majestic, impressive, and as Maud had come to think with Felicia, undeniably handsome, had begged her in the morning to keep several dances for him. The prospect of this among other things had put her in a flutter. She would have preferred some of the ensigns. It seemed a sort of alarming familiarity. Could such a being valse and bend, as ordinary mortals do, to the commonplace movements of a mere quadrille? It was one thing to go spinning round with another school-girl, under the superintendence of Madame Millville, to the accompaniment of her husband's violin: but to be taken possession of by a being like Sutton—to have to write his name down for two valses and a set of Lancers—to know that in five minutes one will be whirling about under his guidance—the idea was delightful, but not without a touch of awe! Sutton, however, quieted these alarms by dancing in a rather ponderous and old-fashioned manner, and finally tearing her dress with his spur. Maud had accordingly to be carried off, in order that the damage might be repaired; and—her mind somewhat lightened by the sense of responsibility discharged and the ice satisfactorily broken—looked forward to the rest of the evening with unmingled pleasure. While her torn dress was being set to rights she scanned her card, saw Sutton's name duly registered for his promised dances, and made up her mind, as she compared him with the rest, that there was no one in the room she liked one-half as well.

But then she had not danced with Desvœux; and Desvœux was now waiting at the door and imploring her not to curtail the rapture of a valse, the first notes of which had already sounded. Desvœux's dancing, Maud speedily acknowledged to herself, bore about the same relation to Sutton's that her Arab pony's canter did to the imposing movements of the latter gentleman's first charger. His tongue, too, seemed as nimble as his feet. He was in the highest possible spirits, and the careless, joyous extravagance of his talk struck a sympathetic chord in his companion's nature.

'There!' he cried, as the last notes of the music died away and he brought his companion to a standstill at a comfortable sofa, 'Such a valse as that is a joy for ever—a thing to dream of, is it not? Some ladies, you know, Miss Vernon, dance in epic poems, some in the sternest prose—Carlyle, for instance—some in sweet-flowing, undulating, rippling lyrics: Yours is (what shall I say?) an ode of Shelley's or a song from Tennyson, a smile from Paradise! Where can you have learnt it?'

'Monsieur Millville taught us all at my school,' said Maud, prosaically mindful of the many battles she had had in former days with that gentleman: 'a horrid little wizened Frenchman, with a fiddle. We all hated him. He was always going on at me about my toes.'

'Your toes!' cried Desvœux, with effusion: 'He wanted to adore them, as I do—sweet points where all the concentrated poetry of your being gathers. Put out that fairy little satin shoe and let me adore them too!'

'No, thank you!' cried Maud, greatly taken aback at so unexpected a request, gathering her feet instinctively beneath her; 'it's not the fashion!'

'You will not?' Desvœux said, with a tone of sincere disappointment. 'Is not that unkind? Suppose it was the fashion to cover up your hands in tulle and satin and never to show them?'

'Then,' Maud said, laughing, 'you would not be able to adore them either; as it is, you see, you may worship them as much as you please!'

'I have been worshipping them all the evening. They are lovely—a little pair of sprites.'

'Stop!' cried Maud, 'and let me see. My shoes

are fairies, and my dancing a poem, and my fingers sprites! How very poetical! And, pray, is this the sort of way that people always talk at balls?'

'Not most people,' said Desvœux, unabashed, 'because they are geese and talk in grooves—about the weather and the last appointment and the freshest bit of stale gossip; but it is the way *I* talk, because I only say what I feel and am perfectly natural.'

'Natural!' said Maud, in a tone of some surprise, for her companion's romantic extravagance seemed to her to be the very climax of unreality.

'Yes,' said Desvœux, coolly, 'and that is one reason why all women like me; partly it is for my good looks, of course, and partly for my dancing, but mostly because I am natural and tell the truth to them.'

'And partly, I suppose,' said Maud, who began to think her companion was in great need of setting down, 'because you are so modest?'

'As to that, I am just as modest as my neighbours, only I speak out. One knows when one is good-looking, does one not? and why pretend to be a simpleton? You know, for instance, how very, very pretty you are looking to-night!'

'We were talking about *you*, if you please,' said Maud, blushing scarlet, and conscious of a truth of which her mirror had informed her.

'Agreeable topic,' said the other gaily; 'let us return to it by all means! Well, now, I pique myself on being natural. When I am bored I yawn or go away; when I dislike people I show my teeth and snarl; and when I lose my heart I don't suffer in silence, but inform the fair purloiner of that valuable organ of the theft without hesitation. That is honest, at any rate. For instance, I pressed your hand to-night, when you came in first, to tell you how delighted I was that you were come to be the belle of the party. You did not mind it, you know!'

'I thought you very impertinent,' said Maud, laughing in spite of herself; 'and so I think you now, and very conceited into the bargain. Will you take me to have some tea, please?'

'With all my heart,' said the other; 'but we can go on with our talk. How nice it is that we are such friends, is it not?'

'I did not know that we were friends,' said Maud, 'and I have not even made up my mind if I like you.'

'Hypocrite!' answered her companion; 'you know you took a great fancy to me the first morning I came to call on you, and Mrs. Vernon scolded you for it after my departure.'

'It is not true,' said Maud, with a stammer and a blush, for Desvœux's shot was, unfortunately, near the mark; 'and anyhow, first impressions are generally wrong.'

'Wrong!' cried the other, 'never, never! always infallible. Mrs. Vernon abused me directly I was gone. She always does; it is her one fault, that prevents her from being absolute perfection. She does not like me, and is always putting me down. It is a great shame, because she has been till now the one lady in India whom I really admire. But let us establish ourselves on this nice ottoman, and I will show you some of our celebrities. Look at that handsome couple talking so mysteriously on the sofa: that is General Beau and Mrs. Vereker, and they are talking about nothing more mysterious than the weather; but it is the General's fancy to look mysterious. Do you see how he is shrugging his shoulders? Well, to that shrug he owes everything in life. Whatever happens, he either shrugs his shoulders, or arches his eyebrows, or says "Ah!" Beyond these utterances he never goes; but he knows exactly when to do each, and does it so judiciously that he has become a great man. He is great at nothing, however, but flirtation; and Mrs. Vereker is just now the reigning deity.'

'No wonder,' cried Maud. 'How lovely she is! such beautiful violet eyes!'

'Yes,' said the other, with a most pathetic air,

'most dangerous eyes they are, I assure you. You don't feel it, not being a man, but they go through and through me. She always has a numerous following, especially of boys, and has broken a host of hearts, which is all the more unfair, as she does not happen to possess one of her own.'

'She must have a heart, with those eyes and such a smile,' objected Maud.

'Not the least atom, I assure you,' said the other. 'Nature, in lavishing every other grace and charm upon her, made this single omission, much, no doubt, to the lady's own peace of mind. It is all right in the present instance, because Beau does not happen to have any heart either.'

'I don't believe you in the least,' said Maud, 'and I shall get my cousin to take me to call upon her.'

'You are fascinated, you see, already,' said Desvœux, 'though you are a woman. You will find her a perfect Circe. Her drawing-room is an enchanted cell hung round with votive offerings from former victims. She lives on the gifts of worshippers, and will accept everything, from a sealskin jacket to a pair of gloves. I used to be an adorer once, but I could not afford it. Now I will introduce you.' Thereupon he presented Maud in due form.

General Beau arched his handsome brow, and said, 'Ah! how dy'e do, Miss Vernon?' in his inscrutable way; and Mrs. Vereker, who, as a reigning beauty, felt an especial interest in one who seemed likely to endanger her ascendency, was bent on being polite. She gave Maud the sweetest of smiles, scolded Desvœux with the prettiest little pout for not having been to see her for an age; and, if she felt jealous, was determined, at any rate, not to show it. She observed, however, with the eye of a connoisseur, how Maud's hair was done, and took a mental note of a little mystery of lace and feathers, just then the fashionable head-dress, which she thought would be immensely becoming to herself. She pressed Maud affectionately to come some day to lunch and inwardly resolved to spoil the pretty *ingénue* of her novelty.

Mrs. Vereker was a type of character which Indian life brings into especial prominence and develops into fuller perfection than is to be found in less artificial communities. Herself the child of Indian parents, whom she had scarcely ever seen, with the slenderest possible stock of home associations, accustomed from the outset to have to look out for herself, she had come to India while still almost a child, and in a few months, long before thought or feeling had approached maturity, had found herself the belle of a Station, and presently a bride. Then circumstances separated her frequently from her husband, and she learnt to bear separation heroically. The sweet incense of flattery was for ever rising about her, and she learnt to love it better every day. Any number of men were for ever ready to throw themselves at her feet and proclaim her adorable, and she came to feel it right that they should do so. She found that she could conjure with her eyes and mouth and exercise a little despotism by simply using them as Nature told her. The coldness of her heart enabled her to venture with impunity into dangers where an ardent temperament could scarcely but have gone astray: she, however, was content so long as she lived in a stream of flattery and half-a-dozen men declared themselves heartbroken about her; strict people called her a flirt, but friends and foes alike declared her innocence itself.

Beau was devoting himself to her partly because her good looks gave him a slight sense of gratification, partly because he considered it the proper thing to be seen on confidential terms with the handsomest woman in the room, partly to have the pleasure of holding his own against the younger men.

Desvœux, delighted with his new-found treasure, was only too happy to leave a quondam rival in possession of the field, and to have a decent excuse for abandoning a shrine at which it was no longer convenient to worship.

CHAPTER X.

THE WOES OF A CHAPERON.

The time is out of joint—O cursed spite,
That ever I was born to set it right!

FELICIA came home from the ball in far less high spirits than her *protégée.* Things had not gone as she wished, nor had Maud behaved at all in the manner which Felicia had pictured to herself as natural and appropriate to a young lady making her *début* in polite society. Instead of displaying an interesting timidity and clinging to her chaperon for guidance and protection, Maud had taken wing boldly at once, as in a congenial atmosphere, had been far too excited to be in the least degree shy and had lent herself with indiscreet facility to a very pronounced flirtation. Felicia began to realise how hard it is to make the people about one be what one wants them to be, and how full of disappointment is the task of managing mankind, even though the fraction operated upon be no larger than a wayward school-girl's heart. Maud, whose rapidly-increasing devotion to Sutton had for days past been a theme of secret congratulation in Felicia's thoughts, had been behaving all the evening just in the way which Sutton would, she knew, most dislike, and showing the most transparent liking for the person of whom, of all others, he especially disapproved. Sutton, too, Felicia considered, was not comporting himself at all as she would have had him: he lavished every possible kindness on Maud, but then it was less for Maud's sake than her own; he would have done, she felt an annoying conviction, exactly the same for either of her little girls; and though he agreed with her in thinking Maud decidedly picturesque, and in being amused and interested in the fresh, eager, childlike impulsiveness of her character, his thoughts about her, alas! appeared to go no further.

'Why that profound sigh, Felicia?' her husband asked, when Maud had gone away to bed, leaving the two together for the first time during the evening. 'Does it mean that some one has been boring you or what?'

'It means,' said Felicia, 'that I am very cross and that Mr. Desvœux is a very odious person.'

'And Maud a very silly one, *n'est-ce pas?* Did not I tell you what a deal of trouble our good-nature in having her out would be sure to give us? Never let us do a good-natured act again! I tell you Maud is already a finished coquette and, I believe, would be quite prepared to flirt with me.'

'I am sure I wish she would,' said Felicia in a despairing tone. 'Do you know, George, I do not like these balls at all?'

'Come, come, Felicia, how many valses did you dance to-night?' her husband asked incredulously, for Felicia was an enthusiastic Terpsichorean.

'That has nothing to do with it,' she said. 'All the people should be nice, and so many people are not nice at all. It is too close quarters. There are some men whose very politeness one resents.'

'Courtesy with a touch of traitor in it,' said her husband, 'for instance?'

'For instance, General Beau,' said Felicia. 'He looks up in the pauses of his devotions to Mrs. Vereker and turns his eyes upon one as if to say, "Poor victim! your turn will be the next."'

'I saw you playing "Lady Disdain" to him with great success to-night,' her husband answered. And indeed it must be confessed that Beau's advances to Felicia, with whom he was always anxious to stand well, were received by that lady with a slightly contemptuous dignity, very unlike her usual joyous cordiality.

'Yes,' said Felicia; 'General Beau's compliments are more than I can stand. But, George, what can I do with Maud? Is not Mr. Desvoeux insufferable?'

'Well,' said her husband, 'if a man's ambition is to be thought a *mauvais sujet*, and to dress like a shopboy *endimanché*, it does not hurt us.'

'But it may hurt Maud,' said Felicia, 'if, indeed, it has not hurt her already. Oh dear, how I wish she was safely married!'

From the above conversation it may be inferred that the responsibilities of her new charge were beginning to weigh upon Felicia's spirits. Sutton too slow, and Desvœux too prompt, and Maud's fickle fancies inclining now this way, now that—what benevolent custodian of other people's happiness had ever more harassing task upon her hands?

It is probable, however, that had Felicia's insight or experience been greater, the position of affairs would have seemed less fraught with anxiety. Maud's liking for Desvœux was a sentiment of the lightest possible texture; its very lightness was, perhaps, its charm. With him she was completely at her ease and experienced the high spirits which being at one's ease engenders. She was certain of pleasing him, but careless whether she did so or not. His extravagant protestations amused her and were flattering in a pleasant sort of way, and his high spirits made him an excellent companion; but nothing about him touched her with the keen deep interest that every word or look of Sutton's inspired, or with the same strong anxiety to retain his friendship. Desvœux might come and go, and Maud would have treated either event with the same indifference; but if Sutton should ever begin to neglect her, she was already conscious of a sort of pang which the very idea inflicted.

Upon the whole it is probable that Felicia's apprehensions were groundless. Not the less, however, did she feel disconcerted and aggrieved when the very next morning after the ball Desvœux made his appearance, in the highest possible spirits, evidently on the best terms with Maud and politely ignoring all Felicia's attempts to put him down. He was, as it seemed to her, in his very most objectionable mood, and she felt glad that, at any rate, her husband was at home and that she was not left to do battle by herself. She resolved to be as unconciliatory as possible. As for Maud it never occurred to her to conceal the pleasure which Desvœux's arrival gave her, and she soon let out the secret that his visit had been prearranged.

'I did not think that you really would come, Mr. Desvœux; it is so nice of you, because we are both of us far too tired to do anything but be idle, and you can amuse us.'

'You forget, Maud,' said Vernon, 'that Desvœux may be too tired to be amusing.'

'And I,' said Felicia, with a slight shade of contempt in her tones, 'am too tired even to be amused. I feel that Mr. Desvœux's witticisms would only fatigue me. I intend to give up balls.'

'Then,' said Desvœux, with an air of admiring deference which Felicia felt especially irritating, 'balls will have to give up me. I should not think it in the least worth while to be a steward and to do all the horrid things one has to do—polish the floor and audit the accounts and dance official quadrilles with Mrs. Blunt—if our chief patroness chose to patronise no more. A ball without Mrs. Vernon would be a May morning without the sunshine.'

'Or a moonlight night without the moon,' said Felicia: 'Allow me to help you to a simile.'

'You see he *is* tired,' said Vernon, 'poor fellow, and for the first time in his life in need of a pretty phrase.'

'Not at all,' said Desvœux, with imperturbable goodnature; 'I am constantly at a loss, like the rest of the world, for words to tell Mrs. Vernon how much we all admire her. It is only fair that the person who inspires the sentiment should assist us to express it.'

'But,' cried Maud, 'you are forgetting poor me.

Who is to take care of me, if you please, in the balls of the future?'

'Yes, Felicia,' said Vernon, 'you cannot abdicate just yet, I fear. As for me, I feel already far too old.'

'Then,' cried Desvœux, 'you must look at General Beau and learn that youth is eternal. How nice it is to see him adoring Mrs. Vereker, and to remember that we, too, may be adored some thirty years to come!'

'Beau's manner is very compromising," said Vernon; 'it is a curious trick. His first object, when he likes a lady, is to endanger her reputation.'

'Yes,' answered Desvœux, 'he leads her with a serious air to a sofa or hides himself with her in a balcony; looks gravely into her eyes and says, "How hot it has been this afternoon!" or something equally interesting; and all the world thinks that he is asking her to elope at least.'

'His manners appear to me to be insufferable,' Felicia said, in her loftiest style; 'just the sort of familiarity that breeds contempt.'

'Poor fellow!' said Desvœux, who knew perfectly that Felicia's observations were half-intended for himself, 'it is all his enthusiasm. He is as proud of every fresh flirtation as if it were a new experience—like a young hen that has just laid its first egg. He always seems to me to be chuckling and crowing to the universe, "Behold! heaven and earth! I have hatched another scandal." Now,' he added, 'Miss Vernon, if ever you and I had a flirtation we should not wish all the world to "assist," as the French people say, should we? People might suspect our devotion, and guess and gossip; but there would not be this revolting matter-of-fact publicity; and we should be for ever putting people off the scent: I should still look into the Misses Blunt's eyes, still dance a state quadrille with their mamma, still talk to Mrs. Vereker about the stars, still feel the poetry of Miss Fotheringham's new Paris dresses: you would continue to fascinate mankind at large; only we two between ourselves should know how mutually broken-hearted we had become.'

'That is a contingency,' Felicia said, in a manner which Desvœux understood as a command to abandon the topic, which, happily, there is no need to discuss.' The conversation turned to something else; but Felicia made up her mind more than ever that their visitor was a very impertinent fellow, and more than ever resolved to guard Maud's heart from every form of attack which he could bring to bear against it. No protection could, she felt, be half so satisfactory as the counter-attraction of a lover who would be everything that Desvœux was not, and whom all the world acknowledged to be alike *sans peur* and *sans reproche.*

CHAPTER XI.

FRIENDS IN COUNCIL.

After short silence then,
And summons sent, the great debate began.

A BODY constituted of as discordant elements as the three members of the Salt Board was not likely to remain very long at peace with itself; and for weeks past, Blunt's increasing truculence of deportment had warned his colleagues of an approaching outbreak.

Since his successful raid upon the Board's accounts this gentleman had made the lives of Fotheringham and Cockshaw a burden to them. His insatiable curiosity plunged in the most ruthless manner into matters which the others knew instinctively would not bear investigation. He proposed reforms in an offhand manner which made poor Fotheringham's hair stand on end; and the very perusal of his memoranda was more than Cockshaw's industry could achieve. He had a sturdy cob on which he used to ride about in the mornings, acquiring health and strength to be disagreeable the entire day, and devising schemes of revolution as he went. Poor Cockshaw's application for the Carraways had been refused; General Beau had got the appointment and was actually in course of a series of valedictory visits to various ladies whom he believed broken-hearted at his departure. Fotheringham grew greyer and sadder day by day and prepared himself as best he might to meet the blows of fate in an attitude of dignified martyrdom. Matters at last reached a crisis in a proposal of Blunt's, brought out in his usual uncompromising fashion and thrust upon the Board, as Fotheringham acknowledged with a shudder, with a horrid point-blank directness which rendered evasion and suppression (the only two modes of dealing with questions which his experience had taught him) alike impossible. In the first place Blunt demonstrated by statistics that not enough salt was produced at the Rumble Chunder quarries to enable the inhabitants to get enough to keep them healthy. Nothing could be more convincing than his figures: so many millions of people—so many thousands of tons of salt—so much salt necessary per annum for each individual, and so forth. Then Blunt went on to show that the classes of diseases prevalent in the Sandy Tracts were precisely those which want of salt produces; then he demonstrated that there was wholesale smuggling.

From all this it followed obviously that the great thing wanted was to buy up existing interests, develop the quarries, improve the roads, and increase the production. If this were done salt might be sold at a rate which would bring it within the reach of all classes, and yet the gains of Government would be increased. This was Blunt's view. The opposite party urged that to vary the salt-supply would interfere with the laws of political economy, would derange the natural interaction of supply and demand (this was one of Fotheringham's favourite phrases), would depress internal trade, paralyse existing industries, cause all sorts of unlooked-for results and not benefit the consumer a whit; and that, even if it would, ready money was not to be had at any price. Blunt, however, was not to be put off with generalities and claimed to record his opinions, that his colleagues should record theirs, and that the whole matter should be submitted to the Agent. Cockshaw gave a suppressed groan, lit a cheroot, and mentally resolved that nothing should tempt *him* into writing a memorandum, or, if possible, into allowing anybody else to do so. 'For God's sake,' he said, 'don't let us begin minuting upon it; if the matter must go to Empson, let us ask him to attend the Board, and have it out once for all.' Now Mr. Empson was at this time Agent at Dustypore. The custom was that he came to the Board only on very solemn occasions, and only when the division of opinion was hopeless; then he sat as Chairman and his casting-vote decided the fortunes of the day.

The next Board day, accordingly, Empson appeared, and it soon became evident that Blunt was to have his vote.

Fotheringham was calm, passive, and behaved throughout with the air of a man who thought it due to his colleagues to go patiently through with the discussion, but whose mind was thoroughly made up. The fight soon waxed vehement.

'Look,' said Blunt, 'at the case of cotton in the Kutchpurwanee District.'

'Really,' said Fotheringham, 'I fail to see the analogy between cotton and salt.' This was one of Fotheringham's stupid remarks, which exasperated both Empson and Blunt and made them flash looks of intelligence across the table at each other.

'Then,' Blunt said with emphasis, 'I'll explain the analogy. Cotton was twopence-halfpenny per pound and hard to get at that. What did we do? We laid out ten lakhs in irrigation, another five lakhs in roads, a vast deal more in introducing European machinery and supervision; raised the whole sum by an average rate on cotton cultivation —and what is the result? Why, last year the outcome was more than double what it was before, and the price a halfpenny a pound lower at least.'

'And what does that prove?' asked Fotheringham, who never could be made to see anything that he chose not to see; 'As I said before, where is the analogy?' Blunt gave a cough which meant that he was uttering execrations internally, and took a large pinch of snuff. Fotheringham looked round with the satisfied air of a man who had given a clencher to his argument, and whose opponents could not with decency profess any longer to be unconvinced.

'I am against it,' said Cockshaw, 'because I am against everything. We are over-governing the country. The one thing that India wants is to be let alone. We should take a leaf out of the books of our predecessors—collect our revenue, as small an one as possible, shun all changes like the devil —and let the people be.'

'That is out of the question,' said Empson, whom thirty years of officialdom had still left an enthusiast at heart; '"Rest for India" is the worst of all the false cries which beset and bewilder us; it means, for one thing, a famine every ten years at least; and famines, you know, mean death to them and insolvency to us.'

'Of course,' said Fotheringham, sententiously, with the grand air of Æolus soothing the discordant winds; 'when Cockshaw said he was against everything, he did not mean any indifference to the country. But we are running up terrible bills; you know, Empson, we got an awful snubbing from home about our deficit last year.'

'Well, but now about the Salt,' put in Blunt, whose task seemed to be to keep everybody to the point in hand; 'this is no question of deficit. I say it will pay, and the Government of India will lend us the money fast enough if they can be made to think so too.'

'Well,' said Cockshaw, stubbornly lighting another cheroot, and getting out his words between rapid puffs of smoke, 'it won't pay, you'll see, and Government will think as I do.'

'Then,' replied Blunt, 'you will excuse me for saying Government will think wrong, and you will have helped them. Have you examined the figures?'

'Yes,' said Cockshaw, with provoking placidity, 'and I think them, like all other statistics, completely fallacious. You have not been out here, Blunt, as long as we have.'

'No; but the laws of arithmetic are the same, whether I am here or not.'

'Well,' observed Fotheringham, 'I really do not see—forgive me, pray, for saying it—but, as senior member, I may perhaps be allowed the observation

—I really do not see how Blunt can pretend to know anything about our Salt.'

'There is one thing I know about it,' said Blunt to Empson as they drove home together from the Board; 'whatever it is, it is not Attic!'

While thus the battle raged within, Desvœux, who had come with the Agent to the Board, took an afternoon's holiday, and found himself, by one of those lucky accidents with which Fortune favours every flirtation, in Mrs. Vereker's drawing-room, where Maud had just arrived to have luncheon and to spend the afternoon.

Now Mrs. Vereker was a beauty, and, as a beauty should, kept a little court of her own in Dustypore, which in its own way was quite as distinct an authority as the Salt Board or the Agency itself. Her claims to sovereignty were considerable. She had the figure of a sylph, hair golden and profuse and real. She had lovely, liquid, purple eyes, into which whoever was rash enough to look was lost forthwith; and a smile—but as to this the position of the present chronicler, as a married man and the father of a family, renders it impossible for him to describe it as it deserved. Suffice it to say that, even in a faded photograph, it has occasioned the partner of his bosom the acutest pangs, and it would be bad taste and inexpedient to say more than that gentlemen considered it bewitching, while many married ladies condemned it as an unmeaning simper of a very silly woman.

Mrs. Vereker affected to be greatly surprised at Desvœux's arrival, and even to hesitate about letting him in; but the slight constraint of her manner, and the flush that tinged her cheek, suggested the suspicion that the call was not altogether fortuitous.

'How provoking,' she said, when Desvœux made his appearance, 'that you should just come this morning to spoil our *tête-à-tête!* Don't you find, Miss Vernon, that whatever one does in life, there is invariably a man *de trop?*'

'No,' cried Desvœux gaily; 'Providence has kindly sent me to rescue you both from a dull morning. Ladies have often told me that under such circumstances it is quite a relief to have a man come in to break the even flow of feminine gossip. Come, now, Miss Vernon, were you not pleased to see my carriage come up the drive?'

'No, indeed,' said Maud; 'nothing could be more *mal à propos.* Mrs. Vereker was just going to show me a lovely new Paris bonnet, and now, you see, we must wait till you are gone!'

'Then, indeed, you would hate me,' answered Desvœux; 'but happily there is no necessity for hat, as I happen to be a connoisseur in bonnets, and Mrs. Vereker would not be quite happy in wearing one till I had given my approval. She will go away now, you will see, and put it on for us to look at.'

'Is not he conceited?' said Mrs. Vereker, raining the influence of a bewitching smile upon her guests, and summoning, as she could at pleasure, the most ingenuous of blushes to her cheeks; 'he thinks he is quite a first-rate judge of everything.'

'Not of *everything*,' said the other, 'but of some things—Mrs. Vereker's good looks, for instance—yes, from long and admiring contemplation of the subject! It would be hard indeed if one could not have an opinion about what has given one so much pleasure, and, alas! so much suffering!'

Desvœux said this with the most sentimental air, and Mrs. Vereker seemed to take it quite as a matter of course.

'Poor fellow!' she said; 'well, perhaps I will show you the bonnet after all, just to console you; am I not kind?'

'You know,' said Desvœux, 'that you are dying to put it on. Pray defer your and our delectation no longer!'

'Rude and disagreeable person!' cried the other. 'Suppose, Miss Vernon, we go off and look at it by ourselves and have a good long chat, leaving him alone here to cultivate politeness?'

'Yes,' cried Maud, 'let us. Here, Mr. Desvœux,

is a very interesting report on something—Education—no, Irrigation—with nice tables and plenty of figures. That will amuse you till we come back.'

'At any rate, don't turn a poor fellow out into such a hurricane as this,' said Desvœux, going to the window and looking into the garden, where by this time a sand-storm was raging and all the atmosphere thick and murky with great swirls of dust. 'I should spoil my complexion and my gloves, and very likely be choked into the bargain.'

'But it was just as bad when you came, and you did not mind it.'

'Hope irradiated the horizon,' cried Desvœux; 'but it was horrible. I have a perfect horror of sand—like the people in "Alice," you know—

They wept like anything to see
  Such quantities of sand.
"If this were only cleared away,"
  They said, "it would be grand."
"If seven maids with seven mops
  Swept it for half a year,
Do you suppose," the Walrus said,
  "That they could get it clear?"
"I doubt it," said the Carpenter,
  And shed a bitter tear.

And I shall shed a bitter tear if you send me away. At any rate, let me stay to lunch, please, and have my horses sent round to the stable.'

'Shall we let him?' cried Mrs. Vereker teasingly. 'Well, if you do, you will have nothing but poached eggs and bottled beer. There is a little pudding, but only just big enough for Miss Vernon and me.'

'I will give him a bit of mine,' said Maud. 'I vote that we let him stay, if he promises not to be impertinent.'

'And I will show him my bonnet,' cried the other, whose impatience to display her new finery was rapidly making way. 'It is just as well to see how things strike men, you know, and my *caro sposo*, among his thousand virtues, happens to be a perfect ignoramus on the point of dress. He knows and cares nothing about all my loveliest things.'

'Except,' said Desvœux, 'how much they cost. Well, there is a practical side which somebody must know about, I suppose, and a husband is just the person; but it is highly inartistic.'

'How did you know that I was here?' Maud asked, when Mrs. Vereker had left the room. 'And why are you not at the Agency doing your lessons?'

'Because we have an aviary of little birds at the Agency,' answered Desvœux, his manner instantly becoming several shades quieter and more affectionate, 'and one of them came and sung me a tune this morning, and told me to go and take a holiday and meet the person I like the best in the world.'

'Now,' said Mrs. Vereker, gleefully re-entering the room, with a cluster of lace and flowers artistically poised upon her shapely little head, 'is not that a duck, and don't I look adorable?'

'Quite a work of art,' cried Desvœux, with enthusiasm. 'Siren! why, already too dangerously fair, why deck yourself with fresh allurements for the fascination of a broken-hearted world? I am convinced Saint Simon Stylites would have come down from his pillar on the spot if he could but have seen it!'

'And confessed himself a gone coon from a moral point of view,' laughed Mrs. Vereker, despoiling herself of the work of art in question. 'And now let us have some lunch; and mind, Mr. Desvœux, you can only have a very little, because, you see, we did not expect you.'

Afterwards, when it was time for Maud to go, it was discovered that no carriage had arrived to take her home. 'What can I do?' she said, in despair. 'Felicia will be waiting to take me to the Camp. George. promised to send back his office-carriage here the moment he got to the Board.'

'Then,' said Desvœux, with great presence of mind, 'he has obviously forgotten it, and I will drive you home. Let me order my horses; they are quite steady.'

Maud looked at Mrs. Vereker—she felt a burning wish to go, and needed but the faintest encouragement. Felicia would, she knew, be not well pleased; but then it was George's fault that she was unprovided for, and it seemed hardly good-natured to reject so easy an escape from the embarrassment which his carelessness had produced.

'I would come and sit in the back seat, to make it proper,' cried Mrs. Vereker, 'but that I am afraid of the sun. I tell you what: I will drive, and you can sit in the back seat, Mr. Desvœux; that will do capitally.'

'Thank you,' said Desvœux, with the most melancholy attempt at politeness and his face sinking to zero.

'Indeed, that is impossible!' cried Maud. 'I know you want to stay at home. I will go with Mr. Desvœux.' And go accordingly they did, and on the way home Desvœux became, as was but natural, increasingly confidential. 'This is my carriage,' he explained, 'for driving married ladies in: you see there is a seat behind—very far behind

—and well railed off, to put the husbands in and keep them in their proper place—quite in the background. It is so disagreeable when they lean over and try to join in the conversation; and people never know when they are *de trop*.'

'Ah, but,' said Maud, 'I don't like driving with you alone. I hear you are a very terrible person. People give you a very bad character.'

'I know,' answered her companion; 'girls are always jilting me and treating me horribly badly, and then they say that it is all my fault. I dare say they have been telling you about Miss Fotheringham's affair,.and making me out a monster; but it was she that was alone to blame.'

'Indeed,' said Maud, 'I heard that it made her very ill, and she had to be sent to England, to be kept out of a consumption.'

'This was how it was,' said Desvœux; 'I adored her—quite adored her; I thought her an angel, and I think her one still, but with one defect—a sort of frantic jealousy, quite a mania. Well, I had a friend—it happened to be a lady—for whom I had all the feelings of a brother. We had corresponded for years. I had sent her innumerable notes, letters, flowers, presents, you know. I had a few things that she had given me—a note or two, a glove, a flower, a photograph, perhaps—just the sort of thing, you know, that one sends——'

'To one's brother,' put in Maud. 'Yes; I know exactly.'

'Yes,' said Desvœux, in the most injured tone, 'and I used to lend her my ponies, and, when she wanted me, to drive her. And what do you think that Miss Fotheringham was cruel, wild enough to ask? To give back all my little mementoes, to write no more notes, have no more drives; in fact, discard my oldest, dearest friend!—I told her, of course, that it was impossible, impossible!' Desvœux cried, getting quite excited over his wrongs: '"Cruel girl," I said, "am I to seal my devotion to you by an infidelity to the kindest, tenderest, sweetest of beings?" Thereupon Miss Fotheringham became quite unreasonable, went into hysterics, sent me back a most lovely locket which I had sent her only that morning; and Fotheringham *père* wrote me the most odious note, in his worst style, declaring that I was trifling! Trifling, indeed! and to ask me to give up my——'

'Your sister!' cried Maud; 'it was hard indeed! Well, here we are at home. Let me jump down quick and go in and get my scolding.'

'And I,' said Desvœux, 'will go to the Agency and get mine.'

Stolen waters are sweet, however; and it is to be feared that these two young people enjoyed their *tête-à-tête* none the less for the consideration that their elders would have prevented it if they had had the chance.

CHAPTER XII.

A CHAPTER OF DISCLOSURES.

For his thoughts,
Would they were blank sooner than filled with me!

MAUD did not exactly get a scolding, but Felicia looked extremely grave. Maud's high spirits were gone in an instant; the excitement which had enabled her to defy propriety hitherto deserted her at the door; the recklessness with which Desvœux always infected her had driven away with him in his mail-phaeton, and left her merely with the disagreeable consciousness of having acted foolishly and wrongly. Felicia knew exactly how matters stood and scarcely said a word. Her silence however was, Maud felt, the bitterest reproach.

'Scold me, scold me, dear,' she cried, the tears starting to her eyes; 'only don't look like that and say nothing!'

'Well,' said Felicia, 'first promise me never again to drive alone with Mr. Desvœux.'

'After all,' suggested Maud, 'it is a mere matter of appearances, and what do they signify?'

'Some matters of appearance,' said Felicia, 'signify very much. Besides, this is something more than that. It is bad enough for you to be *seen* with him—what I really care about is your *being* with him at all.'

'But,' said Maud, 'he is really very nice: he amuses me so much!'

'Yes,' answered the other, 'he amuses one, but then it always hurts. His fun has a something, I don't know what it is, but which is only just not offensive; and I don't trust him a bit.'

'But,' Maud argued, 'he is great friends with George, is he not?'

'Not great friends,' said Felicia; 'they were at college together, and have worked in the same office for years, and are intimate like schoolboys, and George never says an unkind word of any one; but I do not call them friends at all.'

'No?' said Maud, quite unconvinced, and feeling vexed at Felicia's evident dislike for her companion. 'Well, he's a great friend of mine, so don't abuse him, please.'

'Nonsense, child!' cried Felicia, in a fright. 'You don't know him in the least, or you would not say that. To begin with, he is not quite a gentleman, you know.'

'Not a gentleman!' cried Maud, aghast, 'he seems to me a very fine one.'

'As fine as you please,' said Felicia, 'but not a thorough gentleman. Gentlemen never say things that hurt you or offend your taste. Now with Mr. Desvœux I feel for ever in a fright lest he should say something I dislike; and I know he *thinks* things that I dislike.'

'I think you are prejudiced, Felicia. What he says seems to me all very nice.'

'Perhaps it is prejudice,' Felicia answered, 'but I think it all the same. I feel the difference with other people; Major Sutton, for instance.'

'He is your ideal, is he not?' cried Maud, blushing and laughing, for somehow she was beginning to feel that Felicia had designs upon her.

'Yes,' Felicia said in her fervent way; 'he is pure and true and chivalrous to the core: he seems to me made of quite other stuff from men like Mr. Desvœux.'

'He is all made of solid gold,' cried Maud, by this time in a teasing mood, 'and Mr. Desvœux is plaster-of-Paris and putty and pinchbeck, and everything that is horrid. But he is very amusing, dearest Felicia, all the same, *and very nice.* I will not drive with him any more, of course, if you do not like it.'

Thereupon Maud, in a somewhat rebellious frame of mind, was about to go and take her things off, and was already half-way through the doorway when she turned round and saw Felicia's sweet, serene, refined brow wearing a look of harassment and annoyance, and a sudden pang of remorse struck her that she should, in pure mischief, have been wounding a tender heart and endangering a friendship, compared with which she felt everything else in the world was but a straw in the balance. She rushed back and flung her arms round her companion's neck. 'Dearest Felicia,' she said, 'you know that I would fly to the moon rather than do anything you did not like or make you love me the tiniest atom less. I want to tell you something. You think, I know, that I am falling in love with Mr. Desvœux. Well, dear, I don't care for him *that!*'

Thereupon Maud clapped two remarkably pretty hands together in a manner highly expressive of the most lighthearted indifference, and Felicia felt that at any rate he might console herself with the reflection that Maud was as yet quite heart-whole, and that, so far as Desvœux was concerned, Sutton's prospects were not endangered. The certainty, however, that Desvœux had selected Maud for his next flirtation, and that she felt no especial repugnance to the selection, made Felicia doubly anxious that her chosen hero should succeed, and her *protégé* be put beyond the reach of danger as soon as possible. But then Sutton proved provokingly unamenable to Felicia's kind designs upon him.

His continued bachelorhood was a mystery of which not even she possessed the key. It was not insensibility, for every word, look, and gesture bespoke him more than ordinarily alive to all the charms which sway mankind. It certainly was not that either the wish or the power to please were wanting; nobody was more courteous at heart, or more prompt to show it, or more universally popular: nor could it be want of opportunity; for, though he had been all his life fighting, marching, hurrying on busy missions from one wild outpost to another, on guard for months together at some dangerous spot where treachery or fanaticism rendered an explosion imminent; yet the busiest military life has its intervals of quiet, and the love-making of soldiers is proverbially expeditious. Was it, then, some old romance, some far-off English recollection, some face that had fascinated his boyhood, and forbade him, when a man, to think any other altogether lovely? Could the locket, which formed the single ornament where all else was of Spartan simplicity, have told a tale of one of those catastrophes where love and hope and happiness get swamped in hopeless shipwreck? Was it that, absolutely unknown to both parties, his relations to Felicia filled too large a place in his heart for any other devotion to find room there? Was it that a widow sister who had been left with a tribe of profitless boys upon her hands, and to whom a remittance of Sutton's pay went every month, had made him think of marriage as an unattainable luxury?

Sutton, at any rate, remained without a wife, and showed no symptom of anxiety to find one. To those venturesome friends who were sufficiently familiar to rally him on the subject he replied, cheerfully enough, that his regiment was his wife and that such a turbulent existence as his would make any other sort of spouse a most inconvenient appendage. Ladies, experienced in the arts of fascination, knew instinctively that he was unassailable, and even the most intrepid and successful gave up the thoughts of conquest in despair. To be a sort of privileged brother to Felicia—to be the children's especial patron and ally—to sit chatting with Vernon far into the night with all the pleasant intimacy of family relationship, seemed to be all the domestic pleasures of which he stood in need. 'As well,' Felicia sighed, 'might some poor maiden waste her love upon the cold front of a marble Jove.'

Such was the man upon whom Felicia had essayed her first attempt at match-making; and such the man, too, whom Maud, though she had buried the secret deep in the recesses of her heart—far even out of her own sight—had already begun to love with all the passionate violence of a first attachment.

CHAPTER XIII.

DESVŒUX MAKES THE RUNNING.

Free love, free field—we love but while we may:
The woods are hushed, their music is no more;
The leaf is dead, the yearning past away,
New leaf, new life—the days of frost are o'er.
New life, new love, to suit the newer day:
New loves are sweet as those that went before,
Free love, free field—we love but while we may.

FELICIA was beginning to find Maud a serious charge, and to be weighed down in spirit by the responsibility involved in her protection. It would have been easy enough to tell her not to flirt; but it was when Maud was unconscious and self-forgetful that she fascinated the most; and how warn her against the exercise of attractions of which she never thought and the existence of which would have been a surprise to her? When, on the lawn, Maud's hat blew off and all her wealth of soft brown hair tumbled about her shoulders in picturesque disarray, and she stood, bright and eager and careless of the disaster, thinking only of the fortunes of the game, but beautiful, as every creature who came near her seemed to feel—when she was merriest in the midst of merry talk, and made some saucy speech and then blushed scarlet at her own audacity—when her intensity of enjoyment in things around her bespoke itself in every look and gesture —when the pleasure she gave seemed to infect her being and she charmed others because she was herself in love with life, how warn her against all this? You might as well have preached to an April shower!

Desvœux, too, was not a lover likely to be easily discouraged or to let the grass grow beneath his feet. Both from temperament and policy he pressed upon a position where advantages seemed likely to be gained. Despite the very coolest welcomes Felicia began to find him an inconveniently frequent visitor. An avowed foe to croquet, he appeared with provoking regularity at her Thursday afternoons, when the Dustypore world was collected to enjoy that innocent recreation on the lawn, and somehow he always contrived to be playing in Maud's game. Even at church he put in an unexpected appearance, and sate through a discourse of three-quarters of an hour with a patience that was almost ostentatiously hypocritical. Then he would come and be so bright, natural and amusing, and such good company, that Felicia was frequently not near as chilling to him as she wished and as she felt that the occasion demanded. He was unlike anybody that Maud had ever met before. He seemed to take for granted that all existing institutions and customs were radically wrong and that everybody knew it. 'Make love to married women? Of course; why not—what are pretty married women for? Hard upon the husbands? Not a bit; all the unfairness was the other way: the husbands have such tremendous advantages, that it is quite disheartening to fight against such odds: tradition and convention and the natural feminine conservatism all in favour of the husbands; and then the Churchmen, as they always do, taking their part too: it was so mean! No, no; if the husbands cannot take care of themselves they deserve the worst that can befall them.' Or he would say, 'Go to church! Thank you, if Miss Vernon sings in the choir and will say "How d'ye do?" to me as she comes out, I will go and welcome; but otherwise, *ça m'embête*, as the Frenchman said. I always was a fidget, Miss Vernon, and feel the most burning desire to chatter directly any one tells me to hold my tongue; and then I'm argumentative and hate all the speaking being on one side; and then—and then,—well, on the whole, I rather agree with a friend of mine, who said that he had only three reasons for not going to church—he disbelieved the history, disapproved the morality and disliked the art.'

Maud used to laugh at these speeches; and though she did not like them nor the man who made them, and understood what Felicia meant by saying that Desvœux's fun had about it something which hurt one, it seemed quite natural to laugh at them. She observed too, before long, that they were seldom made when Felicia was by, and that Desvœux, if in higher spirits at Mrs. Vereker's than at the Vernons' house, was also several shades less circumspect in what he said, and divulged tastes and opinions which were concealed before her cousin. More than once, as Felicia came up Desvœux had adroitly turned the conversation from some topic which he knew she would dislike; and Maud, who was guilelessness itself, had betrayed by flushing cheeks and embarrassed manner the fact of something having been concealed.

On the whole, Felicia had never found the world harder to manage or the little empire of her drawing-room less amenable to her sway. Her guests somehow would not be what she wished. Desvœux, though behaving with marked deference to her wishes and always sedulously polite, pleased her less and less, Maud's innocence and impulsiveness, however attractive, frequently produced embarrassments which it required all Felicia's tact to overcome. Her husband, laconic and indolent, gave not the slightest help. Another ground on which she distressed herself (very unnecessarily, could she only have known) was, that Sutton, among other performers on Felicia's little stage, played not at all the brilliant part which she had mentally assigned him. The slightly contemptuous dislike for Desvœux which Felicia had often heard him express, and in which she greatly sympathised, though veiled under a rigid courtesy, was yet incompatible with cordiality, or good cheer; and Desvœux, whose high spirits nothing could put down, often appeared the pleasanter companion of the two. Sutton, in fact, had on more occasions than one come into collision with Desvœux in a manner which a less easy-going and light-hearted man would have found it difficult to forgive. Once, at mess, on a Guest-night, Desvœux had rattled out some offensive nonsense about women, and Sutton had got up and, pushing his chair back unceremoniously, had marched silently away to the billiard-room in a manner which in him, the most chivalrous of hosts, implied a more than ordinarily vehement condemnation. Afterwards Desvœux had been given to understand that, if he came to the mess, he must not, in the Major's presence at any rate, outrage good taste and good morals by any such displays. Then, at another time, there was a pretty young woman—a sergeant's wife—to whom Desvœux showed an inclination to be polite. Sutton had told Desvœux that it must not be, in a quietly decisive way which he felt there was no disputing, though there was something in the other's authoritative air which was extremely galling. He could not be impertinent to Sutton, and he bore him no deep resentment; but he revenged himself by affecting to regard him as the ordinary 'plunger' of the period—necessary for purposes of defence and a first-rate leader of native cavalry, but socially dull, and a fair object for an occasional irreverence. Sutton's tendency was to be more silent than usual when Desvœux was of the party. Desvœux, on the other hand, would not have let Sutton's or the prophet Jeremiah's presence act as a damper on spirits which were always at boiling-point and a temperament which was for ever effervescing into some more or less indiscreet form of mirth. The result was that the one man quite eclipsed the other and tossed the ball of talk about with an ease and dexterity not always quite respectful to his less agile senior. One night, for instance, Maud, in a sudden freak of fancy, had set her heart upon a round of story-telling. 'I shall come last of course,' she said, 'as I propose it, and by that time it will be bedtime; but, Major Sutton, you must tell us something about some of your battles, please, something very romantic and exciting.'

Sutton was the victim of a morbid modesty as to

all his soldiering exploits and would far rather have fought a battle than described it. 'Ah,' he said, 'but our fighting out here is not at all romantic; it is mostly routine, you know, and not picturesque or amusing.'

'Yes, but,' said Maud, 'tell us something that *is* picturesque or amusing: a hairbreadth escape, or a forlorn hope, or a mine. I love accounts of mines. You dig and dig for weeks, you know, and then you're countermined and hear the enemy digging near you; and then you put the powder in and light the match, and run away, and then—now you go on!'

'And then there is a smash, I suppose,' laughed Sutton; 'but you know all about it better than I. I'm not a gunner—all my work is above-ground.'

'Well, then,' cried Maud, with the eager air of a child longing for a story, 'tell us something above ground. How did you get your Victoria Cross, now?'

Maud, however, was not destined to get a story out of Sutton.

'There was nothing romantic about *that*, at any rate,' he said. 'It was at Mirabad. There was a cannon down at the end of the lane which was likely to be troublesome, and some of our fellows went down with me and spiked it. That was all!'

'Excuse me, Miss Vernon,' said Desvœux; 'Sutton's modesty spoils an excellent story. Let me tell it as it deserves.' And then he threw himself into a mock-tragical attitude.

'Go on,' said Maud, eagerly.

'The street-fighting at Mírabad,' said Desvœux, with a declamatory air, 'was the fiercest of the whole campaign——'

'What campaign?' asked Sutton.

'The Mírabad campaign,' replied the other, with great presence of mind, 'in eighteen hundred and —, I forget the year—but never mind.'

'Yes, never mind the year,' said Maud; 'go on.'

'The enemy fought us inch by inch, and lane by lane; from every window poured a little volley; every house had to be stormed, hand-to-hand we fought our way, and so on. You know the sort of thing. Then, as we turned into the main street, puff! a great blaze and a roar, and a dense cloud of smoke, and smash came a cannon-ball into the midst of us—five or six men were knocked over—Tomkin's horse lost a tail, Brown had his nose put out of joint, Smith was blown up to a second-storey window—something must be done. But I am tiring you?'

'No, no,' cried Maud, 'I like it—go on.'

'Well, let me see. Oh yes, something must be

done. To put spurs to my Arab's sides, to cut my way down through the astonished mob, to leap the barricade (it was only eight feet high, and armed with a *chevaux de frise*), to sabre the six gunners who were working the battery, was, I need hardly say, the work of a moment. Then—a crushing blow from behind, and I remember nothing more, till, a month later, I found myself, weak and wounded, in bed; and a lovely nun gave me some gruel, and told me that Mírabad was ours! "Where am I?" I exclaimed, for I felt so confused, and the nun looked so angelic, that I fancied I must have gone to heaven. My companion, however, soon brought me to earth by—*et cætera et cætera et cætera.*'

'That is the sort of thing which happens in "Charles O'Malley,"' said Sutton; 'only Lever would have put Tippoo Sahib or Tantia Topee on the other side of the barricade, and I should have had to cut his head off and slaughter all his bodyguard before I got out again.'

'And then,' said Maud, 'the nun would have turned out to be some one.'

'But,' said Desvœux, 'how do you know that the nun did *not* turn out to be some one, if only I had chosen to fill up those *et cæteras?*'

'Well,' said Sutton, who apparently had had

enough of the joke 'that part of the story I will tell you myself. The nun was a male one—my good friend Boldero, who took me into his quarters, looked after me for six weeks, till I got about again, and was as good a nurse as any one could wish for.'

'I should have liked to be the nun,' Maud cried, moved by a sudden impulse which brought the words out as the thought flashed into her mind, and turning crimson, as was her wont, before they were out of her mouth.

'That is very kind of you,' said Sutton, standing up, and defending her, as Maud felt, from all eyes but his own; 'and you would have been a very charming nurse and cured me, I dare say, even faster than Boldero. And now, Desvœux, go and sing us a song as a *finale* to your story.

Maud knew perfectly well that this was a mere diversion to save her from the confusion of a thoughtless speech and turn Desvœux's attention from her. It seemed quite natural and of a piece with Sutton's watchful, sympathetic care to give her all possible pleasure and to shield her from every shade of annoyance. A thrill of gratitude shot through her. There was a charm, a fascination, in protection so prompt, so delicate, so kind, compared with which all other attractions seemed faint indeed. That evening Maud went to bed with her heart in a tumult, and wept, she knew not wherefore, far into the night—only again and again the tears streamed out—the outcome, though as yet she knew it not, of that purest of all pure fountains, an innocent first love.

CHAPTER XIV.

TO THE HILLS!

However marred, and more than twice her years,
Scarred with an ancient sword-cut on the cheek,
And bruised and bronzed,—she lifted up her eyes,
And loved him with that love which was her doom.

SUMMER was beginning to come on apace; not summer as English people know it, the genial supplement to a cold and watery spring, with just enough heat about it to thaw the chills of winter out of one; but summer in its fiercest and cruellest aspect, breathing sulphurous blasts, glowing with intolerable radiance, begirt with whirlwinds of dust—the unsparing despot of a sultry world. The fields, but a few weeks ago one great 'waveless plain' of ripening corn, had been stripped of their finery, and were now lying brown and blistering in the sun's eye. The dust lay deep on every road and path and wayside shrub, and seized every opportunity of getting itself whirled into miniature siroccos. More than once Maud and Felicia had been caught, not in a sweet May shower, stealing down amid bud and blossom and leaving the world moist and fresh and fragrant behind it, but in rough, turbulent clouds of rushing sand, which shut out the sunshine and replaced the bright blue atmosphere with the lurid glare of an eclipse. Felicia's flowers had begun to droop, nor could all her care rescue the fresh green of her lawn from turning to a dingy brown. Already prudent housekeepers were busy with preparations against the evil day so near at hand. Verandahs were guarded with folds of heavy matting, to shut out the intolerable light that would have forced a way through any ordinary barrier; windows were replaced by fragrant screens of cuscus-grass, through which the hot air passing might lose a portion of its sting; and one morning, when Maud came out, she found a host of labourers carrying a huge winnowing-machine to one side of the house, the object of which was, Vernon informed her, to manufacture air cool enough for panting Britons to exist in.

Day by day some piece of attire was discarded as too intolerably heavy for endurance. The morning ride became a thing of the past, and even a drive at sunset too fatiguing to be quite enjoyable. Maud felt that she had never—not even when Miss Goodenough had locked her up for a whole summer afternoon, to learn her 'duty to her neighbour'—known what exhaustion really meant till now.

The children were turning sadly white, and Felicia began to be anxious for their departure to the Hills. Maud would of course go with them, and Vernon was to follow in a couple of months, when he could get his leave. Much as she hated leaving her husband, Felicia was on the whole extremely glad to go. The state of things at home disturbed her. Maud's outspoken susceptibility, Desvœux's impressionable and eager temperament, Sutton's unconsciousness of what she wanted him to do—the combination was one from which it was a relief in prospect to escape to the refuge of a new and unfamiliar society. Felicia's buoyant and hopeful nature saw in the promised change of scene the almost certainty that somehow or other matters would seem less unpromising when looked at from the summits of Elysium.

For Elysium accordingly they started. Three primitive vehicles, whose battered sides and generally faded appearance spoke eloquently of the dust, heat and bustle in which their turbulent existence was for the most part engaged, were dragged one afternoon, each by a pair of highly rebellious ponies, with a vast deal of shouting, pushing, and execrating, into a convenient position before the hall-door, and their tops loaded forthwith with that miscellaneous and profuse supply of baggage which every move in India necessarily involves, and which it is the especial glory of Indian servants to preserve in undiminished amplitude. Suffice it to say, that it began with trunks and cradles, went on with native nurses, and concluded with a goat. Vernon sat in the verandah, smoking a cheroot with stoical composure and interfering only when some pyramid of boxes seemed to be assuming proportions of perilous altitude. He was to travel with them, establish them at Elysium, and ride down sixty miles again by night—a performance of which no Dustyporean thought twice. Maud, to whom one of the creaking fabrics was assigned in company with the two little girls, found that (the feat of clambering in and establishing herself once safely accomplished) the journey promised to be not altogether unluxurious. The Vernons' servants were experienced and devoted, and every detail of the journey was carefully foreseen. The interior of the carriage, well furnished with mattresses and pillows, made an excellent bed; a little army of servants gathered round to proffer aid and to give the Sahibs a passing salaam; friendly carriages kept rolling in to say 'Good-bye.' Sutton, who had been kept away on business, galloped in at the last moment and seemed too much occupied in saying farewell to Felicia to have much time for other thoughts. 'Good-bye,' he said, in the most cheery tone, as he came to Maud's carriage, and 'Good-bye, Uncle Jem!' shouted the little girls, waving their adieux as best they might under the deep awning; and then, after a frantic struggle for independent action on the part of the ponies, they were fairly off and spinning along the great, straight, high road which stretches in unswerving course through so many hundred miles of English rule.

The little girls were in the greatest glee, and busy in signalling Uncle Jem for as long as possible. Maud, somehow, did not share their mirth: for the first time Sutton had seemed unkind, or near enough unkind, to give her pain. This ending of the pleasant time seemed to her an event which friendship ought not quite to have ignored. She looked back upon many happy hours, the brightest of her life; and the person who had made them bright evidently did not share her sentimental views about them in the least. Partings, Maud's heart told her, must surely be always sad; yet Sutton's voice had no tone of sadness in it. 'Stay—stay a little!' she could have cried with Imogen,

> Were you but riding forth to air yourself,
> Such parting were too petty—

True, they were to meet in a few weeks; but yet—but yet!

'You've dot a big tear on your cheek,' said one of her companions, with the merciless frankness of childhood.

'Have I?' said Maud. 'Then it must be the dust that has gone into my eyes. How hot it is! Come, let us have some oranges!'

By this time evening was fast closing in, and Maud's cheeks were soon safe from further observation. Before long her and her companions' eyes were fast closed by that kindly hand which secures to the most troubled of mankind the boon that one-third, at any rate, of existence shall be spent in peace. When they awoke the stars were shining bright, but the sky was already ruddy with the coming dawn, and Maud could see the giant mountain forms looming, cold and majestical, in the grey air above them. They alighted at a little wayside inn, and found delicious cups of tea (the Indians' invariable morning luxury) awaiting them. Maud had sufficiently recovered her spirits to make a bold inroad on the bread and butter.

A mist hung about the country round, and it was a delightful, home-like sensation to shrink once again, as the cold mountain blasts came swirling down, throwing the wreaths of vapour here and there, and recalling the delicious reminiscence of a

November fog. In a few moments the horses were ready, the children and nurses packed into palanquins, and the upward march began.

These morning expeditions in the mountains are indescribably exhilarating. At every step you breathe a fresher atmosphere and feel a new access of life, vigour and enjoyment. Sweet little gushes of pure cold air meet you at the turnings of the road and bid you welcome. The vegetation around is rich, profuse and — long-forgotten charm — sparkling everywhere with dew. There has been a thunderstorm in the night, and the mountain-sides are streaming still: little cataracts come tumbling clamorously beside your path; below you a muddy stream is foaming and brawling and collecting the tribute of a hundred torrents to swell the great flood that spreads away miles wide in the plain, and glitters in the far horizon. As the path rises you get a wider view, and presently the great champaign lies below, flashing and blinking in the morning's rays. Miles away overhead a tiny white thread shows the road along which in an hour or two you will be travelling, and a little speck at the summit, the cottage where your mid-day rest will be. Behind you lie heat, monotony, fatigue, hot hours in sweltering courts, weary strugglings through the prose of officialdom, the tiresome warfare against sun and dust; around you and above, it is all enchanted ground; the air is full of pleasant sounds and sweet invisible influences; the genius of the woods breathes poetry about the scene, the mountain nymphs are dancing on yonder crest, and Puck and Oberon and Titania haunting in each delicious nook. Well may the first Englishman, who toiled panting hitherwards from the reeking realms below, have fancied himself halfway to Paradise and have christened the crowning heights Elysium. Maud, at any rate, leaving the rest of the party behind, rode forward in an ecstasy of enjoyment.

. . . . . .

They spent the hot hours of the day in a sweet resting-place. Years afterwards the calmness of that pleasant day used to live in Maud's recollection; and though many scenes of bustle and trouble and fevered excitement had come between herself and it, yet the very thought of it used to soothe her. 'I have you, dear,' she would say to Felicia, 'in my mind's picture-gallery, set in a dozen different frames—scenes in which you played a part—and this is my favourite. I love you best of all in this; it cools and gladdens me to look at it.'

The scene, in fact, was a lovely one. On one side rose a vast amphitheatre of granite, rugged, solemn, precipitous; downwards, along the face of this, a careful eye might trace from point to point the little path up which the party were to make to-morrow's march. This mountain ridge separated them from the Elysian hills, and seemed to frown at them like some giant bulwark reared to guard the snowy solitudes beyond from human intrusion. On the other hand, fold upon fold, one sweet outline melting into another—here kissed by soft wreaths of cloud, here glittering clear and hard in the flood of light—stretched all the minor ranges, along which for fifty miles the traveller to the Elysians prepares himself for the final sublimity that lies beyond. In front, where the mountains parted, lay sweltering in the horizon, and immeasurably below them, the great Indian plain, spread out as far as eye could follow it—a dim, glistening, monotonous panorama—varied only when occasionally a great river, swollen with the melting snows above, spread out for miles across the plain and twinkled like an inland lake as the sun's rays fell upon it—and the whole suggested intolerable heat.

The hillside around was covered thick with forest growth of tropical luxuriance. On the heights above, a clump of rhododendrons glowed with a rosy glory; here, on a rugged precipice, a storm-stricken deodar spread its vast flat branches as if to brave the storm and the lightning strokes such as had before now seamed its bark. The path below was overhung with a dense growth of bamboo, each stem a miracle of grace, and growing at last to an inextricable jungle in the deep bosom of the mountain gorge. Mountain creepers in fantastic exuberance tossed wildly about the crag's side or hung festooning the roadside with a gorgeous natural tapestry. A hundred miles away the everlasting snow-clad summits, which had stood out so clear in the grey morning, when they first emerged from their couch of clouds, were fading into faintness as the bright daylight poured about them. Just below the spot on which their camp was pitched there was a little spring and a drinking-place, and constant relays of cattle came tinkling up the road and rested in the tall rocks' shadow for a drink, while the weary drivers sat chatting on the edge. Every now and then weird beings from the Interior, whose wild attire and unkempt aspect bespoke them as belonging to some aboriginal tribe, were to be seen staggering along under huge logs of timber felled in the great forests above and now brought down to the confines of civilisation for human use. It was a new page in Nature's grand picture-book, and full of charm. Maud, who was always very much alive to the outer world, was greatly impressed. Her nerves were overwrought. She took Felicia's hand and seemed to be in urgent need of imparting her excited mood to some one.

'How beautiful this is!' she cried; 'how solemn, how solitary! Already all the world seems to be something unsubstantial, and the mountains the only reality.'

Felicia threw herself back upon the turf and gave a great sigh of relief.

'I love these delicious gusts of air,' she said, 'fresh and pure from the snow-tops.'

'Yes,' cried Maud; 'how serene and grand they look! No wonder the Alpine tourists go crazy about them and break their necks in clambering about them, bewildered with pleasure:

> '"How faintly flushed, how phantom fair,
> Was Monte Rosa hanging there!
> A thousand shadowy pencilled valleys
> And snowy dells in a golden air!"

'And here is a whole horizon of Monte Rosas! I should like to stop a month here and devote myself to sketching.'

While they were chatting in the shade, a native lad, who had been standing on a neighbouring knoll, came running down to a picketed pony and began hurriedly to prepare him for departure.

'What Sahib's horse?' Vernon asked with that imperative inquisitiveness that the superior race allows itself in India.

'Boldero Sahib,' replied the breathless groom; and before many minutes more 'Boldero Sahib' himself began to be apparent on the opposite hill-side.

'The impetuous Boldero,' cried Vernon, 'riding abroad, redressing human wrongs, and doing his best, as usual, to break his neck, as if there could by any possibility be anything worth hurrying about in the plains below. Now, Maud, you will see a real philanthropist in flesh and blood.'

Presently the tiny distant object had shaped itself into a man and horse, and in a quarter of an hour more Boldero came clattering into the yard, had slung himself out of the saddle in a moment, and was already preparing to mount his new horse, when he discovered the Vernons and was introduced to Maud.

He seemed to have broken like a whirlwind into the repose of the party. His servants were evidently well experienced in their master's movements; the saddle had been speedily shifted and the fresh horse was already ready for a start. Boldero drank off a great beaker of cold water. Maud's first impression was that he looked extremely handsome and extremely hot, and in better spirits and a greater hurry than she had ever seen any one in in her life. Vernon, after first greetings, had speedily resumed his attitude of profound repose and evidently had no intention of being infected with bustle.

'Come, Boldero,' he said, 'do, for goodness' sake, send away your horse and wait here and have some lunch, instead of flying off in such a madman's hurry. India, which has already waited several thousand years for your arrival to reform her, can, no doubt, dispense with you for twenty minutes more; and fortune does not send good meetings every day.'

'Yes, Mr. Boldero,' said Felicia, 'and I have just been making a salad, which I am delighted you have arrived to admire; and I daresay you have half-a-dozen new ferns to show me.'

'I am pledged to be at Dustypore to-morrow, and ought to be ten miles further on my way by this time,' said Boldero. 'However, there is a glorious moon all through the night, and this delightful Doongla Gully seems set as a snare to beguile one into loitering by the way. What a sweet little oasis it is among all the gloom of the mountains!'

'Now, Maud,' said Vernon, 'I'll give you an idea of what the virtuous civilian does. He rides all night, he works all day.'

'Or rather,' said Boldero, who had as much dislike as the rest of the army of good fellows to being the topic of conversation, 'by night he dances, by day he plays at Badminton. My visit to the Viceroy was nothing except for the solemnity of the affair.'

'Well,' answered Vernon, 'and now you come just in time to give my cousin a lesson in water-colours. You must know, Maud, that Mr. Boldero carried off the prize at Elysium for a mountain-sketch last year. Now, Boldero, be good-natured and tell her the mystery of your sunset skies, which, though I deny their fidelity, are, I must admit, as beautiful as the real ones.'

'Will you?' said Maud, her eyes flashing out and her colour coming at the mere thought of what she especially desired.

'Will I not?' Boldero said, with alacrity. 'What pleasanter afternoon's work could fortune send one?' And thereupon Maud's sketch-book was produced.

'Did you ever see such a daub?' she cried. 'It looks worse now it is dry than when I did it. It is so provoking! I feel the scenes—I have them all beautifully in my mind, and then come those horrid, hard, blotchy heaps. Just look at this odious mountain! Alas! alas!' Maud went on ruthlessly blotting out her morning's work, which, to tell the truth, did not deserve immortality.

'You made it a little too blue,' said her tutor. 'See, now; I will tone it down for you in a minute.'

'No, no,' cried Maud, 'let us have something

fresh, that I have not desecrated by a caricature. Here, this in front of us will be lovely.'

'See,' said Boldero; 'we will have that nice bit of dark shade with that ragged deodar, and that jolly little cloud overhead.'

Maud's face glowed with pleasure, and her companion's last thought of getting in time to Dustypore disappeared.

Before the sketch was done the evening shadows were already fast climbing up the mountain's side; the valley's short day was over; cold masses of vapour were gathering about the crags; and the moon, that was to light the traveller through his night-long journey, was sailing, pale and ghost-like, overhead. Boldero waved them a last farewell as he disappeared round the opposite hillside, and seemed to Maud's excited imagination like some knight-errant riding down into the gloom.

CHAPTER XV.

A DISTRICT OFFICER.

> Their aches, hopes,
> Their pangs of love, with other incident throes,
> That nature's fragile vessel doth sustain
> In life's uncertain voyage——

BOLDERO was one of the Queen's good bargains. His mind teemed with schemes for the regeneration of mankind. Disappointment could not damp his hopefulness, nor difficulty cool his zeal; he was an enthusiast for improvement and the firmest believer in its possibility. Against stupidity, obstinacy, the blunders of routine, official *vis inertiæ*, he waged a warfare which, if not always discreet, was sufficiently vigorous to plague his opponents: 'See,' cries Mr. Browning's philanthropist,

> I have drawn a pattern on my nail
> And I will carve the world fresh after it—

Boldero's nails were absolutely covered with new patterns, and the little bit of the world on which he was able to operate was continually being carved into some improved condition. Nature having gifted him with courage, high spirit, resource, inventiveness, enterprise, and—precious gift!—administrative effectiveness, and Fortune and the Staff Corps having guided his steps from a frontier regiment to a civilian appointment in the Sandy Tracts, his importance was speedily appreciated. Wherever he looked at the machinery about him he saw things out of gear and working badly, and his mind was forthwith haunted with devices to improve them. He saw material, money, time wasted; wheel catching against wheel and producing all sorts of bad results by the friction; office coming to dead-lock with office; one blundering head knocking against another; wants to which no one attended; wrongs which no one avenged; sufferings to which no hand brought relief. Some men see such things and acquiesce in them as inevitable or relieve themselves by cynical remarks on the best of all possible worlds. Boldero felt it all as a personal misfortune and was incapable of acquiescence.

Thus he was for ever discovering grievances, which, when once discovered, no one could deny. His reports to Government sent a little shudder through the Chief Secretary's soul. The Salt Board regarded him with especial disfavour. Cockshaw cursed him for the long correspondence he involved.

Fotheringham thought him dangerous, rash, Quixotic. Even Blunt accorded him but a scanty approval, Blunt's view being always the rough, commonplace and unsentimental, and Boldero's projects involving a constant temptation to expenditure. But the Agent was a finer judge of character than any of them, and his keen eye speedily detected Boldero's rare merits and his fitness for responsible employment. Boldero had more than justified the Agent's hopes, and accordingly moved rapidly up from one post to another.

He was now acting as chief magistrate of the district next to Dustypore. Here his energetic temperament had the fullest play. He built, he planted, he drained. Sunrise found him ever in the saddle. He drove his Municipal Committee wild with projects of reform—water-supply, vaccination, canals, tanks, and public gardens. He fulminated the most furious orders, plunged into all sorts of controversies, was always waging war in some quarter or other, and manufactured for himself even a hotter world than Nature had provided ready-made. He offended the doctors by invading the hospitals and pointing out how the patients were killed by defective arrangements; the Chaplain, by objecting to the ventilation of the church and the length of the sermons; the Educational Department by a savage tirade on the schools, and the General in command by a bold assault on the drainage of the barracks. Altogether a bustling, joyous, irrepressible sort of man, and, as the Agent knew, a perfect treasure in a land where energy and enthusiasm are hard to keep at boiling heat, and where to get a thing done, despite the piles of official correspondence it gets buried under, is a result as precious as it is difficult of achievement.

When he first came to India he had been for a couple of years in Sutton's regiment, and at the time of Sutton's illness the two had almost lived together. The intimacy so formed had ripened into a cordial friendship, and Boldero had thus become a not unfrequent visitor at the Vernons' house, where, though her husband pronounced him an enthusiastic bore, Felicia ever accorded him a kindly welcome.

He had now, however, carried away with him that which speedily cured him of enthusiasm, or, rather, forbade him to feel enthusiastic about anything but one. With his accustomed earnest precipitancy he had fallen deeply in love with Maud the first moment he had seen her, and all his afternoon had been spent in that paradise which springs into sudden existence beneath a happy lover's feet. Maud had been delighted with him for being so handsome, so good-natured, and the latest comer. And, then, was not he Sutton's friend, whose care and kindness had brought him from Death's door? Maud thought of this with a gush of interest and rained the sweetest and most gracious smiles upon him in consequence. Those bright looks pursued him down the mountain's side, through the livelong night, and next day into court and office and all the hundred businesses of a busy official's day. So bright were they, even in recollection, that all the brightness seemed to have faded out of everything else. The details of his District, lately so full of interest, had become the dreariest routine. Improvements which, when last he thought of them, seemed of vital importance, faded away into uselessness or impossibility. A great pile of papers stood, ranged upon the study table, inviting disposal. A week ago Boldero would have fallen upon them, like a glutton on some favourite repast, and driven through them with alacrity and enjoyment. Now he had not the heart to touch them. A week ago the plains, with all their drawbacks, were pleasanter far, for a healthy man, than the indolent comforts and dull frivolities of a Hill station. Now, alas! Elysium was the only place where life—any life, that is, which deserved the name—was to be had.

Meanwhile, the object of his devotion was conscious only of having had a very pleasant afternoon and added one more to an already ample list of agreeable acquaintances. By the time she arrived at Elysium next day, Boldero had faded into indistinctness, and his chance meeting with them figured in Maud's thoughts only as one, and not the most striking, incident of a journey which had been to her full of things new, interesting and picturesque.

CHAPTER XVI.

ELYSIUM.

For they lie beside their nectar, and their bolts are hurled
Far below them in the valleys, and the clouds are lightly curled
Round their golden houses, girdled with the gleaming world.

THE conquering races, who in one age or another have owned the fair plains of Hindostan, have successively made the discovery that there are portions of the year when their magnificent possession had best be contemplated from a respectful distance. Some monarchs retired for the summer to the exquisite Cashmir valleys: others to cool plateaux in the far interior. The latest administrators of the country have solved the problem by perching, through the hot season, on the summits of a craggy range, and by performing the functions of Government at an altitude of 7000 feet above the sea.

The fact that the highest officials in the country, having a large amount of hard work to do, should prefer to do it in an invigorating mountain atmosphere, rather than amid swamps, steam and fever in the plains below, is not, of course, surprising. The only matter of regret is that the obvious advantages, public and private, of an European climate for half the year can, from the nature of things, be enjoyed by so tiny a fraction of the official world. As it is, the annual removal of the Government to its summer quarters gives rise too often to a little outburst of unreasonable, though not unnatural jealousy; and Indian journalists, who are necessarily closely pinned to the plains, are never tired of inveighing against the 'Capua' of the British rule. The truth is, however, that if Hannibal's soldiers had worked half as hard at Capua as English officials do at Elysium, nothing but good could have resulted from their sojourn in that agreeable resting-place. Of the holiday-makers it may safely be said that, in nine cases out of ten, they have earned, by long months of monotonous, laborious, and often solitary life, a good right to all the refreshment of body and soul that a brief interval of cool breezes, new faces, and an amusing society can give them. The 'Jack' of the Civil Service is often a dull boy because the stern *régime* of 'all work and no play' is too rigorously enforced upon him. Let no one therefore grudge him his few weeks of rest and merry-making, or mock at the profuse homage with which the goddess Terpsichore is adored by her modern votaries on the Himalayan heights.

Elysium, indeed, enchants one on the first approach. You clamber for weary miles up a long, blazing ascent, where even the early morning sun seems to sting and pierce. As the road turns, you enter suddenly a sweet depth of shade formed by thick growths of ilex and rhododendron, from the breaks in which you look out at ease upon the blazing day beyond. Dotted all about the road, above and below, perched on every convenient rock or level ridge of soil, or sometimes built up on a framework of piles, are the homes of the Elysians; not, alas! the ideals which the imagination would conceive of the abodes of the blest, but seaside lodgings, of a by no means first-rate order, with precipices, clouds and rain, instead of sea. Presently the road fails at a great chasm in the mountain-side, and the horses' feet clatter over a frail-looking structure of planks and scaffolding, which clings to the mountain's edge. This is merely a landslip, an event too common even to be observed. Each heavy rainfall, however, washes an appreciable fraction of the Elysian summits to the depths below and leaves the craggy sides barer and steeper than ever. Then, emerging from the ilex grove, the traveller passes to a little Mall, where the fashionable world assembles for mutual edification, and the tide of life, business and gaiety flows fast and strong.

There is something in the air of the place which bespeaks the close neighbourhood of the Sovereign rule, the august climax of the official hierarchy. Servants, brilliant in scarlet and gold, are hurrying hither and thither. Here some Rajah, petty monarch of the surrounding ranges or the fat plains below, attended with his mimic court and tatterdemalion cavalry, is marching in state to pay his homage to the 'great Lord Sahib.' Here some grand lady, whose gorgeous attire and liveried retinue bespeak her sublime position, is constrained to bate her greatness to the point of being carried —slung like the grapes of Eschol—on a pole, and borne on sturdy peasants' shoulders to pay a round of the ceremonious visits which etiquette enjoins upon her. Officers, secretaries, aides-de-camp come bustling by on mountain-ponies, each busy on his own behest. The energetic army of morning callers are already in the field. A dozen palanquins, gathered at Madame Fifini's, the Elysian 'Worth,' announce the fact that as many ladies are hard at work within, running up long-bills for their husbands and equipping themselves for conquest at the next Government House 'At home.' Smartly-furnished shops glitter with all the latest finery of Paris and London, and ladies go jogging along on their bearers' shoulders, gay enough for a London garden-party in July. In the midst of all,—the solid basis on which so huge a structure of business, pomp and pleasure is erected,—clumps the British

Private, brushed, buttoned and rigid, with a loud, heavy tread, which contrasts strangely with the noiselessly moving crowd around him and bespeaks his conscious superiority to a race of beings whom, with a lordly indifference to minute ethnological distinctions, he designates collectively as 'Moors.'

Some servants were waiting at the entrance of the place to conduct the Vernons to their home, and before many minutes the travellers were standing in the balcony, looking out on the steep slopes of green foliage below them and the noble snow-ranges which bounded the entire horizon. Maud soon rushed off to explore the house; and Felicia made her way to the garden, to see how many of last summer's plants the winter had spared to her. Presently she came in, with dew-bedrenched sleeves and gloves and an armful of sparkling roses, geraniums and heliotropes, and deposited them joyously in a heap on the table.

'There,' she cried, 'is my first fruit-offering. Bury your face in them, George, and do homage, as I have been doing, to the Genius of the Hills! Come here, babies, and be crowned.'

Felicia knelt down and stuck the children's hair full of flowers, till each looked as gaudy as a little Queen of May. Her husband came and stood over them and watched the scene.

'Now,' he said, 'Felicia, you ought to be quite

happy—you have your children and your flowers to adore at once.'

'And my husband,' said Felicia, looking up at him, with her sweet, radiant smile. 'And, oh dear, how I wish you had not to go down again to-night! Do you know, George, I mind each separation worse than the last? Next summer we will send the children straight to "The Gully," and we will stay comfortably together.'

Maud came back in the highest spirits. 'Look here,' she said, showing a handful of snow, and fingers red and blue with unaccustomed cold—'how nice it is to feel it once again! And what nectar the air is! And, George, actually, strawberries!'

'Yes,' said Vernon, 'and cream, and plenty of both. Is it not enchanting?'

'You shall have some flowers too, dear,' cried Maud, who seldom missed an opportunity of petting Felicia and letting her love run out in some pretty act or speech. 'See, this rose was made for me to deck you with. Does she not look charming, George?'

'Hush!' said George; 'we shall make her and the little girls too as vain as possible. Now, as I suppose nobody means to crown me, I vote that you go and get ready for breakfast, and I will prepare Maud a plate of strawberries-and-cream, by way of beginning the feast.'

That morning lived ever afterwards in Maud's thoughts as one of the times when the world looked brightest to her. Everything was full of excitement, interest and keen pleasure. If from time to time a thought of Sutton set her heart beating, it was more that she had learnt to worship him as an ideal of all that was most charming in man than that his absence cost her any serious regret. It had given her a pang to part and to feel how little of a pang it had given him. He had been almost unconscious of her departure; he had been certainly quite, quite indifferent to it. Such insensibility was a little speck on the otherwise spotless perfection; but Maud's heart was too light for this to weigh it down for long. A long, charming vista of enjoyment was opening before her. Half-a-dozen people, she knew, were awaiting her arrival with impatience and thought Elysium not quite Elysium till she was there. Before the morning was over there would come, so her prophetic soul announced, kind familiar faces, all the brighter for her presence, with all sorts of delightful projects, often talked of beforehand, now to come into actual fruition; rides, picnics, dances, theatricals, and (thrilling thought!) a fancy ball, at which Maud had already found herself twenty times whirling in anticipated valses, each more enchanting than the last. Who could contemplate such a prospect with equanimity? or whose heart have room for gloomy thoughts with so many bright dreams to crush them out?

Then presently there came a note from Mrs Vereker, bidding her a cordial welcome and threatening her high displeasure if Maud's first visit was not to her. To Mrs. Vereker's accordingly they went, and found her in a little cottage, romantically stuck into a cleft in the rocks, with a cataract of honeysuckle tumbling all about a wooden porch, and a view of the mountains which even her adorers, burning to behold herself, were yet constrained to stop and look at. There was a little court, with a wooden railing to guard the edge and geraniums blazing all about it, where a succession of enthusiasts' ponies waited while their owners did homage within. Through that convenient cranny in the foliage the deity, unseen, could spy the approaching visitor and decide betimes whether she would be 'at home' or not. Now she was unquestionably at home and met them at the door with merry greetings. She led them in and showed them her drawing-room, the very home of innocence and refined propriety. 'My husband does not wish me to mope when he is away,' she said, with a charming simple smile; and, to do her justice, in this respect, at any rate, she obeyed his wishes. If the loveliest, freshest bonnets, the daintiest gloves, the most picturesque mountain costumes, a succession of bewildering head-dresses, could rescue a widowed soul from melancholy, Mrs. Vereker had no right to gloom. Nor was hers the only nature that was cheered, for all mankind conspired to assure her that she was the most bewitching of her sex. Turn where she would she found a host of willing courtiers, who thought their assiduous services well rewarded with a single smile. She looked at the world through her beautiful purple eyes, and saw it prostrate at her feet.

Even Felicia was captivated, despite her own convictions; and Vernon alone of the party declared her a little ogling hypocrite, and pronounced himself unable to understand how any one could think her even pretty.

CHAPTER XVII.

A BATTLE ROYAL.

Impiger, iracundus, inexorabilis, acer——

LEAVING the celestials to their business and pleasures in the upper regions, the Historic Muse must now descend into the plains and record the wrath of Blunt and the more than Homeric combats which, stirred by Até in her most malignant mood, that irrepressible official waged against his luckless compeers at the Board. The outbreak was horribly inopportune. The weather was becoming disagreeably hot; Cockshaw was looking up his rifles and fishing-rods for a month's run into Cashmir; Fotheringham was preparing to retire behind his cuscus entrenchments and æstivate in placidity till the moment arrived for going to the Hills. But the black soul of Blunt was impervious to climatic influences; his craving for information became more insatiable, his contempt for Fotheringham's platitudes and Strutt's tall writing less and less disguised. The further Blunt looked into the Rumble

Chunder affair the keener grew his sense of the feeble, roundabout, inaccurate, unthorough way in which it had been treated by every one who had essayed to take it in hand. 'The way to handle nettles,' he said, roughly, 'is to take tight hold of them and bear what stinging you get and have done with it.'

Neither Fotheringham nor Cockshaw were in the least disposed to handle official nettles or to admit the force of Blunt's logic as applied to themselves.

'Some nettles,' Fotheringham said, with dignified composure, 'will not bear handling at all. Many of our Indian maladies you will find, Blunt, require a course of treatment always unpopular with ardent physicians, that, namely, of being left alone.'

'Ay,' said Cockshaw, blowing a great stream of smoke from his mouth, as if he wished he could treat Blunt and his schemes in like fashion; 'leave well alone, Blunt. What the deuce is it you are driving at?'

'I'll tell you what I am driving at,' said Blunt, 'I want to be out of the muddle in which we have been going on all these years, just for want of a little explicitness and courage.'

'Excuse me,' said Fotheringham testily; 'I am not aware that the conquerors and administrators of the Sandy Tracts have ever been accused of deficiency in courage, at any rate.'

'Of course not,' answered the other; 'no one supposes anything of the sort; but what I mean is that no one has faced the consequences of that confounded Proclamation of the Governor-General in a plain, business-like way, and seen what it really comes to.'

Now the Governor-General's Proclamation was regarded in official circles at Dustypore with a sort of traditional awe, as something almost sacred. Fotheringham had often spoken of it as the Magna Charta of the Sandy Tracts, and Strutt generally quoted it in the peroration of his Annual Report. Nothing, accordingly, could be less congenial to his audience than Blunt's coarse, offhanded, disrespectful way of referring to it. Fotheringham's whole nature rose in arms against the idea of this rash, irreverential intruder handling with such jaunty freedom and contempt the things which he had all his life been accustomed to treat and to see treated with profound respect. The moment had now come when to put up with Blunt any longer would, he thought, be simple weakness; the cup of Blunt's misdeeds at last was full; and Fortheringham, his patience fairly at an end, pale and excited, spoke, and spoke in wrath.

'I must beg,' he said, in a tone of aggrieved dignity which Blunt especially resented, 'to remind our junior colleague that there are some things of which his inexperience of the country renders it impossible for him to be a competent judge, and of which, when he knows them better, he will probably think and speak with more respect. This Rumble Chunder Grant is one of them. Cockshaw and I have been at work at it for twenty years: we know the places, the people, the language, the feeling it excites, the dangers it may provoke. The Proclamation, which Blunt is pleased to describe as "confounded," was, we know, a high-minded, well-considered act of a great statesman and has been the foundation stone of all peace, prosperity, and civilisation in the province. It all seems clear to you, my good sir, because—forgive me for saying it—you do not see the intricacies of the matter, and are incapable of appreciating its bearings. For my part'——

'Come, come, Fotheringham,' said Cockshaw, who had been looking nervously at his watch and knew that it wanted only seven minutes to the hour at which his afternoon game of racquets should begin, 'don't let us drift into a quarrel. As to speaking rudely of the Proclamation, it is as bad as the man who damned the North Pole, you know—no harm is done to any one by that. Blunt is not so nervous about the matter as we are, because he has not had such a deal of bother over it as we have had. My idea is that we have gone into it of late quite as far as we can just now. Suppose we drop it for the present and take it up again in the cold weather?'

'I object altogether,' Blunt said, in a dogged way, which made Cockshaw give up his chance of racquets that day as desperate. 'That system of postponements is one of the objectionable practices which I especially deprecate. Whenever any of us comes across a thing which he does not fancy, or cannot or will not understand, he puts it into his box and burkes it, and no more is heard of it for a twelvemonth. I would sooner take the chance of going wrong than the certainty of doing nothing.'

'And I,' answered Cockshaw, lighting a new cheroot with the remaining fraction of his old one, 'would sooner take the risk of a little delay than the certainty of going wrong, as you will do to a moral certainty if you are in such a devil of a hurry.'

'Please, Cockshaw,' said Fotheringham, to whom his colleague's cheroots and bad language were a chronic affliction, 'do not lose your temper. For my part, I was going to observe when you interrupted me just now, I really do not know what it is that Blunt imagines could be done.'

'This could be done,' Blunt said, 'we could bring things to a head, and know exactly how we stand; ascertain the claims, the rights, and at what prices we could buy the owners of them out.'

'My good sir,' Fotheringham exclaimed, by this time fairly in a passion, 'that is exactly what all of us have been trying to do for the last ten years, and you talk as if it could be done out of hand.'

'And so it could,' cried Blunt, 'if any one would only resolve to do it. I tell you what: let me have Whisp and a few clerks and translators, and hold a local commission, and I will go into the District myself and knock my way through the matter somehow or other.'

'You will find it infernally hot,' said Cockshaw.

'You will have a rising on the frontier,' said Fotheringham, 'mark my words, and come back deeper in difficulties than ever.'

However, Blunt at last got his way and went off trotting on his cob. Cockshaw escaped gleefully to the racquet-court, and Fotheringham sat sadly at the Board-room, conscious of present harassment and impending disaster. Both he and Blunt used to carry away with them to their domestic circles the traces of the conflicts in which they had been engaged: both reached their homes in a truly pitiable state of mind and body whenever this hateful Rumble Chunder Grant affair was on hand: both their ladies knew only too well the days when it formed part of the programme. Blunt used to stamp about and abuse the servants, emphasising his language with various vehement British expletives, quaffing large goblets of brandy and soda-water, as if to assuage an inward fury, and making no secret of his opinion that Fotheringham was a donkey. Fotheringham, on the other hand, retired to his sofa, called for sal-volatile, had both the Misses Fotheringham to bathe his temples with toilet-vinegar, and breathed a hint that poor Blunt was a terribly uncouth fellow, and that it was extremely disagreeable to have to do with people who, not being gentlemen themselves, could not understand what gentlemen felt. Mrs. Fotheringham thought so too, and began, on her part, not to love Mrs. Blunt.

CHAPTER XVIII.

GAUDIA IN EXCELSIS.

Quis non malarum quas Amor curas habet
Hæc inter obliviscitur?

Before many weeks had passed Sutton and Desvœux came up to Elysium for their holidays, and Maud's cup of pleasure began to overflow. Boldero moreover, to the great surprise of every one, discovered that the plains were telling seriously on his constitution, and, despite the lamentations of his Commissioner, who was at his wits' end to find a satisfactory substitute, insisted on carrying out the doctor's recommendation to try a change of air.

'I am sorry you are ill,' the Commissioner said, 'and overworked, but what on earth am I to do without you? No one understands anything about our arterial drainage scheme but you; and who is to open the new cattle fair? And then there is that lakh of saplings we had determined to plant out in the rains—my dear fellow, don't go till October, at any r[illegible]

But Boldero was inexorable: the arterial drainage of the Sandy Tracts, new cattle fairs, and even the delicious prospect of planting out a hundred thousand trees in a region where a tree was almost as great a phenomenon as Dr. Johnson found it in the Hebrides—all seemed to him but as hollow dreams, which fell meaningless on the ear, when compared with the solid reality of a personal romance. To go to Elysium, to see Maud again, to hear her joyous laugh, to watch her eyes light up with pleasure, and the colour coming and going in her cheeks, as each new turn of feeling swayed her this way or that; to hold her hand in his and feel a subtle, electric influence flashing from her to him and stirring every nerve and fibre of his being into new existence; and then to win this sweet creature to himself with a tender avowal of devotion and the sweet coercion of passionate attachment; to bring her to irradiate a dreary, solitary life with youth, beauty, freshness, everything that Boldero now discovered that his own existence wanted; this was the dream which filled his waking and sleeping thoughts, or, rather, this was the reality, and everything else was dream-land, far off, unsubstantial, unsatisfying. What, to a man in this mood, are reclamation schemes and irrigation projects and all the vexatious details involved in improving thankless people against their wills, educating those who do not want to be taught, and aiming at a chimerical Golden Age, which no one is sure can ever come, and which, at any rate, we shall never see? Boldero confessed to himself that a morning's sketching on the mountain's side with Maud was, as far as his interest about the matter went, worth more than all the Golden Ages that poets have sung or philanthropists devised. The utmost concession that the Commissioner could get out of him was that he would go only for a fortnight. And so to Elysium he came among the rest.

There may be natures to whom, according to Sir Cornewall Lewis's dictum, life would be tolerable but for its enjoyments; but the Elysians assuredly are not of the number. They go about pleasure-hunting with a vehemence the stronger and keener for the long period of partial or total abstinence from amusement which most of them have undergone. The soldier who has been for months marching up and down a desert frontier, with no attainable form of excitement but the agreeable possibility of having one's throat cut in the night or a bullet cleverly lodged in one from behind a rock overhead —the engineer who has been for months out in camp with little companionship but that of theodolites and maps—the forest superintendent who has spent a twelvemonth among the deodars in some nameless Himalayan gorge—the civilian who has carried off his bride to a solitary existence in some far-off Mofussil station, where the only European is perhaps an excise officer or policeman—people like these acquire a keen relish for any change of scene and rush into a holiday with the enthusiasm of long-imprisoned schoolboys. Nothing damps their ardour—not even Himalayan rain, which effectually damps everything else. There is a ball, for instance, at the Club House; it is raining cataracts and has been doing so for twenty hours. The mountain paths are knee-deep in mud, and swept by many a turgid torrent rattling from above. Great masses of thunder-cloud come looming up, rumbling, crashing and blazing upon a sodden, reeking world. The night is black as Tartarus, save when the frequent flashes light it up with a momentary glare. The road is steep, rough and not too safe. Carriages, of course, there are none. A false step might send you several thousand feet down the precipice into the valley below. Will all this prevent Jones the Collector and Brown the Policeman and Smith of the Irregular Cavalry putting their respective ladies into palanquins, mounting their ponies like men and finding their way, through field and flood, to the scene of dissipation? Each will ensconce himself in a panoply of indiarubber and require a great deal of peeling before becoming presentable in a ballroom; but each will get himself peeled, and dance till four o'clock. The ladies will emerge from their palanquins as fresh and bright and ambrosial as lace and tarlatan can make them. Mrs. Jones, if she would only tell the truth, has already more than half-filled up her card with engagements. Smith and his wife have never been at a dance since the night he proposed to her at the Woolwich ball, and feel quite romantic at the prospect of a valse together. Mrs. Brown will meet half-a-dozen particular friends who are dying to see her, and whom she is not averse to see. The night outside is Tartarean, certainly, but within there is nothing but light, music and mirth. The band crashes out and drowns the patter of the rain above. The Viceroy, towering like a Homeric chief among his peers, mingles with the throng, and is valsing with Felicia. Boldero has reached the seventh heaven of his hopes, is actually in possession of Maud's hand and has her heart beating close to his own. Desvœux looks reproachfully at her over Mrs. Vereker's shoulder as they go whirling by. A hundred happy hearts are pulsating with excitement and pleasure, drowning the cares of existence in such transient oblivion as may be manufactured out of fiddlers and champagne.

Is this the race which proclaims itself inadept at amusements, and which, historians gravely assure us, loves to take its very pleasures sadly? Are these the melancholy beings whose gloom is supposed to have acquired a still sadder tinge from the sad routine of Eastern life? Say, rather, a race with healthy instincts and conscious energy and the ready joyousness of youth—fittest rulers of a world where much hard work is to be done, where many things tend to melancholy and all things to fatigue.

Boldero, as he rode homewards (only three miles out of his direct course) by the side of Maud's palanquin, through the pelting rain, admitted to himself an almost unlimited capacity for happiness, of which he had till now been unaware.

There were some balls, moreover, when it did *not* rain; when the music, streaming out into the still atmosphere, could be heard miles away across the gorge, and the moon, sailing in a cloudless sky, flooded the mountain-sides with soft pure light. Such a night was that on which the 'Happy Bachelors' entertained their friends. Happy indeed! for the fairest hands in Elysium had been busy twining wreaths and arranging flowers; and ottomans and sofas and mirrors had been brought from many a despoiled drawing-room, in order that the Happy Bachelors' abode should look as picturesque and comfortable as hands could make it. Whole conservatories of lovely plants had been all the morning marching up the craggy path on peasants' heads.

All Elysium was alert, for the Bachelors were men of taste, 'well loved of many a noble dame;' and, if not otherwise fitted for the Episcopate, at any rate fulfilling the Apostolic requirement of being given to hospitality.

To one person, however, that ball was a period of the darkest disappointment. While the merriment of the evening was raging to its height poor Boldero's heart was growing colder and colder, and all his pleasant schemes were rapidly melting into air. The course of true love always runs delightfully smooth when one person only is concerned and that person's imagination directs it at his will; but how often rude contact with reality brings all our airy castle-building to the ground! Boldero, in his dreams about Maud, had no doubt judged her charms aright; but he had omitted one important consideration, namely, that he was not the only man in the world, and that other people would be likely to think about her much as he did himself. This melancholy fact was now borne in upon him with a cruel vehemence. Maud seemed to be in the greatest request and to smile with distracting impartiality on all who came about her. 'Why did you not ask me sooner?' she said reproachfully when he came to claim a dance, 'my card has been full for ages. Stop—you shall have one of Mr. Desvœux's; he does not matter and he has put down his name for several too many. Shall it be the fifteenth?' Maud asked this in the most artless way and seemingly without a suspicion that Boldero could be otherwise than pleased. Alas! how far otherwise than pleased he felt! The fifteenth! and then only a sort of crumb of consolation from Desvœux's over-ample banquet! How cruel for a man whose heart was beating high with hope, and who had risen to that state of nervous excitement when to propose would have been easier than not! The charmer had come and gone. The next moment Boldero saw her hurrying off with a new partner and laughing just the same joyous, child-like laugh that had been ringing in his ears for weeks. 'What could that idiotic young ensign have said to make her laugh?' How could any one laugh while Boldero found existence rapidly growing into a Sahara around him? What business had Maud to smile so affectionately on each new comer? Then what was this intimacy with Desvœux which enabled her to treat him so unceremoniously? How came he to be putting down his name for what dances he pleased? Boldero moodily denounced the object of his devotion as a flirt of the purest water and not over-particular in her selection of admirers. As for Desvœux, could any really nice girl like such a fop as that? Poor Boldero, in the amiable, sensible condition of mind which jealousy provokes, plunged at once into despair, felt too acutely miserable to dance, and resigned himself, a melancholy wall flower, to the contemplation of enjoyment in which fate forbade him to participate.

Presently Maud came back and put every depreciatory thought about herself to instant flight. There had been some mistake about a quadrille, she said, and her partner was not forthcoming, and so she had taken flight at once. It was so dull dancing with people one did not know; and would it not be nice if it was the fashion to dance only with one's friends? 'And now,' she said, 'do take me outside to look at the moon.' Maud was evidently bent on being kind and gracious; and Boldero, blushing to think what an idiot he had been making of himself, took her out into the balcony, where the Bachelors' industry had worked wonders with ferns and flowers and sofas poetically suggestive of a *tête-à-tête* and all that an artistic Bachelor's soul dreams of as appropriate to balls. There lay the still valley at their feet—all its depths filled with motionless white clouds, that glistened in the moonlight like a silver lake. The twinkling fires of the hamlets opposite were one by one dying out of sight. The solemn pine-shade all around, wherever the moonlight could not pierce, made the rest of the picture seem ablaze with glory. Is there a sweeter, softer radiance in the world than the moonlight of the Himalayas? 'This is enchanting,' Maud said, in great spirits; 'how I should like to sketch it! Why should we not have a moonlight party? And you will do my sketch for me, will you not, Mr. Boldero? Let me get Mr. Desvœux to arrange it; he is great at such things; and we can make him sing to us and play on his guitar, which he does delightfully, while we are drawing—would it not be delicious?'

Boldero, in his heart, doubted the deliciousness of any programme in which Desvœux figured as a performer. He had no time to reply, however, for all too soon—before, as it seemed, he and his companion had well established themselves—the quadrille had ended, and Maud's claimant for the next dance came bustling up; and Maud, who thought moonlight all very well but would not have missed a valse for the world, went gleefully away, smiling her adorer a kind farewell that sent him sevenfold deeper into love than ever.

No proposal, it was clear enough, was destined to be made that night; but would the scheme look hopefuller to-morrow? Boldero lay tossing through the few hours which intervened before to-morrow, already reddening the eastern horizon, came, and could give himself no satisfactory reply. She liked him, certainly; but with how many was this precious privilege shared? He was one of the 'friends' with whom Maud liked to dance; but the list was so long, that all through a long evening he could with difficulty get near her for a minute. She would come with him for a moonlight picnic; but then Desvœux was to arrange it, Sutton, no doubt, to preside, and half-a-dozen more attendant courtiers to swell the little monarch's train. Boldero's manly bosom heaved with sighs. His servant, inexperienced in such symptoms, brought him, unbidden, a large beaker of iced soda-water, as if the flames of love could be extinguished by that innocent beverage.

Maud had, in fact, been very much impressed with Boldero, and, with the frankness of inexperience, had taken good care to let him know it. At this period of her career novelty possessed a wondrous charm and the last admirer had a strong recommendation in being the last. Boldero forgot that at Elysium this fortunate advantage was no longer his. Still Maud smiled upon him, as she did on almost every one who aspired to her smiles. It was not so much fickleness as the keen pleasure of success, the most natural and pleasantest, probably, of all human successes,—the proved capacity to charm mankind. What faint adumbration of love had darkened the sunshine of her heart was all for Sutton; and even this was a sort of transient pang, which the excitement of daily life made it easy to forget. Knowing but faintly what love meant, she mistook, as women often do, the thrill of flattered vanity for solid feeling. Boldero had not disguised his admiration, nor Maud the pleasure which it gave her. Mutual satisfaction had been the natural result. Poor Boldero, who was always rushing at conclusions and unskilled in the tactics of the feminine heart, thought himself at once the happiest of men and gilded his horizon with a bright aurora of matrimonial bliss. Maud meanwhile, by a hundred half-unconscious arts, encouraged the delusion and established the relation of friendly intimacy. When he looked across the room her bright eyes met his and spoke him the heartiest recognition. She would look up wearily from some uncongenial companion and find Boldero watching her, and a glance would sign the pledge of mutual understanding. 'Here is the song you liked,' she had said only the evening before, 'and I like it too;' and then she had sung it, and each note had caught a new charm in being intended especially for his ear. So it was that Boldero had fallen into the too common mistake of impetuous lovers: he thought, poor mortal, that Maud had fallen violently in love with him; the truth being that she was merely rather pleased at the symptoms of his being violently in love with her, and accepted his homage with a light heart, as hardly more than her due.

CHAPTER XIX.

A BRUSH ON THE FRONTIER.

Tell me not, love, I am unkind,
  That from the nunnery
Of thy chaste breast and quiet mind
  To war and arms I fly.

The reign of peace and pleasure was not destined to last through the summer undisturbed. Conflicts, more serious than those which were agitating poor Boldero's breast, broke in upon the tranquil season and caused a hurried dispersion of many of the holiday-makers.

For weeks past the news from the frontier had not been reassuring. Blunt had gone off on his mission to the Rumble Chunder District, dragging the miserable Whisp, who could not ride and hated leaving head-quarters, in his train. He had mastered the whole matter, as he considered, from first to last and was resolved to bring his knowledge to bear with good effect upon the entanglements which his predecessors' ignorance and indistinctness had produced. He saw his way quite clearly and was resolved to have it. Other people had faltered and hesitated; but Blunt was resolved to strike, and to strike hard, and to finish the matter and have done with it once for all. He arrived, accordingly, in no mood to be trifled with, as Mahomed Khan, the first of the Zamindars who had an interview with him, discovered in about two minutes. Now, Mahomed Khan, a wily old gentleman, with a great turn for diplomacy, was deeply interested in the Rumble Chunder question, and had, at different times, interviewed a long succession of 'Sahibs' with reference to it. He had invariably found them long-suffering, conciliatory, anxious to learn and not difficult to puzzle. He had talked to them at ease in his own language and was accustomed to the elaborate courtesy due to the leader of a powerful and not over-loyal clan. His antecedents entitled him to respect. When Sutton was getting his troop together in the Mutiny a word from Mahomed Khan would have put the whole district in a blaze and rendered it impossible to recruit a man. The liking, however, which one good soldier feels for another had carried the day. The old fellow had ridden with fifty followers into Sutton's camp, unstrapped his sword, and, placing it in Sutton's hands, had sworn that he and his would follow him wherever he pleased to lead them. Well had the oath been kept; when some months later the fighting closed, Mahomed Khan's name was recorded as amongst the most deserving of Her Majesty's lieges, and his well-timed loyalty had resulted in a fine grant of fat acres, a conspicuous seat in the Durbar, and, not least in the estimation of men keenly sensitive to honour, a vast deal of complimentary writing and talking on the part of every British official with whom he had to deal. All this flattery had, perhaps, turned the old soldier's head, or, at any rate, had given him no small idea of his importance to the British 'Ráj' and of his claims to the gratitude of British administrators. His rights in the Salt matter had been left in convenient obscurity, and might, not without reason, be considered as tacitly conceded by the Power with whom he was on such affectionate terms.

This, however, was not at all the light in which Blunt saw the matter; he was annoyed at the man's bluster, pomposity and pretence. He was not in the least impressed by a well-worn packet of letters which his visitor produced, in which successive Generals and Commissioners had testified to his deserts; what he wanted was business, and this was essentially unbusinesslike. If Sutton had written, 'You have proved yourself a brave and loyal soldier, and I will ever be your friend,' this was no reason why Mahomed Khan should not pay his salt-dues like other folk, or should object to have his title-deeds rigidly overhauled. 'If it was just, why had Sir John Larrens Sahib never done it?' the old man objected; but Blunt did not care what Sir John Lawrence had done or had not done; what he wanted was his bond, and nothing else would satisfy him.

This was Blunt's first nettle, and he was grasping it firmly, with no doubts as to the propriety of the course. Then, at last, he got tired of the interview, and—fatal blunder for an Eastern diplomat—became abrupt and rude, and began to show his hand. Thereupon Mahomed Khan began to show his teeth and went away in a surly mood with the news, which spread like wildfire among the clansmen, that the Sirkar was going to rule them with a heavy hand; that all old rights were to be cancelled; a grievous land-tax to be imposed, and that a terrible 'Sahib,' of fierce aspect, had arrived to see this objectionable policy carried out.

Then Blunt found the investigation by no means the simple matter he had hoped. Statements, which looked so neat and clean when submitted to the Board and neatly minuted on by Whisp, assumed an aspect of hopeless inexplicability when Blunt had them face to face; and the more he questioned the less he understood. He was armed with powers to examine witnesses, but not a word of truth could be got out of any one. Fine old countrymen, whose noble bearing, well-chiselled features and long flowing beards would have made a fortune in a Roman studio, came before him and told him the most unblushing lies with a volubility and earnestness that fairly staggered Blunt's bewildered comprehension.

To say one thing to-day, the precise opposite to-morrow, and to explain with easy grace that it was a mistake, or that the evidence had been wrongly taken down, seemed to every man whom Blunt interrogated the correct and natural procedure for a person who was being pressed for information which it was inconvenient to produce. Some men remembered everything; others professed the most absolute obliviousness; each contradicted all the rest, except when Government interests were concerned, and then all swore together like a band of conspirators. To make confusion worse confounded, the accounts were kept on a system which none of the Salt Board people understood and which no one else could be induced to explain.

Then, by some fatality, the white ants had always eaten the precise documents of which Blunt stood in need, and the trembling officials produced a tattered mass of dirt and rags and assured him that this was the record which he called for, or rather all that could be found of its remains.

Blunt became, day by day, more profoundly convinced that all men—all the Rumble Chunder men, at any rate—were liars, and let his conviction appear in short speeches and abrupt procedure. The old Zamindars, outraged by discourtesy in the presence of their retainers, came away from his presence quivering with rage and ripe for the first chance of mischief which offered. Blunt found the nettle stinging him sorely, and, like a rough, resolute man, grasped it with all the more unflinching hand. When at last he succeeded in making out a case he dealt out the sternest justice, not, perhaps, without a gratified vindictiveness against the people who had so long baffled and annoyed him. One Uzuf Ali, a large grantee, had been called upon to verify his claims; and this he proceeded to do with the utmost alacrity. He and his forefathers, he protested, had been in possession for centuries—look at the Revenue records, the files of the Courts, the orders of Government. Here, too, was a Sunnud from the Emperor Akbar confirming them in their rights. Twenty witnesses, all disinterested, honourable, unimpeachable, the entire village indeed, would attest the fact of continuous, open, rightful enjoyment from a period as far as memory could go. So the twenty witnesses did; but then appeared a gentleman, one Hosain Khan, on the other side, and blew the pretty story into the air. Uzuf Ali was an audacious impostor, everybody in the country knew that his father had come from Delhi not thirty years ago; he had no more right to an ounce of salt than the 'Commissioner Sahib' himself; the ground over which he claimed his rights was notoriously in the possession of another man: as for the Sunnud of Akbar, it was an obvious forgery, as the Commissioner Sahib might see for himself by merely looking.

Hosain Khan having had his innings, Uzuf Ali returned to the wickets and began to make great play. 'Ask Hosain Khan,' he said, 'if his uncle did not carry off my sister and if some of our people did not kill him for it?'

'Yes,' says Hosain Khan, 'you stabbed him yourself, like a coward as you are, when he lay asleep by his bullocks.'

'And if I did,' cries his opponent, 'did not your father knock out my cousin's brains with a lathee[1] and get sent over the Kala Panee[2] for his pains?'

The controversy waxed ardent; the combatants' voices rose shrill and high; they tossed their black locks and waved their arms, and poured out long streams of passionate family history, long-cherished feuds—deep, never-to-be-forgotten wrongs—interminable complications as to lands and wells, women and bullocks; and Blunt, who understood nothing

[1] Club.

[2] Blackwater, i.e., sea.

but that they had travelled a long way from the Rumble Chunder Grant, sat by in mute and wrathful despair, and began to perceive that the administration of justice to folks so excitable and unveracious as these was no such easy matter as he had once imagined.

Amid all the chaff, however, Blunt had, he thought, got hold of one piece of solid fact: either the Sunnud was a forgery or it was not; and if a forgery, then he resolved to make an example, prosecute Uzuf Ali for his fraud, and turn him summarily out of his pretended rights. A forgery no doubt it was, for the paper bore the British watermark, and you could see the places where the gunpowder had been smeared in hopes of giving it an antiquated look. And so the question was decided, and the order made out, and poor Uzuf Ali, in vain protesting that it was a device of the enemy, left the Commissioner's presence a ruined man.

Ruined men, however, are dangerous things at all times, and especially with an excitable and easily frightened people, who see in their neighbours' fall only an anticipation of their own. The Bazaar was presently in a tumult: angry clusters of talkers gathered in circles round the grain-shops or at the village well, or under the great banyan-tree which spread a wide shade over one end of the street, and discussed past grievances and future disaster. Meanwhile Blunt, not with so light a heart or seeing his way as clearly as usual, had moved his head-quarters a dozen miles away, and begun a new series of investigations with a new set of Hosain Khans and Uzuf Alis, and with precisely similar success.

Before the month was over Fotheringam's words had come true. The Eusuf Khayls, a turbulent tribe of frontier freebooters, were up. A police outpost had been attacked in force one night, and its occupants had made a bad retreat, leaving two of their number on the field. The marauders had ridden through twenty miles of British territory, burning villages, destroying crops, driving away bullocks to their fastnesses in the hills. Blunt, as he came, escorted by a strong detachment, into Dustypore, met the Horse Artillery rattling out towards the disturbed region; and a telegram despatched to Elysium informed Sutton that he was to head a flying column into the enemies' country and that he must be with his regiment without an instant's delay.

CHAPTER XX.

A LAST RIDE.

He turned his charger as he spoke
Upon the river-shore;
He gave the bridle-reins a shake,
Said 'Adieu for evermore,
My love!
And adieu for evermore!'

SUTTON, who was practising '*La ci darem là mano*' with Maud when the telegram arrived, glanced at its contents without stopping the duet and slipped it into his pocket before Maud had even seen it. '*Andiam, Andiam, Andiam,*' she sang joyfully; '*Andiam, Andiam, Andiam*' pealed Sutton's pleasant tenor tones; '*d'un innocente Amor*' sang the two together; so the performance came smoothly to its close. 'And now,' Sutton said, 'I am afraid we must stop our practice for this morning, as I have to go to the Viceroy. I will come and see you on my way back. I may have to go down to Dustypore this afternoon.'

'Down to Dustypore!' Maud cried, in a tone that bespoke the pang of disappointment that shot into her heart, 'I thought that you were to stay all the summer?'

'And so did I,' said her companion; 'but unluckily some of my naughty boys on the Hills out there have been getting into too good spirits, and I must go and look after them. And now for his Excellency.'

Before Sutton had been gone many minutes Desvœux came galloping up the pathway, and found Maud still standing in the verandah, where she had wished Sutton farewell, and where in truth she had been standing in a brown study ever since he went. Desvœux was in the gloomiest spirits, far too much concerned about himself to pay much attention to Maud's troubled looks. 'Have you heard the dreadful, dreadful news?' he said. 'All our holidays are over for the year. There has been an outbreak on the frontier. The troops are already on the march. The Agent is closeted with the Viceroy and goes down this afternoon, and of course poor I have to go along with him. Sutton is to command the expedition, and, I daresay, is off already. Every soldier in the place will be ordered down; and meanwhile what is to become of the fancy-ball?'

'And the moonlight picnic?' cried Maud, suddenly conscious of the necessity of concealing a feeling which she would not for the world have had Desvœux suspect, namely, that Sutton's absence would be to her a calamity which would go far to render balls and picnics alike a matter of indifference.

'Yes,' Desvœux said, with bitter vehemence; 'life is sometimes too unendurably disagreeable, and things go so provokingly as one does not want them. And we were just having such a happy time! And then, I suppose, to make our farewell the sadder, you have chosen this morning to look your loveliest. As for me, the only bits of life I care about any longer are those I spend with you.'

'And with Mrs Vereker,' cried Maud. 'Come, Mr. Desvœux, confess, now, have you not been there just this minute saying the very same thing to her? I'll ask her this afternoon and we will compare notes as to our adieux!'

'Profane idea!' said Desvœux. 'But you are always mocking. You know I care a great deal more about you than you do about me.'

'Impossible,' cried Maud. 'Did I not tell you just now that I was broken-hearted about the picnic? I meant to sit by the waterfall and make you sing us "Spirito Gentil" in the moonlight. It is a cruel disappointment.'

'You are very unkind and very heartless,' said Desvœux in no mood for banter.

'Come, come,' said Maud, 'do not be cross; we will not quarrel just as we are parting.'

'Well, then, be serious.'

'I am serious,' said the other; 'and, seriously, I am sorry that we are to lose you. Poor fellow!'

'Give a poor fellow a present,' said Desvœux, beseechingly; 'that cherry riband that binds the loveliest neck in the world.'

'No, I won't,' said Maud; 'it cost me two rupees only the day before yesterday. There, you may have this rose. Take it, take it, and remember——'

'You are enough to drive a fellow mad,' said Desvœux. 'Who will be the lucky man to find out where your heart is, and whether you have got one?'

Then Desvœux cantered off and Maud retired to her bedroom, locked herself in, threw herself on a couch and indulged in the unusual luxury of a thoroughly good cry. Sutton, quite unconsciously, had made great advances in the occupation of her heart. He had been constantly with her and Felicia; and the more Maud saw of other people, the more convinced she became that he was the paragon of men and with him the only chance of happiness for her. And now he would come back presently, Maud knew, and say a kind, feeling farewell to Felicia and a word or two of politeness to her, and go away on his expedition and take all the sunshine of existence with him, and never have a suspicion of the aching heart he left behind and of the treasure of devotion waiting for him if he chose to have it. Surely there must be something wrong in the constitution of a world where such woes could come to pass.

So while Desvœux, in a sort of half-rage, was hustling his pony down the hillside as if he really did mean to break his neck once for all and have done with a life in which Maud could not continually figure, Maud herself was in affliction for quite another cause; and Sutton, his mind too full of warlike schemes to think of love, was busy with a map spread out on the Viceroy's table, pointing out exactly the route through the Hills which the expedition was to take. Sutton and the Viceroy were the best of friends. They had ridden and shot and slaughtered tigers and bears in each other's company, and each knew and liked the other as a daring, enthusiastic and thoroughgoing sportsman. The Viceroy, himself no mean performer, had seen Sutton dispose of a big boar, turned to bay, on more than one occasion in a way which had filled him with admiration and delight; and when, in rare intervals of business, the Ruler of India allowed himself a day's holiday for a walk through the forest in search of bears or jungle pheasants, no more favourite companion than Sutton ever helped to fill the bag. Each trusted the other thoroughly, and the Viceroy now spoke of the expedition with a cheerful confidence indicative of his conviction that it was in the proper hands. The main plans had been actually settled. The force was to be pushed on as far into the Hills as was practicable. Two strong mule-batteries were provided to keep the mountain-sides clear of a hovering enemy. When they reached the high table-land which lay beyond, a dash was to be made at a village where one of the rebellious tribes was known to be entrenched in force; and when this was seized and destroyed and the rebels for the time dispersed, the little army was to be encamped for a few weeks, by way of demonstration of military power to the refractory mountaineers. 'Good-bye, Sutton,' said the Viceroy, 'and good luck to you and speedy return!' And then, as he went out, kind ladies met him in the hall and wished him a fresh farewell; and Sutton went away, in a glow of excitement and pleasure, to make his preparations for the afternoon's gallop, unconscious of all the sentiment in another person's heart which his departure was stirring into life. He would be gone a fortnight or three weeks, and was, in truth, not sorry for an excuse for a return to his dear soldiers after a month's idleness and holiday-making.

When he came to the Vernons, an hour later,

he found Maud's pony at the door, and herself ready-equipped.

'Would you like a companion for the first stage of your journey?' Felicia said; 'if so, Maud will ride with you, and the children and I will start later, and meet her on the way home.' This was, in fact, a kind device of Felicia's—one of the rash things which people do when they are completely perplexed, in a sort of wild hope that some good may come of it, rather than with any precise design. Felicia had come with distressing distinctness to recognise the full gravity of the position and to feel how dreadfully she had been to blame. She had done all that one woman can to lead another to fall in love, and she had succeeded only too well. Her little scheme of happiness for her two friends was marred by an impediment which she had altogether overlooked. Sutton's obduracy had never occurred to her as a serious impediment, yet now he seemed hopelessly unimpressible. Bitterly Felicia reproached herself for all her part in the transaction; but of what use was self-reproach? There was the terrible result, beyond the reach alike of penitence or redress. Maud's heart, Felicia knew instinctively, was lost—her very silence on the topic betrayed the consciousness of something to conceal. There was a sort of entreating air about her that seemed to cry for pity. More than once Felicia had taken her to her arms and embraced her tenderly—she could not have said why, but yet she knew. Maud, with her joyousness gone, and battling with a silent sorrow, seemed to her to have a touch of pathos which roused all the latent melancholy of Felicia's nature into activity. It was one of those sad things in life before which her fortitude completely failed. Ruefully did she vow, now that vowing was of no use, that her first attempt at match-making should be her last. At any rate she sent the two riders off together on this last ride, in the faint hope that something might occur to bring the tardy wooer to a right frame of mind.

CHAPTER XXI.

MAUD'S SECRET.

——In the glance,
A moment's glance, of meeting eyes,
His heart stood still in sudden trance—
He trembled with a sweet surprise;
All in the waning light she stood,
The star of perfect womanhood.

That summer eve his heart was light,
With lighter step he trod the ground,
And life was fairer in his sight,
And music was in every sound:
He bless'd the world where there could be
So beautiful a thing as she.

THE western horizon was all ablaze, and the sun's rays came slanting through the gloom of the Rhododendron Forest, as Sutton and his companion rode down the mountain-side towards the plains.

Did Felicia's wishes and hopes breathe a subtle influence around them, which drew their hearts together and opened to each the destiny which awaited it? Did the sweet, serious look with which she bade Sutton farewell speak to his eye, for years accustomed to watch for her unspoken commands, of something in which he had failed to please her, to understand her desire, to do or to be exactly what she wanted? Was there some shade of reserve, constraint, dissatisfaction in Felicia's manner that aroused his attention and led him to explore his companion with an anxious curiosity which usually he was far from feeling? Or was it something in Maud, a causeless embarrassment, a scarcely concealed trepidation, a manner at once sad and excited, the flush that, as Desvœux had told her in the morning, gave her cheek more than its accustomed beauty, which, before they had been ten minutes on the road, had sent such a flash of intelligence through Sutton's being,—which came upon him like an inspiration, clear, cogent, indisputable, and only curious in not having been understood before?

Be that as it may, Sutton suddenly found himself in an altogether different mood and in altogether different company to that which he had figured to himself for the first stage of his journey. Maud had all at once become supremely interesting and infinitely more beautiful than he had ever yet conceived her. She was no longer the mere excitable, romantic child, whose nascent feelings and ideas might be watched with half-amused curiosity, but a being whose brightness and innocence were allied with the most exquisite pathos, and who was ready to cast at the first worthy shrine all the wealth of an impulsive, ardent, tender nature. As for Maud, she was too excited, too profoundly moved, too much the prey of feelings of which she knew neither the true measure nor the full force, to be able to analyse her thoughts or to be completely mistress of herself.

Dissimulation was an art of which life had not as yet taught her the necessity, or experience familiarised the use. The unconscious hypocrisy with which some natures from the very outset, perhaps all natures later on in life, veil so much of themselves from the outer world, had never occurred to her as a possible or necessary means of self-protection in an existence which till now had been too simple, childish and innocent to call for concealment. She fixed her clear, honest eyes on her interrogator, whoever he was, be the question what it might, and he knew that it was the truth, pure, simple and complete, that she was telling. Each phase of feeling wrote itself on her expression almost before Maud herself had realised it, certainly long before she knew enough about it to attempt to conceal it from the world. The feeble attempts at deception, which the accidents of life had from time to time forced upon her, had proved such absolute failures as merely to warn her of the uselessness of everything of the kind, even if it had occurred to her to wish to deceive. Her courtesy was the courtesy of sincerity, and she had none other to offer. Those whom she disliked, accordingly, pronounced her rude, and it was fortunate that they were very few in number. Her friends, on the contrary, and their name was legion, read, and knew that they read, to the very bottom of her heart. Now, for the first time in her life, she was distinctly conscious of a secret which it would be misery and humiliation to divulge, but for the custody of which neither nature nor art had supplied her with any effectual means. Silence was the natural resource, but silence is sometimes more eloquent than speech. Whether she spoke or whether she held her peace, Maud felt a terrified conviction that she would betray herself, should it occur to Sutton to pay the least attention to her state of mind.

'There,' Sutton said, pointing to a range of hills just visible in the faint horizon, 'there is the Black Mountain, and there lies the pass where we shall be marching in a day or two. It is such a grand, wild place! I have been along it so often, but have never had leisure to paint it. This time, however, I hope to get a sketch.'

'Tell me,' Maud said, 'the sort of expeditions these are, and what happens, and what kind of danger you are all in.'

'I will tell you,' said her companion. 'They are hot, troublesome, inglorious promenades, over country which lames a great many of our horses and harasses our men. We burn some miserable huts, destroy a few acres of mountain crops and drive off such cattle as the people have not had time to drive away themselves, and, in fact, do all that soldiering admits of in the absence of that most important ingredient of a brilliant campaign, an enemy: *he*, unluckily, is invariably over the hills and far away some hours previous to our arrival.'

Maud felt this account to be on the whole reassuring: 'How soon,' she asked, 'will you come back again?'

'Before you have time to miss me,' said her companion; 'it is an affair literally of days. Besides, Elysium, you will find, is all the pleasanter for having its crowd of soldiers somewhat thinned.'

'It will not be the pleasanter to us,' said Maud, 'for your being gone.'

Her tone took Sutton greatly by surprise.

'You are having a happy time here, are you not?' he asked. 'It seems to me a pleasant sort of life.'

'Yes,' said Maud, emphatically, 'the pleasantest, happiest I have ever known. All life has been bright to me; but there are things in it that hurt one, for all that.'

'Yes?' said Sutton, with a kind inquiry in his tones, for he had never thought of Maud but as the pretty incarnation of enjoyment; 'well, tell me the things which hurt you.'

'The things that have hurt me the most,' said Maud with a sudden impulse of outspokenness, 'are partings. They grieve me, even though I know that they are no real cause for grief. I minded leaving school and my dear mistress more than I can tell, and yet I longed to go. I minded leaving my friends on board ship, and yet I had only known them a month. I minded leaving you at Dustypore when we came away, and now to-day I am sad because you are leaving us.'

'That makes me sad too,' said Sutton, grieved, and yet not wholly grieved, at each new phase of sentiment which the childish frankness of his companion revealed to him; 'but, you know, we soldiers are for ever on the move, and nobody is surprised or sad when we are ordered off. You love Felicia, do you not?'

'Yes,' said Maud, seriously; 'I feel a sort of worship for her. Who could be so sweet, noble and pure without being adored? But then she makes me melancholy too sometimes, because she is so melancholy herself; and, oh, how far above one! Could one ever hope to be half as good? She fills me with love, but love with a sort of despair about it.'

Maud was highly wrought up and feeling strongly and painfully about everything that formed her life. She was full of thoughts that clamoured for expression; and Sutton, she knew not why, seemed the natural and proper recipient; it was so easy almost to confess to him, to trust him with thoughts, hopes, pangs, which instinct said the common eye must never see; to claim from him a sort of gentle, chivalrous protection which no one but he knew how to give.

'Felicia,' Sutton said, 'need fill no one with despair, rather with hopefulness and courage about life. I have known her since she was a child; we two, in fact—children of two sisters, whose marriages had bound them closer in affection to each other—lived for years more as brother and sister than anything else. I have watched her for years gathering strength, calmness, and nobility from going nobly and calmly through the troubles of the world. She seems to me, in the midst of all that is vulgar and base in the world around her, like the Lady in Comus, impervious to everything that could sully or degrade.'

'Ah!' said Maud, 'if one could only go through life in that way—but it is so horribly unattainable. Everything is too difficult, and one is so shamefully weak. I could never be calm or noble in a trouble, like Felicia.'

'Wait till the troubles come,' said her companion kindly; 'you will find how one rises to an emergency. Felicia would not be what she is but for the trials she has borne. But see there is the guard, and here, alas! our pleasant journey together ends. I must travel on alone.'

A few hundred yards below stood Sutton's first relay of horses, and here they were to part. A trooper was waiting to escort Maud on her homeward journey till she rejoined Felicia and the children.

'This,' Sutton said, 'has been a charming ride, though something of a sad one. I shall like to remember it. See, you shall give me that sweet rose you wear, and that shall be my badge in all tournaments to come. In return I will give you something to keep for me. This locket, you know, holds my mother's hair. I never part with it; but I have often thought it a foolish risk to take it on such wild expeditions as this. This time you shall take care of it for me, if you will.

Sutton gave her the locket with the grave, pathetic air which, to Maud's eye, threw a sort of romance over his least important actions. He took her hand and held it in his own, and it seemed as though some sacred pledge were at the moment, with no spoken words, given and received.

Maud never afterwards forgot that little scene—the kind, gentle eyes, the sorrowful furrowed brow, the tender solemn voice; in front the wide mysterious plains, stretching far below, all the horizon still aglow with the expiring glory of the sunset; behind her a cold blue darkening world—the gathering vapours, no longer irradiated, settling in solid masses on the solemn mountain-tops. As she came to a bend in the path she turned to wish her companion a last farewell, for she knew that he was watching her departure. Then she rode homewards through the gloom, moved, agitated, frightened, yet on the whole happier — with a deeper kind of happiness than she had ever known before.

CHAPTER XXII.

LOVE IS BEGUN.

Love is begun—thus much is come to pass;
The rest is easy.

SUTTON rode onward in a condition of happy bewilderment. He recalled the conversation, every word Maud had spoken—her look, her tone: and as he did so the result of the whole seemed to take a deeper hold upon his mind. An afternoon's ride with a pretty girl—what was there in it to a man like Sutton, the experienced companion of so many who had both the power and the will to charm? What was there in this child to whom he had shown the mere ordinary good-nature due to her circumstances, that all of a sudden, he hardly knew whether by her doing or his own, he should find himself completely fascinated? How was it, too, that the first woman with whom he really felt in love should be so different from the ideal which all his life he had set before himself of what was especially lovable? In his childhood he had loved Felicia with the spontaneous and unconcealed attachment of a near relation. Then had followed years of school, long expeditions abroad, a life which soon became adventurous, grave cares, anxieties and interests at a time when most lads are still trifling over their lessons. Sutton had not only to push his own way in life, but to keep guard over others less capable than himself, of whom he found himself, while still a boy, constituted the natural protector. His mother, suddenly left a widow, had looked to him unhesitatingly for counsel, protection and—so Sutton's account book would have testified —supplies, which he was ill able to contribute. Brothers had had to be set a-going, and kept a-going, in that troublesome and anxious process of making a livelihood in a world where no one is in the least want of one's services. Then Fortune and Valour had combined to push Sutton forward as a soldier, and one or two adventures, brilliant because they were not disastrous, made him a reputation which secured him constant employment. When, years later, he had met Felicia again, a newly-arrived bride, in the Sandy Tracts, though he felt towards her the same affection as ever, it had not occurred to him to envy the man who was now lawful possessor of that to which he might have seemed, had circumstances allowed, a natural pretender. He had remained the loyal friend of both. None the less was Felicia the typical conception in his mind of what a woman ought to be.

Her grave, refined serenity; her unstudied dignity of form and gesture; her mirthfulness flashing all about a melancholy mood; her sorrows so acutely felt, so bravely borne, so sedulously concealed; the prompt excitability that made the world full of pleasures and interests to her, and her a moving influence in the world; the tenderness of sympathy which, beginning in the little home centre, spread in increasing circles to all who came within her range of thought or action and enthroned her mistress of a hundred hearts,—made up the type which his imagination had adored. Now he was startled to find himself kneeling at quite another shrine, adoring quite another deity, and adoring it, as he was constrained to confess to himself, with a sudden, vehement devotion, characteristic rather of boyish enthusiasm than of the mature sobriety of middle age.

Anyhow, as Sutton rode into the yard of the little inn where dinner awaited him, he wished, for the first time in his life, that the campaign was well over and himself safe back again at the pacific pursuits on which duty was just now sternly calling him to turn his back.

Here he found the Agent and Desvœux, who had been busy all the afternoon with despatches and were waiting now for the moonlight to allow them to get forward on their journey.

Desvœux, as was always the case in times of difficulty, had risen to the occasion and fully justified the confidence of those who placed a seeming fop in a responsible position. He had been working all day like a slave, and he was now dining like an Epicurean, and in higher spirits than Epicureans mostly are. The Agent, who kept him in thorough order and got an inordinate amount of first-rate work out of him at times, rewarded him by a generous confidence and a liberty of speech in private, which no other subordinate enjoyed. A jaded, weary official, with an uncomfortably lively scepticism as to the usefulness of himself and his system to the world, forced into all sorts of new and uncomfortable conditions, could not but be grateful to an assistant whose spirits, like Desvœux's, were always in inverse ratio to the darkness of surrounding things, whose cynicism was always amusing, and whose observations on the world around and above him, if frequently somewhat impertinent, were never without good sense and insight.

At present both Desvœux and his master were abusing Blunt over an excellent bottle of champagne. Sutton was soon installed at the banquet, which presently began *da capo* on his account.

'We shall have no moon till eleven,' said the Agent; 'so Desvœux and I are amusing ourselves by inveighing against poor Blunt for the kettle of fish he has set a-boiling down below; and which you and your troopers, Sutton, must dispose of as best you can. It is another instance of that bane of the service—zeal. Tallyrand was quite right to insist on no one having any of it.'

'Yes, sir,' said Desvœux; 'Enthusiasm, Experience and Principle may be said to be the three rocks on which we get shipwrecked—enthusiasm, because it gives us affairs like this of Blunt's; experience ——'

'Experience and principle require no illustration,' said the Agent, filling up Sutton's glass and his own. 'I feel how disastrous they are in my own case. But, seriously, one of the difficulties in dealing with a matter is that you always have to rescue it from the clutches of some one who knows too much by half about it, and who takes a host of details for granted of which nobody but himself has the faintest glimmer of understanding. You are right, Desvœux, in naming experience as one of your banes; I qualify it by the addition of an epithet—inarticulate.'

'Oh!' cried Desvœux, gaily, 'one takes that for granted. If men possessed the art of making themselves understood, there would be no difficulty in governing at all.'

'Yes,' said the Agent; 'officials and their reports remind one of cuttle-fish, beings capable of extruding an inky fluid for the purpose of concealing their intentions. And now, Sutton, king of men, tell us how soon you mean to lead the bold Acheans to the fray.'

'As fast as I can march the bold Acheans up. In three days at the furthest I hope to be well into the enemy's country; the mule battery will, I expect, do wonders in bringing about a loyal state of mind, and I may rely on the mules and camels for my commissariat?'

'You may rely,' said the Agent; 'I sent word to Boldero yesterday.' And Sutton knew that on that score, at any rate, he might feel secure.

'Boldero,' cried Desvœux, 'has no doubt by this time impressed every donkey in the province and has a cavalcade of camels awaiting us. The job will, it is to be hoped, have driven Miss Vernon out of his poor bleeding heart. Here is to her good health.'

'And here's to Mrs Vereker's,' cried Sutton, who felt an urgent need of an immediate change in the conversation.

'Cruel, cruel Sutton,' cried Desvœux, 'to suggest the mournful thought. Let me see; it is half-past ten. I left at noon. I grieve to think that I have been forgotten an entire afternoon. Mrs. Vereker's recollections, I believe, never survive a repast. Luncheon, no doubt, swept me from her thoughts.'

'Desvœux,' said the Agent, 'you are a very unfeeling young man. I believe I am rather in love with Mrs. Vereker myself.'

'Then, sir, I presume you will wish me to transfer my attentions elsewhere; but meanwhile let me dream of the paradise I have quitted—

> In the clear heaven of her delightful eye
> An angel guard of loves and graces lie;
> Around her knees domestic duties meet——'

'So that,' interposed the Agent, 'as you look at her face, and not at her knees, you naturally see more of the loves and graces than of the domestic duty.'

'Indeed, sir,' cried Desvœux, 'she is all that a wife and mother should be.'

'Very well,' said the Agent; 'then go and order the horses and let us be off.'

CHAPTER XXIII.

A STRAY SHOT.

——A barren strand,
A petty fortress and a dubious hand——

THE expedition, though in no way distinguishable from twenty others, did not prove such a mere promenade as Sutton had anticipated. The whole country-side was in a nasty, excitable mood. The news of Blunt's injudicious proceedings had spread far and wide, and the prospect of endangered rights turned the wavering scale with wild clans, whose loyalty at the best of times was anything but proof against a seeming danger or a fancied wrong.

Every landholder whose title Blunt had impugned proved a centre of disaffection; and even where there was no reason for hostility the example of unruliness was infectious. Many a stalwart hillsman, coerced for years into uncongenial tranquillity, felt the old pulses throb within him, and his heart beating high at the prospect of a fight; unearthed some primitive weapon—sword or matchlock or lance—from its hiding-place beneath the floor of his hut, mounted on a wiry pony and made his way over the mountains to the scene of action. Several more outrages, of which the District officers knew the significance too well, had already been reported. Everything predicted a storm, and a pretty severe one.

Indian life is like a strange, dark sea, full of invisible currents, strange tides, unsuspected and unexplained influences. The waters, which look so smooth and lifeless, may be stealing silently along and hurrying the hapless vessel to its doom. Magnetic streams, inappreciable to the nicest scrutiny, pour this way or that and disturb the most accurate calculations. Storms gather and lower and burst when all looks most serene; a little cloud rises in the quarter where danger is least expected, and in a few minutes the ship is tossing, a crushed and staggering wreck, in the midst of a tornado.

Just before the great outbreak of 1857 the ruler of India had occasion to remark on the absolute tranquillity of the Empire and on the peaceful prospects of a reign which stood, as the facts proved, on the very crisis of its fate, and whose annals were presently to be written in characters of blood. Men who live in such a world as this become sensitive to its symptoms, and adepts at interpreting them. The magistrates knew well enough—they could scarcely have said why—that mischief was at work. Police officers on remote stations wrote uneasily and hinted at the advisability of reinforcements. Strange, weird beings, whose unkempt locks and half-crazy visages bespoke for them the *prestige* of especial sanctity, thronged about the bazaars, the wells, the spreading tree where travellers halted for rest and talk. A famous Fakir went through the District haranguing excited audiences on the kindred duties of piety and rebellion against an impious ruler. Then the first drops of the storm began to fall. One morning the collector of a neighbouring town was sitting in his verandah; in front a pair of saddled horses were being led up and down; by his side was a tea-table, with letters, business papers and the frugal repast which ushers in the Indian official's day. At his feet two little children sat at play. From inside a lady's voice cried that she would be ready for a start in two minutes. Presently an animated bundle of rags, hair and dirt, came grovelling up with a petition. The misery of the creature was its passport, and the sentry who stood by, at a signal from the officer, let it pass. Then came a whining, rambling, unintelligible story of grievance; and then, as the listener's eye for a moment wandered from the speaker, a sudden rush—the flash of a concealed dagger—a groan—a heavy fall, and the Englishman lay dead on the ground with a cruel Pathan knife-wound through his heart. The assassin stood fiercely at bay, exulting in his accomplished vow to slay a 'Feringhee,' and trying his best to stab the sentry who approached him. They cut him down as he stood; and before noon that day rumour had whispered in a hundred villages that Allah's will had been done, and that the Jehad, or Sacred War, was forthwith to commence.

To strike quickly, effectually, and with an air of absolute confidence in the result, is in such cases the safest policy. A symptom of hesitation, an hour's delay, would ensure disaster. The spark, which one moment might be stamped under foot, the next would be a consuming fire, forbidding all approach.

Sutton's business was, he well understood, to teach these lawless spirits (which no conqueror has ever yet succeeded in taming) a stern lesson of obedience, and to teach it them quickly, sharply, and in the mode most likely to impress the popular imagination. If all went well the business would be over in a week, and the refractory clansmen our good friends and subjects till temper, forgetfulness, or an official blunder produced another outburst. If things went ill—but this is a contingency upon which the administrators of British India cannot afford to calculate and which Sutton's temperament and good fortune alike had long accustomed him to ignore.

When he rode into the camp he found everything in readiness and everybody in the highest spirits. Boldero had impressed a fine array of camels and bullock-carts, and had organised a commissariat train more than sufficient for the wants of the expedition. The mule battery had arrived in perfect order. The little knot of officers who were to join the expedition gave a hearty welcome to a leader whose very presence seemed to them the best guarantee of success. In a minute the news spread through the camp that the 'Colonel Sahib' had arrived, and the men, whom he had led so often to victory, glowed at the thought that the well-loved and well-trusted leader was once again in the midst of them and that something stirring was certainly at hand. The little force was to encamp that night at the bottom of the pass along which for the next two days their route would lie; then they would come to a high level table-land, where the enemy was (so the scouts said) entrenched, and where the serious part of the business might be expected to begin.

Occasions such as these were the parts of Sutton's life in which hitherto he had felt himself most at home, and which he had, in fact, enjoyed the most keenly. He had been very successful, and had, he knew, been not undeserving of success. This was the thing in life which he could do pre-eminently well, and the doing it gave him a thrill of pleasure, which lasted all through the duller parts of his existence. Yet now things seemed changed to him. He had looked forward to this expedition with enthusiasm; it had taken in every way the shape which he wished; and now, when the hour was come, it had brought no sense of pleasure with it. Sutton was startled at his own lack of zeal. The lads who were having their first apprenticeship in actual soldiering, were, he felt, far more soldier-like about it than he was. He could not sleep that night, and strolled about the camp amid all the old accustomed sights and sounds; the long array of human sleeping forms, each one motionless and corps-like; the lines of tethered horses; the sentinels pacing stolidly up and down and challenging the passer-by in the still, clear air; the bullocks encamped by their carts, serenely chewing through the peaceful hours undisturbed by the thought of pokes and shoves which awaited them on the morrow. It was all very familiar, and brought back many a like occasion of former years; and yet there was, Sutton knew, a difference: the world was no longer the same; a new current of thought and feeling had set in and disturbed all the old associations. His afternoon ride had metamorphosed his entire being. Maud's sweet impassioned air as she had wished him farewell; her serious, soft, pathetic tones; her last look as she turned to go, the sort of earnest rapture which her eyes bespoke; the unspoken pledge which had been exchanged between them; these were the matters which preoccupied his thoughts and left but scant room in them for the business which he had in hand. He found himself, accordingly, uninterested, unenthusiastic, and, for the first time in his life, completely sceptical as to the usefulness of his employment. Every man, philosophers tell us, is seized at some period of his career with a misgiving as to whether his life-task is not a delusion. Is it worth the long, painful endeavour, the patient waiting, the resolute hopefulness which a successful career demands? Life seems, as it did to the sailors of Ulysses, a wearisome, endless affair,

For ever climbing up the climbing wave;

Is it certain that the end for which we struggle so earnestly is good for ourselves or for any one? Sutton had such a mood just now strong upon him. He had been all his life soldiering; a hundred time-honoured phrases had declared it the finest profession in the world; but what did it come to? To be chasing a pack of lawless savages about a country scarcely less savage than themselves, and inflicting a chastisement which no one supposed would be more than temporarily effectual. To drill a handful of freebooters into something sufficiently like discipline to render them effectual as an instrument of destruction; to march up a pass and stamp out the first germs of civilised life by burning a few wretched crops and crumbling hovels; to fire at an enemy always well out of reach, and then march down again; what was there in all this to deserve the thought, the devotion, the sacrifice of life itself, which men so freely gave in its pursuit? Had not life something better worth living for than this? Were not the civilians right who sneered at soldiering as a meet occupation for brainless heads and hands for which, if not kept thus wholesomely employed, Satan was sure to find some less desirable occupation? Thus it came to pass that of all the men who marched in the expedition its leader was the one who was least in love with it.

Two days later Sutton had warmed into his work and was in better spirits. The march had been delightful. The splendid military road, which coiled in and out among the folds of the mountain, robbed the journey alike of anxiety and fatigue. Nothing gives a pleasanter sense of power and triumph over nature than these great engineering exploits. You canter along a splendid road with easy gradients, a scarcely perceptible ascent; there is a precipice above, a precipice below, and no spot anywhere on which, till the hand of science came to make it, a human foot could rest. Every now and then a distant vista reminds you that you are climbing some of the wildest and steepest hill sides in the world. The mountaineers may well cower and fly before a foe who begins with so impressive an achievement, and who cuts his way—resistless as fate itself—across the rocky brow of barriers which it seems half-mad, half-impious to try to scale.

The expedition, Sutton found, was in every way complete. His own regiment was always ready to march at twenty minutes' notice, and the General at Dustypore seemed to have been equally well prepared. The air, despite the hot sun, was fresh and exhilarating; the men were in the very mood for brilliant service. Besides, a peasant who had just been brought in from the district told them that, ten miles across the plain which now stretched away in gentle undulations before them, the enemy was entrenched in strength and intended to show fight. The village had been fortified, the man said, with a wall of earth and stones, and the fighters would be found behind it.

'Then, gentlemen,' cried Sutton, who was standing with a knot of officers at his tent door when the news arrived, 'I propose that we attack them to-night. If we let them have a day to do it in, these scoundrels will give us the slip.'

In half an hour the whole force was on the march. The day was delightfully fresh; the mountain-mists gathered overhead and formed a welcome shelter from the blazing sky. Sutton had his troopers on either flank; then came the tiny battery, looking more like playthings than the grim realities the Armstrongs proved; in the midst of a long line of Native Infantry. The men marched with a will and with the exciting consciousness that in the afternoon there was to be a fight. At noon, when there was a halt to rest the force, the outline of the village wall might be clearly seen, and those who had telescopes could make out an occasional figure creeping stealthily about. There was a little rising ground some half-mile from the village, and here Sutton determined to establish his battery. The tiny telescope-like tubes soon did their work, and the main gate of the village fell inwards with a crash; the mud wall crumbled and fell wherever it was touched, and a thick cloud of dust showed where each ball had lodged. In ten minutes the village was in flames, and Sutton's little army was advancing on it at a run. Presently they got within musket-shot, and bullet after bullet came singing through the air. Sutton was riding, with a trumpeter on the right, half-a-dozen yards in advance of his men; the ground, though firm and safe, grew rougher as they neared the village; and the troops' line was somewhat broken. By this time they could make out the mud wall which had been thrown up in front of the village and measure the paces between it and them. It was a mere nothing, but the men were going at it faster than they should. Two horses were struck and fell heavily just as their riders were pulling them together for the jump. Half-a-dozen more refused: then came the usual scene of rearing, plunging, and dismounted men. There was an instant's check, but only an instant's, for Sutton and the trumpeter were over, and the first dozen men who followed them had knocked the wall level with the ground. Sutton had speedily disposed of two of the hillsmen, who fired their pistols in his face and made at him with their swords; and had galloped up to help the trumpeter, who was having a hard time of it with a Sawar, mounted on a nimble little horse and evidently a competent and practised swordsman. The man turned on his noble antagonist and made a cut which left a deep dent on Sutton's sword-handle. The native had, however, met with more than his match. The others got over just in time to see Sutton cut him down, and his horse gallop wildly off with an empty saddle.

The men gave a shout and galloped forward. Then some one from a neighbouring window took a lucky shot. Sutton was at the moment giving an order and pointing with his sword in the direction indicated. His sword flew out of his hand, his arm fell powerless, and his horse, rearing up, fell back upon him. His native aide-de-camp dragged him out from under the horse, which was lying shot through the heart across him. Half-a-dozen men carried him to the rear. Ten minutes later, when the village had been cleared and the troop returned from the pursuit, they found him lying in a crimson pool, insensible, with a broken arm and a bullet-wound in his side, the red stream from which the surgeon, kneeling beside him, was endeavouring in vain to staunch.

CHAPTER XXIV.

THE GULLY.

I know not if I know what true love is;
But if I know, then if I love not him,
Methinks there is none other I can love.

PERHAPS the thing which more than any other exasperated Fotheringham about this unlucky frontier outbreak was the cool way in which Blunt took it. He quite ignored all responsibility in the matter. This was more than Fotheringham could forgive. When he had to come post-haste back to Dustypore, with his tail, so to speak, between his legs, leaving the country in a blaze behind him, with an escort of cavalry to protect him from the animosities which his proceedings had provoked, the least that could be expected of him was to wear the penitent air of a man who has had his own way and come to grief. Blunt, however, was as unabashed and uncompromising as before, and it had never, it was evident, crossed his mind that he could be the person to blame. The whole affair was gall and wormwood to Fotheringham: it was improper, incongruous, and a shock to his perceptions of the eternal fitness of things. It never ought to have happened—never, so his fine instincts told him, would have happened—but for this rough, self-confident, inexperienced outsider. It came too at the most horrid time of year, just when almost every one was at the hills and the few whose ill-luck compelled them to remain in the plains were exhausted with the summer and in need of repose. The Misses Fotheringham and their mamma had been all the summer at Elysium, and poor Fotheringham had been meaning to join them for a few weeks' autumnal holiday; and this was now out of the question. This in itself was no small grievance. And then, on public grounds, Fotheringham felt the outbreak a sort of stain on himself and the institution which he cared most about. The Salt Board might be to others a mere abstraction, but he had worked at it and in it till he had come to regard it with a sort of fondness. Now Blunt's mismanagement exhibited the Board in a perfectly false light, as political incendiaries. The Rumble Chunder Grant was made to figure as a stone of stumbling and rock of political offence, instead of, as its advocates felt it to be, a sort of moral buffer on which any little unpleasantness which the wear and tear of government engendered, was allowed to vent itself in safety. Fotheringham had exactly foretold the result, and felt, it must be supposed, that kind of melancholy satisfaction which the most good-natured prophets of evil cannot but experience when their prophecies come true. He was too much of a gentleman to say to Blunt, 'There! I told you so,' in so many words; but this was what he *felt;* and this sort of inward triumph joined together with the other and graver aspects of the affair to make him treat Blunt in a manner, which, no doubt, the latter gentleman, pachydermatous as he was, found the reverse of soothing.

Cockshaw, too, in his idle way, was greatly put out and not at all inclined to make himself pleasant. He smoked more cheroots than ever—was more impatient of discussion—fidgeted worse when Fotheringham was settling down into nicely-rounded periods and getting real relief from doing so, and altogether did not behave as Fotheringham felt that he ought at a trying time.

Of his two colleagues Cockshaw had come to dislike Blunt by far the worst. Fotheringham, he knew, was an ass; but then he had known him as such ever since they were at Haileybury together as lads, and his being asinine seemed all right and proper in the natural course of things. With all his feebleness he had a sort of chivalry about him, a pride in his order, an enthusiasm about his work, a professional sympathy with his colleagues, which bound him to his brother-civilians. Blunt was a stranger to all this and was known to talk about the Civil Service in a way that made Cockshaw long to knock him down and give him a thrashing, as he would have done to a rude schoolfellow years ago. An article appeared in the 'Edinburgh Review' about the Government of India, which Cockshaw felt certain from its style was Blunt's, and which spoke of the administrators of the country with undisguised contempt. There was a phrase about 'one dead level of mediocrity,' which some angry Governor-General had used, and which the article quoted with an approval which Cockshaw could neither forgive nor forget. The Rumble Chunder Grant was quoted as a specimen of the gigantic messes which ensue, when second and third rate men have the management of first-rate questions. The local Governments were described as costly bureaux, with all the natural defects of a bureau and some peculiar evils of their own to boot—now meddlesome and fussy, now indolent and obstructive, frequently unprincipled and insubordinate. The three separate War establishments were disposed of with a sneer as the most expensive folly in existence. The vile corruption which characterised the East India Company in its earlier days, the scandalous exhibitions of public and private wickedness which fired the righteous wrath of Burke, had, the writer admitted, been rendered impossible by the increased communication with home and the generally improved tone of English manners; but Indian Governments had long remained the home of jobbery. The stringent remedy of the Competitive System had been necessary to deal with the accumulated dulness with which years of licensed favouritism had crowded the ranks of the service. On the whole it was not true, or anything like true, that India was well administered. The wonder, however, was, considering the class of men to whom the job had been entrusted, that it had ever got administered at all.

'D—— his impudence!' exclaimed Cockshaw with all the fervour of an indignation which had been gaining strength through a dozen pages of unpalatable reading; and the expression may be taken as representing in a concise formula the view which Cockshaw had come to take of his colleague's mental attitude, and of the respect or consideration to which he and his proposals were entitled.

The meetings of the board grew very stern and stiff. Unluckily, too, at this very time the Board's Annual Report had to be written, and the conflicting views of the members as to the cause of the disaster could scarcely fail to be brought prominently forward. It was one of the occasions which Strutt had been accustomed to treat historically, and which called, he felt, for something grander than Whisp's businesslike and unpretentious style. 'My good sir,' he would say, 'I have no time to read history: I am *making* it.' In the good old days, when Strutt had his own way, he would have knocked the affair off in half-a-dozen well-rounded, vague, magniloquent phrases; have left the connection of the Board with the whole thing in obscurity; have congratulated the Government on the excellent behaviour of the troops; applauded the accuracy and range of the Armstrong battery, and paid Providence a handsome compliment on the fortunate turn which events had taken.

But now Strutt felt a painful misgiving that this sort of thing would not do. When he began the paragraph—'The sun of the official year has set in blood,' he saw Blunt's horrid cynical look, and knew that he would never stand it. Any allusion to Providence—and Strutt felt that one was quite essential to anything like a proper peroration—Blunt would, he was sure, ruthlessly draw his pen through. Nor was it only as to matters of taste and style that Strutt felt embarrassed. Fotheringham would, he was certain, deprecate any reference to a connection between the outbreak and the Rumble Chunder Grant. 'Policy,' he would say, in a mysterious way, 'calls for reticence. We may be misconstrued, but we cannot afford to show all the world our hand; we don't want the hillmen to imagine that we admit them to have a grievance.' Blunt, on the other hand, would be for having it all down in black and white—for describing the outbreak as the natural result of indistinctness, cowardice and idleness. Altogether Strutt felt that his lines had been cast in rough places, and began to agree with Fotheringham that outsiders like Blunt were a mistake.

While things stood thus, one of those events occurred which form so constant a characteristic of Indian life and add so formidable a contribution to the difficulties of government. How is it possible to have continuity of action, settled policy, completeness of design, when existence is so shifting that no man who begins a work is likely to see its close? Promotion or leave or the chances of health keep the hierarchy of Indian officials for ever on the move. One man goes home to Europe, and his departure involves the change of a dozen others, each of whom is waiting anxiously for an advance and is entitled to step into his fellow's shoes. One of these vicissitudes befell the Board, for poor Fotheringham fell violently ill, and for some time seemed likely to create a permanent vacancy. A week's fever left him a skeleton, but a live one, and his only chance of re-established health was immediate flight for home. Accordingly, in fewer hours than it takes an English lady days to determine where she will spend her summer holiday, the Fotheringham establishment had moved off the scene. The fine barouche—the Australian carriage-horses—the lovely Arabs on which the Miss Fotheringhams took their morning exercise—the pretty garden where their mamma received society to tea and croquet—the dining-room where the Senior Member had regaled his friends—the library where he assailed his enemies—the piano at which the young ladies sang tremulous duets—the arm-chair in which Fotheringham had sate and thought or seemed to think—all became matters of the past. A neat paper, copied out by the elder Miss Fotheringham and containing the scanty catalogue of an Indian official's worldly belongings, was circulated in the Station, each item at so many rupees for those who liked to buy. Before the week was over the house was stripped, the simple treasures were scattered to a dozen new possessors, and the Fotheringhams, as the Arab folds his tent and glides silently away, had departed. The waters of the official life rolled smoothly over them, and next day the 'Dustypore Gazette' announced with laconic severity that Mr. Snaply had on such and such a morning taken over charge, as Member of the Salt Board, from Mr. Fotheringham, during the absence of the latter on sick leave, or pending further orders.

Now Snaply was known as the crossest man in the Service, and it cheered poor Fotheringham, who was almost too ill and weak to care about anything, to know that his *locum tenens* would not allow Blunt to repose on a bed of roses if he could help it.

Felicia, meanwhile, had carried Maud off to the

'Gully,' a mountain retreat some twenty miles away, where purer air and a less constrained life were to be had than at Elysium. It was, in fact, nothing more than one of a cluster of log-huts, built years before, when a working party of soldiers had been cutting one of the grand military roads that traverse the mountains in these parts, and sold off-hand, when the work was done, for what they would fetch to the first comer. Felicia and her husband had been encamped in the neighbourhood, and had fallen in love with the wildness of the place, the exquisitely pure air, the huge towering pines, which gave the scene a character of its own, and, moreover, with the unfamiliar idea of owning a part of the Himalayas in freehold.

For a few hundred rupees, accordingly, Vernon had become possessor of the huts and some adjoining acres, and since then Felicia's embellishing hand had worked wonders. Nature, as if in gratitude for unaccustomed devotion, lent herself in a lavish mood to beautify the little structure. A profuse growth of creepers festooned the porch; a delicious piece of turf, bright, smooth and soft, and broken only by one or two projecting crags, stretched down the mountain-side in front; inside the rough deodar paling the beds were all ablaze with English flowers that not even Felicia's tenderness could coax into healthiness in the plain below.

'These are my invalids,' Felicia said, to whom this spot was always full of charms: 'I send them up with the babies to breathe a little wholesome air. Shut your eyes, Maud, and smell this—cannot you fancy yourself in a sweet English wood in June?'

There were other beauties, moreover, about the place than those of an English summer. They were hanging in a little picturesque nook of safety, but all around them was sublime. Storms gathered and crashed and spent their fury as if this was their very home where they could play at ease. An inky mass came lowering over the heights above and shed itself in one angry deluge on the mountain-side; the thunder crashed in fierce echoes from crag to crag, and all the heavens blazed from end to end as the fearful fiery zig-zags came darting out of the gloom; then the tempest would pass away and nothing be heard but the distant rumble and the hundred muddy torrents roaring downwards. The great folds of mist came swirling up the precipice, wrapping everything for a few moments in gloom; then they would pass on, and presently again the sky be serene and bright, and the reeking mountains sun themselves gleefully in the brightness and warmth that were everywhere present.

'It is beautiful,' Maud said, 'but too grand to be quite pleasant; it is rather awful. That black mountain opposite, with its army of skeleton deodars, makes me shudder.'

Across the gorge the forest had been burnt—the first rude attempt by the mountaineers at reclaiming the soil. For weeks together these blazing patches may be seen on the hillside, hidden in a cloud of smoke by day, and at night lighting up the landscape with a lurid, fitful glare. When, by a change in the wind or sudden downpour, the conflagration ceases, nothing remains but a gloomy array of charred stumps, with here and there some monstrous stem towering above, which the flames, though they were able to kill, have not succeeded in devouring. Then among the ruins of the forest comes the primitive cultivator, with his tiny plough and scrambling goat-like bullocks, and wrings a scanty crop of oats or potatoes from each ridge and cranny of the rocky steep; and so the reign of agriculture has begun. The effect, however, from the picturesque point of view is weird and gloomy; it was so, at any rate, in Maud's thoughts, for she ever after associated it with the first piece of really bad news that had ever come to her in the whole of her sunshiny existence. A note arrived one morning from Vernon at Dustypore, and Felicia read it out before she was well aware of its import. He was just starting, Vernon said, for the head-quarters of the expedition. 'There has been a fight, and the entrenched village has been carried by a *coup de main*, and——'

'And what?' said Maud, who felt herself turning deadly cold and her heart beating so that she could scarcely speak, 'Go on, Felicia, please.'

'"Sutton, I fear, has had a serious wound and a fall from his horse. I am going out to look after him. More news to-morrow."'

Maud rose and fled, without a word, to her bedroom, to deal with this agitating piece of news as best she might. She did not feel sure enough of her composure to trust herself to the chances of a break-down even before Felicia. There was something in herself, she knew, that she did not wish even Felicia's eye to read. To Felicia her husband's letter spoke only of the fortunes of their common friend; to Maud it was, as a quick, agonising pang told her, an affair of life or death. A serious wound — a fall from horseback — terrible, vague words that might mean anything — that might mean something that would eclipse all Maud's existence in the gloom of a lifelong disaster. She had thought over their last ride together often; but she knew now, and now only, to the full what it had really been to her. She had recalled his last acts and words—they had been sweet and tender words, such as would keep their fragrance through a lifetime; but, supposing that they were to be really last words, the long farewell of a man who was going to his doom! Maud sat still, crushed and stunned at this first brush of misfortune's passing wing: a dark shadow, black and fateful as the storms which came raging up the valley, seemed to be gathering across her life. Life itself seemed to hang on a slender thread, the tidings which to-morrow's messenger should bring —perhaps even now life was over for her.

Felicia did not leave her long in solitude; she came in presently, with her kind considerate air, knowing and feeling all, as Maud instinctively was aware, but speaking only just what should be spoken, and guarded by a delicate tact (rare attribute of only the most finely-moulded natures) from the possibility of a word too much.

'Courage,' she said; 'I know the meaning of George's letter too well to be frightened. To-morrow, dear Maud, there will be good news for both of us.'

Maud took her companion's hand in a helpless, imploring way that went to Felicia's very heart; but, if her life had depended on it, no spoken word would come.

There are some things in life, some desperate chances, some horrible possibilities of suffering, which seem to strike one mute. Maud seemed now to have come across some such crisis of existence. She followed Felicia about; they took the children for a walk; she went almost unconsciously about the little routine of their home life; all the time she seemed to herself in a sort of dreadful dream; she turned faint and chill as the messengers now and again came clambering up the gorge, each with his fresh item of news from the world below, some one of them, as she knew must be the case, carrying with him the sentence of her fate.

'It makes my blood run cold,' she told Felicia afterwards, 'to see one of them coming even now.'

Sutton's words of farewell to her were not, however, destined to be his last. The next day a good friend at Government House sent them across the Hills a copy of a telegram from head-quarters, which showed that Sutton's life was at any rate in no immediate danger. Then came a letter to Felicia from her husband. He had been up to head-quarters, he said, and stayed two days with Sutton. He was a good deal knocked about; there was a bullet lodged in his side, which had been troublesome, and he had been much bruised by his horse rolling across him. But there was no danger; in a week or two he would be able to move, and meanwhile he was in splendid air, and well looked after.

Then Maud went to her precious locket once again, and wept over it tears of joy, gratitude and love. The mists had cleared away, the world was irradiated with happiness and hope; even the blackened hillside opposite had caught a ray of sunshine and seemed to smile back at her. She felt a very child again in the lightness of her heart; and Felicia, in a graver but not less happy mood, breathed a deep prayer of fervent gratitude that the calamity so near and terrible had passed away, leaving this young bright life as bright as ever.

CHAPTER XXV.

AN INVALID.

> How do I love thee? Let me count the sums.
> I love thee to the depth and breadth and height,
> My soul can reach, when feeling out of sight
> For the ends of Being and Ideal Grace——

When, a month later, Sutton was carried into Dustypore, he was, as any one would have felt, a fit subject for romance, and Maud was just in the mood to appreciate all that was romantic about him to the full. She had been thinking about this event and fancying it, and dreaming about it for weeks past, poor child, till it had become for her the very climax of existence. As the time for its realisation drew near she had been haunted by nervous apprehensions as to whether she had not misinterpreted Sutton's words of kindness at that last interview, and whether the moment of disillusionment might not be now arriving. Sutton, so a morbid mood suggested, might have meant nothing; or his words, perhaps, proved only a passing tenderness, engendered by the special circumstances of the hour: her fancy, perhaps, had dressed up a few careless expressions into something serious. But there came a truer voice which said that it was not so; that Sutton was not a man of careless words or a transicut mood, and that a pledge had been given, though without actual spoken vow, which he assuredly would redeem on his return. On the whole then, though not absolutely without a misgiving, Maud was joyous and courageous, and her heart was light within her. She, however, felt herself becoming greatly embarrassed and excited as the hour of Sutton's arrival drew near. The most needless blushes came flushing into her cheeks; the simplest things seemed difficult to answer. Felicia knew, Maud was certain, pretty well how matters stood; knew at any rate that there was something between her and Sutton: yet Maud had never summoned up courage to inform her what it was, nor had Felicia chosen to inquire. It was rather agitating, accordingly, that Felicia should now be about to have an opportunity of judging for herself how matters stood.

Then Sutton arrived, too suffering from his wound to be moved except in a palanquin; and was got, with a great deal of trouble and pain apparently, to the sofa in Vernon's study, which was turned into his sitting-room for the time being, and where the invalid was to spend the day. Here he lay, a close prisoner, as feeble as a bad wound and a month's fever could make him, and quite in a condition for judicious nursing. A man in such a plight wants company—pleasant, gentle, noiseless, unexciting, feminine if possible; he wants to be read to, and sung and played to; he wants cooling drinks, which, when mixed and administered by a hand like Felicia's, are more than nectar; he wants those delicious idle gossips, for which the healthy busy side of life so seldom provides either the opportunity or the mood. If a man lack these, an illness is a dreary affair; if he has them, it may bring him the pleasantest hours of his life.

All these pleasant conditions now attended the fortunate Sutton's convalescence. Felicia welcomed him with a joyful cordiality and devoted herself with enthusiasm to the task of making his imprisonment as little wearisome as might be. Vernon stole an hour from his office to read him the 'Pall Mall Gazette;' Maud found herself busy with the rest, a willing attendant on the happy warrior in his hour of weakness. Everybody made a great deal of him. Felicia's little girls, coming with much modesty and many blushes, brought him a nosegay apiece and kissed his hand with a sort of affectionate reverence. His face was wan and thin, and marked with lines of suffering; but the sweet, kind smile was still the same, and the honest eyes and finely-chiselled brow. On the whole Maud found him handsomer and ten times more touching than ever before. She knew, too, before they had been a minute in each other's company that all was well with her. The time of separation, uncertainty, distress, was done: happiness, greater than she had ever dreamed of, was already hers. Her foot stood already on the crowning ridge of existence, and all the horizon blazed with the golden clouds of Hope and Joy.

One effect that Sutton always had upon her she was especially conscious of just now: she had no feeling of shyness with him, such as she felt with all the world beside; he stirred her being too profoundly for any slighter feeling to find a place. Shyness deals with the superficial, slighter outcomings of life. Sutton seemed to transport her to another world of thought and feeling: thoughts too high and feelings too intense to heed the mode of their expression. The consequence was, that it seemed quite natural to Maud for her to be waiting on him; who had so good a right as she to that pleasant duty?

Then presently Felicia went away with the children, and the two were again, for the first time, alone together.

'Come,' Sutton said, changing his manner instantly, 'sit down by me and tell me all that has happened since we parted on the mountain's side. You missed me a little, I hope?'

'Yes,' said Maud, simply, looking at him with fearless, trusting eyes; 'your going was the end of all our pleasure—we went away to the Gully, and then came your accident and some dreadful days of anxiety. Since then everything has seemed a sort of dream.'

'It has seemed a dream to me sometimes,' said Sutton, 'as I lay and wondered whether the happiness I fancied for myself was real or fable. Things befall one so suddenly in life, and strokes of good or ill fortune take one so by surprise, that one distrusts one's own belief about them, and cannot fancy that the old life which went before has been all transfigured. Now, however, that I see you and hear you and have you about me, I begin to feel it was not a dream after all.'

'It was no dream,' said Maud, in her serious way; 'here is your locket, which I have been keeping for you since we parted.'

'No,' said the other, giving back the proffered locket and keeping the hand which gave it in captivity; 'you shall keep it now, if you will, for good and all; that is, if you have a fancy for an old soldier, wounded and battered as you see me. Here I shall be or weeks, I suppose, a burden on the friends who are good-natured enough to be my nurses. You will have to tend me, as Elaine did Launcelot in his cave.'

'I will,' Maud said, wrapped into a mood which left her scarcely mistress of herself; 'my love is as great as hers was. I have been living all these weeks only that I might see you again. I must have died if you had not come back, or come back other than I hoped.'

The die was cast—the words were spoken; they came out naturally, spontaneously, almost unconsciously before Maud had time to know what she was about, or to judge of the wisdom and propriety of what she was saying. They were the truth; they were what she had been feeling and saying to herself for weeks past; they were the true outcoming of her honest heart; and yet no sooner were they spoken than Maud felt an awful conviction that they had better have been left unsaid; they were more, far more, than anything which had been said on Sutton's part to her. Was it wrong, unwomanly, indecorous, thus to have declared herself and torn the veil from her feelings without waiting for a lover's hand to remove it? The thought rushed in upon her with an agonizing distinctness; the blood came rushing to her cheeks and forehead; her very hand which Sutton was holding in his own, emaciated and bloodless, was blushing too. She could say nothing, she could do nothing but stay, helpless, having made her confession, and wait for Sutton to rescue her.

As he lay there, holding her hand in his, clasping it with a firm, tender grasp, which seemed to be expressive of all she wanted, Felicia came into the room. Maud stood there, scarlet, and moved not, nor did Sutton seem inclined that she should.

'Felicia,' he said, 'you are the good angel of us both, and this moment would have been incomplete without you. Maud has just consented to become my wife.'

Felicia took Maud to her arms in a sort of rapture of happiness; her heart was too full for speech. It was a delightful relief from the anxiety and distress which had been weighing upon her all the summer and which had of late grown into an acute pang. She felt grateful to both parties, who had at last brought about the result for which she had wished so anxiously and of which she had somehow begun to despair.

Maud, on her part, felt it natural that Sutton should, at a trying emergency, have protected her skilfully, considerately, efficiently from the embarrassment into which her outspokenness had betrayed her; it was like himself to do so, and typical of the sort of feeling of confidence with which he always inspired her. There was a delightful sense of safety and protection in being with him. How should her heart not beat high at the thought that this safety and protection would evermore be hers!

CHAPTER XXVI.

DESVŒUX IN DESPAIR.

All through, love
Protested in a world of ways save one
Hinting at marriage——

THE news of Maud's engagement was naturally a congenial topic for gossip in Dustypore. The romantic circumstances under which it had come about lent themselves readily to the superaddition of any details, necessary, in the teller's opinion, in order to bring the story to the correct pitch of embellishment. Everybody considered Maud a lucky girl; some cynics remarked that once again Sutton had shown himself the most courageous of mankind; and Mrs. Vereker said, sentimentally, that she feared poor Desvœux would *this time* be really broken-hearted. There was some satire lurking in the words 'this time,' because the present occasion was by no means the first on which the same sort of thing had occurred. Desvœux's was one of those inconveniently adjusted temperaments to which no woman is completely delightful till she has become unattainable. His relations to the opposite sex did not as a general rule appear to involve anything of a seriously pathetic order; but no sooner was a girl engaged to some one else than he awoke to the terrible discovery that he was deeply in love with her himself and deeply aggrieved by her betrothal to another. He was known not to be a marrying man; he made no secret of his dislike of matrimony as an institution; still he greatly resented other people's marriages. Whenever any ladies of his acquaintance got married he used to send them the most lovely bridal presents, with beautiful little gilt-edged notes on the finest satin paper, politely intimating that he was broken-hearted. Sometimes his feelings were too much for prose and his melancholy would break out into epigrammatic versicles; sometimes the gift bore only an inscription eloquent in its reticence—'*Le don d'un triste célibataire*,' or '*Avec un soupir*.' The presents, however, were so very pretty (for Desvœux's tastes were of the extravagant order), that their fair recipients, for the most part, were glad enough to take them, sighs, poetry and all, without inquiring too rigidly into the giver's actual frame of mind. As most of the young ladies who had for some years past been married at Dustypore had experienced something of the sort, they probably compared notes and reassured each other as to the probability of a disease, from which Desvœux had already more than once recovered, not proving fatal on any subsequent occasion.

Maud's engagement, however, touched Desvœux more nearly than any previous blow of the same description. Her joyous, childish beauty, the readiness of her wit, the quickness of her replies, the great fun which they always had whenever Fortune was kind enough to throw them together, Maud's unconcealed appreciation of himself, despite the coquettish airs in which she now and then indulged; the ready frankness which invited intimacy so pleasantly—all had gone deep into Desvœux's heart, and he had grown to feel a sort of proprietorship in them, which it vexed him terribly to feel suddenly at an end. He felt certain that Maud liked him very much; and certain, doubly certain now, that he intensely admired her. No one else, he felt bitterly, had an equal right to do so. That Sutton, too, should be the fortunate rival made defeat all the bitterer. Sutton's good qualities were precisely those which Desvœux could least appreciate; his military prowess did not impress him in the least; his chivalry touched no corresponding chord; his ideas of duty seemed pedantic, his feelings about women an anachronism.

If there was one thing in which it was especially irritating that such a man should have carried the day, it was in the ascendancy over women, which Desvœux considered as his especial forte. He piqued himself not a little on his knowledge of the sex, his insight into their weaknesses, his experienced tact in dealing with them to the best account. He had established what he considered a perfectly satisfactory footing with Maud, and had spent no little time, trouble, and sentiment in the process. It was a cruel humiliation to be rudely displaced from this agreeable eminence by a mere commonplace soldier, who had lived all his life in a camp and talked about women like a child.

Women are, Desvœux came bitterly to feel, inscrutable, and the cleverest or stupidest of mankind alike puppets in their hands when they have a passion to gratify or a secret to conceal. Anyhow, the news of Maud's engagement set his heart a-beating and sent his spirits down to zero. He was dining with the officers in the Fort when the announcement was made. One of them had been calling at the Vernons', and had heard the interesting fact from Felicia's own lips. 'Honneur aux braves!' cried Desvœux, with ostentatious merriment, tossing off his glass; 'here's to their very good healths.' He was an adept at concealing his feelings, but a near observer might have seen that his hand trembled so that it was with difficulty he could carry his glass to his lips, and that, despite his jovial tones, he had turned deadly pale.

'I am glad she has come into the Army, at any rate,' said some one.

'Of course,' said Desvœux; 'it is the old story. "J'aime beaucoup les militaires." What chance have we poor civilians when a red jacket is in the field?'

'And what, pray,' said one of the guests, a new arrival, 'is the lady's name?'

Desvœux had risen from the table, and was moving towards the billiard-room. 'Her name,' he said, stopping in the act of lighting a cigar, 'is that of the rest of her sex—frailty.'

'Desvœux is hard hit this time,' observed one of a little knot who lingered behind the rest over their wine; 'he really loved her.'

'Fiddlededee!' said another. 'Desvœux love her, indeed!'

'He will have to drop all that now,' observed a third; 'Sutton would wring his neck for him or pitch him out of the window, if he as much as dared look at her!'

The fact, however, was that, conceal it as he would, Desvœux was hard hit. His usual expedient of buying a handsome wedding present and writing the lady some poetry quite broke-down. Maud's bright eyes and glowing cheeks, her beautiful upper lip—now full of pretty scorn, now melting into a smile that was sweetness itself—haunted him in his dreams. He lit his pipe, he raged about the room, he denounced the perfidy of womankind, he read all the most horrible passages in all the worst French novels in his possession, he quoted all the fiercest cynicism of Chamfort and Rochefoucauld in vain; there was Maud, enthroned unquestioned mistress of his heart, and it was labour lost to endeavour to displace her.

In course of time Desvœux lashed himself into a highly uncomfortable state of mind and became perfectly convinced that Maud had treated him most cruelly. Accordingly, when next they met, his appearance was suggestive of a Byronic gloom of the very deepest dye; his handkerchief was tied with the negligence which spoke of shattered hopes, and his general demeanour was that of a man for whom the world was over. Maud was really in consternation at her friend's metamorphosis and felt herself growing inconveniently shy. She was conscious of an instinctive apprehension that Desvœux was going to bring about a scene. His face of martyrdom was a study in the completeness of its woe.

'You expect me to wish you joy,' he said, 'and so I do. May all bright things attend you wherever you go, and wherever you are! The news of your engagement surprised and hurt me, of course.'

'Surprised and hurt you, Mr. Desvœux!' cried Maud, with increased alarm, 'I can't think why it should do that or why you should look so very odd and—untidy.'

'Cannot you?' cried the other, stalking about the room and fanning the flame of his excitement; 'I suppose not; you women are all so heartless.'

'No, we are not,' said Maud; 'and if we were, I do not see that you, of all people in the world, have any right to complain. Come now, tell me what is the matter. Has the Agent been scolding you?'

'The Agent!' cried Desvœux, in tones of the profoundest disgust; 'you little traitress, don't you know as well as possible that there is only one thing in the world that could really hurt me, and that you have done it?'

'I!' exclaimed Maud, in horror. 'I'm sure I am very sorry. You must try and forget me.'

'Try and fly to the moon!' said Desvœux; 'I shall remember you all my life, to my cost, as the most bewitching little piece of mischief in existence. Why am I so unfortunate? I wish to goodness I had never seen you.'

'I am sure,' said Maud, fervently, 'I wish to goodness you never had, since it makes you so unhappy. But remember, if you please, that I had no idea of what you were feeling. You never told me, you know.'

'Who was to guess that Sutton would be so abominably precipitate? I thought he was safe with his soldiers and out of harm's way. Besides, I told you! Why, you knew as well as possible that I adored you. Don't you remember how I squeezed your hand at the last Government House ball?'

'And don't you remember,' cried Maud, indignantly, 'how I refused to dance a single round dance with you all the evening in consequence, and only gave you a Lancers to prevent your being laughed at?'

'I only wish you could feel my heart beating,' said Desvœux, feeling that interesting organ, and apparently horrified at its activity.

'That is because you will go stamping about the room in that absurd way instead of sitting still and talking quietly. Come now, Mr. Desvœux, come and sit down and wish me joy kindly and pleasantly, or I never will speak to you again.'

'Little tyrant!' said the other, doing as he was bid as meekly as could be wished; 'and to think that you should be growing lovelier every day and more charming, if possible, and all for Sutton! Speak to me, indeed! Why, you will not dare open your mouth for fear of a scandal. Sutton will make you cut me, you will see, as an old admirer.'

'Indeed,' said Maud, upon whom Desvœux's flattery always told with some effect, 'I have not the slightest intention of giving up my old friends. Why should I? Only you will not make love to me, of course.'

'Oh, of course not,' said the other, with a laugh. 'But tell me now, are you not a wee bit sorry for a poor fellow who is breaking his heart about you?'

'Breaking his fiddlestick!' cried Maud, bursting out laughing. 'Why, Mr. Desvœux, you don't, I assure you, know what you say. It is very kind of you to like me, and admire me, and so forth, and I am very much obliged.'

'Don't, don't, for heaven's sake, talk like that,' cried the other; 'it is not kind of me at all to be over head and ears in love with you, but just my misfortune. But, tell me: they teased you into it, did they not?'

'Teased me into it!' cried Maud, tossing her head indignantly; 'how little you know!'

'Yes,' said the other, positively, 'it is obvious. You are an orphan—you have that sweet, interesting, dependent look that orphans have; and Mrs. Vernon made it up; set Sutton to flirt with you; everybody observed that much last summer; and then, no doubt, told you that you had been flirting and were bound to accept him. Why didn't you pluck up heart of grace and say "No"?'

'Because I plucked up heart of grace to say "Yes." Do you think that Colonel Sutton is a sort of man who needs any one to help his wooing?'

'I do,' said Desvœux, with provoking persistency, 'and Mrs. Vernon gave him every assistance. I only wish she would have done half as much for me.'

'Well, then,' cried Maud in a passion, 'if you must know, it was I that proposed to him—not he to me; and I adore the tip of his little finger more than all the other men and women in the world. Now do you think they teased me into it?'

'No; but if you begin with so much enthusiasm you will come to dislike him very much before long. His little finger indeed! And here am I left out in the cold! What am I to do?'

'Write and consult Mrs. Vereker,' said Maud. From which unfeeling remark it may be inferred that she believed less in Desvœux's broken-heartedness than he was inclined to do himself.

'Well,' said her companion, with a resigned air, which Maud felt had a touch of reproachful dignity in it, 'laugh at me as you will. I love you, and always shall.'

'Nonsense!' said Maud. 'Here comes my cousin. I have a great mind to tell her, and get her to comfort you.'

The interview was over. Maud had stuck to her programme, which was to treat Desvœux with an airy indifference and his protestations with ostentatious disbelief. Nevertheless his words were not without effect. Had she been less inexperienced Maud would have known that she had allowed him to leave off in a most dangerous position; that of an admirer whose homage was sufficiently congenial to be allowed a hearing; whom it was within her power to have at any moment at her feet, and who, whether rightly or wrongly, felt he had some show of right to be aggrieved and disappointed at her declared preference for another man.

There was another person, however, besides Desvœux to whom the news of Maud's engagement gave a serious shock.

One of Sutton's first acts, after Maud and he had mutually ascertained each other's views, was to scribble a line to Boldero, announcing the joyful event; and he had done so, too full of his own happiness to pay much attention, even had he known more than he did, to the view his friend might take of it. All that he knew was that

Boldero, like all the world, was a great admirer of his future wife. This was but natural, and Sutton without the least misgiving accepted the position. 'My dear old boy,' he wrote, 'you will, I know, be pleased to hear a good piece of news of me, to make up for my bad luck the other day. Come over as soon as you can and wish me joy. Meanwhile, remember, of course, that you must be my groomsman.'

'His groomsman!' Boldero sat, pale and speechless and stunned by the sudden overthrow of all his hopes. The day-dream of his existence was ended by this stern awakening. Life—all that part of life, at least, which is worth living—was, he felt bitterly, over for him. It was, to use Heine's expressive figure, as if some one had climbed up a celestial ladder, rolled up the bright blue sky and taken down the sun. Only the dismal scaffolding, the dust, the gloom remained. Maud, though she had never quite encouraged him to hope, had never bidden him despair, and figured, we may be certain, the lovely chatelaine of all his castles in the air. He found out now to his cost how full his thoughts had been of her. And now it was all over. His pleasant hope lay shattered on the ground. The blow was hard to bear; none the easier, perhaps, that it was his dearest friend's hand that struck it.

Being, however, a man of pluck and determination, he sat down courageously, wrote a cheery note of congratulation to the fortunate winner of the prize, promised his services as groomsman or anything else which Sutton wished, and then ordered his horse and rode twenty miles to an outlying village, where there was a troublesome boundary dispute to be settled, which he had had in his eye for weeks past as wanting a visit from the Collector.

CHAPTER XXVII.

CHRISTMAS AT DUSTYPORE.

Truth is the strong thing. Let man's life be true—
And love's the truth of mine—time prove the rest!

CHRISTMAS had arrived, and Christmas was a festival observed at Dustypore with all the emphasis proper to men who had carried their Lares and Penates beneath a foreign sky, and were treasuring in alien regions the sacred fire of the paternal hearth.

The weather was cold enough to realise all that English tradition requires as 'seasonable' in the way of climate. For weeks past, great bullock-carts, piled high with gnarled heaps of jungle-wood, had been creaking along the dusty tracks from the outlying villages and supplying the Station with materials for Christmas-fires of appropriate magnificence. The air was deliciously clear, crisp and invigorating: the searching wind came with its breath frozen from the Elysian snows and left a hoary rime on all the country's face. English habits began to resume their sway: people were glad to forego the morning ride, and came down to breakfast at half-past nine with red noses and blue fingers and—romantic reminiscence of European life—extremely bad colds in their heads.

Dustypore surrendered itself to holiday-making. The Salt Board suspended its sittings. The vehement Blunt, finding that no work was to be got out of any one for love or money, started off into the country with his rifle after black-buck and jungle-partridges. The courts were closed for a fortnight, and judges and collectors devoted themselves to sweeping off long arrears of morning calls. Contingents of visitors from all the surrounding out-stations came pouring in to share the festivities: every house was full and more than full; for, by the hospitable usages of India, when your spare rooms are filled you order tents to be pitched in the garden, and enlarge your encampment as each new guest arrives. An Indian house is, therefore, viewed as to its capacities for hospitality, extremely elastic, and just now every house in Dustypore had its elasticity tested to the uttermost. Felicia was renowned as a hostess; and there were half-a-dozen friends whose winter holiday would have lost half its charm if spent anywhere but beneath her roof. There was a mixture of joyousness and pathos in these Christmas gatherings which suited her temperament exactly, and showed her in her sweetest, most attractive mood. Her guests invariably went away with cheered spirits and lightened hearts and a little store of remembered kindness to last them through the dreary months to come. Nor was Felicia alone in her good intentions. Everybody set about keeping Christmas with heroic good-nature. The Agent gave a ball in the state apartments in the Fort. The Dustypore Hunt had a home meet and a lunch. The 'Tent Club' organised a pig-sticking expedition for the keener sportsmen. The volunteers had a gala-day, and were formed into a hollow square and panegyrised by the General of the Division on their loyalty and discipline. Everybody attempted something for the edification of everybody else.

The Vernons gave some private theatricals, and Felicia and Maud made a great success as Portia and Nerissa in the 'Merchant of Venice.' Desvœux, who was entrusted with the part of Shylock, heroically shaved off his moustache and transformed himself into the most frightful of old Israelites, with a hook-nose and beard of diabolical aspect. The way in which he rolled his eyes when Gratiano exclaimed 'Now, infidel, I have thee on the hip!'

had twice caused Maud to explode in irrepressible laughter at rehearsals and very nearly caused a break-down among the actors at the final performance. Altogether it was very like home, and very pleasant, as all the party felt.

These Indian festivities are, perhaps, none the less festive, and certainly the more touching, for the fact that at least half the holiday-makers have a dark, sad corner in their hearts which has to be hidden from the world's eye and to be ignored in the common intercourse of life. Separation is the dark cloud which hangs over an Indian existence: husbands and wives, mothers and children, forced asunder, perhaps at the very time when union is most delightful, and living (how maimed and sad a life!) in the absence of all that is best-beloved. They put a brave face upon it, but the heartache is there all the same. What a strong pulse of love and tenderness and sorrow goes throbbing week by week across half the world from the wives and children at home to the lonely exile, struggling bravely with his fate in the far-off Indian station: what dear, ill-spelt, round-hand, stupid letters, which yet are wept over with such passionate pleasure and treasured with such pious care! People have a cheap tariff for telegraphing back to India their safe arrival in England, with a rupee extra for saying that the traveller 'is better.'

What a story it tells of anxious men in India toiling over work, with their hearts far away with the shattered, invalid lady or flickering child's life, carried away to cool regions in hopes of saving it!

Take, for instance, little Major Storks, who was stage-manager for the Vernons' theatricals and sang a comic song between the acts. He is a grizzly, wizen, well-tanned, wiry little fellow, but has, under that rough exterior, as brave and tender a heart as ever beat. He is in charge of the Rumble Chunder Canal and bestows on it all a lover's assiduity: for it he thinks, he writes, he plans, he labours early and late: he rides about in the most demented fashion until the sun has dried him up into a perfect mummy. He knows the Canal's ways and manners—how much water it ought to pour per second; how much it *does* pour; which of the bridges are infirm; where the silt is accumulating; where the water is being wasted or stolen. He drives his subordinates frantic by a zeal in which they cannot participate and a thoroughness which they cannot shirk. To the world outside he seems the merest drudge. To-day, however, he is in paradise. It is Christmas morning and the mail has brought him a goodly budget of letters, all redolent of home and tender conjugal love, and—precious alleviation of exile—photographs of half-a-dozen little Storks. He sits now, with all his family before him, with tears of joyful satisfaction in his eyes. What comely lads! what sweet, ingenuous little girls! what dear, familiar looks, the legacy of a youth that has passed away, greeting him from every little portrait! In a moment Storks' soul quits its shabby tenement of clay and its hot surroundings, and is away in England with wife and children—the wife, whose heart has ached for many a dreary year of separation—the children, who have been taught to love him with a sort of romantic piety, all the more for being far away—the pleasant, cool, idle life in England, which lies afar off, a sort of Promised Land, if ever his long, rough task in India can get itself performed. Then, in the fulness of his heart, he will put on his shabby uniform and order round his shabby dogcart, and go and show his treasures to Felicia, who will, he knows, have a quick sympathy for his pleasure and his pain; and when the two act in a charade that night, each will know that all is not as merry as it seems, but that, under a stoical calmness, lie thoughts and hopes and pangs which stir the very depths of man's being, and which require all the help that sympathy and kindliness can give.

The last and most interesting occasion of the holidays was one in which Sutton and Maud played a leading part. Sutton had a two months' Inspection march before him, and no better sort of honeymoon could be desired. The country through which they were to go was wild but very picturesque. Sutton's duties would never take him away for more than a few hours; and camp life is idyllic in its freedom, unconstraint and tranquillity. Existence has something charming about it when each morning's ride takes you through new scenes to a new home, in which you live as comfortably for the next twenty-four hours as if you had been there all your life. Maud was in rapture at the prospect, nor was her happiness lessened by the arrival of the most perfect Arab to be found in Bombay—her husband's wedding gift to her—on which her long journey was to be performed. To Sutton these weeks seemed the fitting threshold of the new and brighter existence into which he was about to pass. Each day Maud bound herself closer to his heart by some sweet act or word, some unstudied outpouring of devotion, childish in its simplicity and unconsciousness, but womanly in its serious strength; some sympathetic note which vibrated harmoniously to his inmost soul. 'To be with you, dear,' he said, 'is like travelling through a lovely mountain country, where each turn in the road opens up a fresh delight: you charm me in some new fashion every hour.'

To this sort of remark Maud had no need of any

other reply than that easiest and most natural of all to feminine lips, which dispenses with the necessity of spoken words. Her kisses were, we may be certain, eloquent enough to Sutton's heart, irradiated for the first time with a woman's love and beating high with a courageous joyfulness and hope.

By the end of January Sutton was well enough to be emancipated from the pleasant thraldom of an invalid's sofa; nor could his march be any longer delayed. One afternoon, accordingly, the little world of Dustypore assembled to see the brave soldier and the beautiful girl made man and wife. Boldero came in from the District and performed his part as groomsman with creditable stoicism. No one—Maud and Sutton least of all—had the least idea that he was assisting at the sacrifice of all his hopes.

Desvœux preserved his tragic demeanour to the last, presented Maud with a diamond pendant which must have gone far into his quarter's income, and refused obstinately to return thanks for the bridesmaids—a task which was traditionally assigned to him in Dustypore, and which, on all ordinary occasions, he accepted with alacrity and performed with success.

CHAPTER XXVIII.

MORNING CLOUDS.

——The little rift within the lute——

SUTTON brought back his bride in April, all the better, as it appeared, in health and spirits for her two months' expedition. The beautiful rose of her cheeks had a tinge of brown which spoke only of healthy exercise in the open air. Everybody pronounced her prettier, brighter and more charming than ever. She was in the highest spirits to be back, and Sutton seemed pleased to bring her and to be once more amongst old friends.

To all who saw them, except Felicia's observant eye, they seemed everything which a newly-wedded pair should wish to be. But Felicia felt less confident of their happiness. Whether Maud's letters had unconsciously sounded a little note of distress, or whether it was that she knew both their natures so well and how they ought to harmonise, that the least approach to discord caught her ear—something, at any rate, made her aware of the existence of a subtle disquietude between Maud and her husband. The discovery, or rather the suspicion, filled her with a distress which she attempted in vain to ignore. She found herself joining languidly and insincerely in the chorus of gratulation which the Dustypore community set up over the happy couple. When Mrs. Vereker came to call, rustling in the loveliest of new dresses, and poured out a little stream of gossiping remarks—how pretty it was to see them together, and what a charming lover Sutton made, and was not Maud a picture of a girl-wife?—Felicia responded with a coldness which puzzled her visitor and which Felicia was conscious of trying in vain to conceal. Something, her fine instinct told her, was amiss. One alarming symptom was the obvious relief which Maud found in her society, and the profuse tenderness and affection which she displayed whenever there was no one else to see. She lavished on her a sort of unconscious fondness, for which Felicia looked in vain in her behaviour to her husband. With him her affection seemed constrained, conscious, too deferential to be natural and happy. There was about Maud, when she and Felicia were alone together, a joyous self-abandonment to animal high spirits, which was for ever flowing out into some pretty childish act of fun or affection, but which vanished at the appearance of

Sutton or any other onlooker. She became a girl again—she sang, she danced, she got into the wildest games with the children—she let off her excitement and mirth in a thousand natural acts. Then Jem would come in, and it all seemed to die away. When visitors arrived, and Felicia had presently more on her hands than was at all to her taste, Maud would seem to enjoy it and to get amused and interested; then, as the door closed upon the strangers, she would come and throw her arms round Felicia and caress her, as if her one feeling about the visit was that it had been an inconvenient restraint on love which was wanting every moment to express itself in some outspoken fashion; 'I love you the best, the best of all,' she would say impetuously.

'Of all women,' Felicia put in.

'Of all women and of all men too, except Jem,' Maud answered; 'yes, and I believe I love you better even than Jem; anyhow, I love you.'

More than once, too, Felicia detected little manœuvres on Maud's part to walk or drive with her and to quit her husband's society in order to do so. Altogether Felicia felt frightened, anxious and sad about her friends: and Vernon, who always knew her melancholy moods and could generally guess their cause, in vain endeavoured to console her with the assurance that all was right and that Sutton's had been a wise and happy choice.

The truth was that the march had not been altogether a success. A great authority on such matters has said that people often endanger the permanent happiness of married life by putting too severe a strain upon it at its outset. Now a two-month's *tête-à-tête* is a serious strain. Life wants something besides mere affection to make it run smoothly: it wants the ease and comfort of familiarity, the freedom of tastes ascertained to be congenial, the pleasant usages of common action. The first year of wedded life is, no doubt, a series of experiments in getting on; two wheels, however nicely fitted, are likely to rub a little at some point of contact or other. And then Paradise itself would lose its charm if it were all the same; and the days on Maud's first journey had a distracting resemblance. Her eyes ached with the interminable horizon of dust and sand, the scrubby brushwood, the lonely crumbling tomb, the rare clumps of palms, the scuffling, bellowing herds of cattle. Sutton's cook, whom his master in his simple tastes believed a prodigy of culinary skill, used to send up the same dishes with depressing monotony, and, do what she would, Maud could not like them. Then some marches were over terribly rough ground, and her Arab made stumbles that took her breath away, though she was ashamed to say so. But it was not the little things which really mattered. Her husband's very nobility of nature oppressed her. A hundred times she had felt how good he was, how true, how really great, how chivalrous in his devotion, how tenderly considerate, and yet—and yet—something more unheroic would perhaps have been sometimes a relief. When the most ineffably stupid young officers rode across from some neighbouring station and plunged with cheerful volubility into the gossip of last season at Elysium, there was, Maud felt, something welcome in the humbler companion and the more trivial theme. Then, too, the solitary days oppressed her. Sutton had often outlying posts to visit and would accomplish them by starting off three or four hours before Maud was awake and making a *detour*, so as to meet her at their new halting-place at breakfast. On these mornings Maud had the company of an escort of troopers, her greyhound Punch, and her own thoughts, which were apt to get gloomy. Even Punch, she fancied, thought it a bore, and went along in a dejected fashion. Sometimes Sutton's work could not be so quickly disposed of, and he would be detained till the evening, and then the solitary day seemed sad and interminably long. More than once the tears had come unbidden to her eyes. Did Sutton forget her? Never for an instant, her heart told her clearly enough; but he did not perhaps sufficiently realise the wants and wishes, the flickering, uncertain spirits, the wayward moods, the causeless melancholy of one who, though invested with the dignities of womanhood, was in character and powers in reality still a child.

Then, though Sutton was never in the slightest degree imperative, and though her every spoken wish was law, Maud was conscious sometimes of being kept in better order than she liked and being forced up to a standard which was inconveniently high. Her husband spoke little of his tastes; no word from him ever assumed the resemblance of a command; yet Maud not unfrequently felt that a secret pressure was constraining her to something that was not exactly congenial; she knew with an almost distressing distinctness what her husband liked and disliked, and the knowledge was something of a burden. She was conscious when she hurt him; sometimes from mere waywardness she chose to do it, but she hurt herself in the process as much as him. She had given him her heart and made him all her world, and was glad to have done so. None the less there was sometimes an undefined pang about her self-devotion; she became restless, anxious, uncertain in her moods, and the tears seemed to lie near the surface and would spring to light, in unwary moments, at trifles too slight to cause their flow.

Then on some matters her husband's tastes and

hers were by no means in harmony. On one occasion Desvœux had seized the opportunity of the Agent's camp being in the neighbourhood and had ridden across and travelled a couple of marches with them. Maud had looked forward to seeing him with pleasure and greeted his arrival with marked animation. The visit turned out as pleasant as she had expected; but the pleasure was marred by a secret conviction of her husband's disapproval. Nothing could quench Desvœux's light-heartedness or impede the easy flow of his amusing small-talk. Sutton, however, did not seem to find it amusing, and assumed, quite unconsciously, a dignified air, which Maud felt to be rather awful, though Desvœux was, as usual, imperturbable in his gaiety. His spirits, however, were better, and she was more at her ease to be infected by them when Sutton was not by. It vexed her to the heart to know that it was so, but so she knew it was.

The morning that Desvœux went away was one of Sutton's busy days, and Maud was alone when their guest bade her farewell. 'Good-bye,' she said, with a sort of sigh; 'how I wish you could have stopped and ridden with me this morning! I shall be alone all day and feel that I am going to have a fit of low spirits.'

'And so am I,' said Desvœux, 'a very bad fit

indeed, which will last till next time we meet. Good-bye.'

Maud saw him turning pale, as he used to do when he got excited, and heard the eager tremble in his voice. He held her hand for an instant as if he could not bear to give it up, and looked at her with a look that was earnest and reproachful and, Maud felt, very, very sad. Then Desvœux had left without another word, but how eloquent may silence sometimes be!

Was she smiling or crying, and did she really want his company; and was she neglected and miserable? Desvœux had galloped away with his heart in a tumult from queries such as these, cursing the cruel fate which obliged him to be at his master's camp, full thirty miles away, with endless boxes of despatches ready for disposal before to-morrow morning.

Thus it was that Maud's early married life had not been without its morning clouds and sorrows. Then, as people do when they are unhappy, casting about for a cause of her unhappiness, she began to reproach herself. The old doubts of her fitness, her worthiness for her position, her power to retain her husband's love, began to haunt her. 'Ah me!' she sometimes felt inclined to cry, 'I fear that I am [illegible] wife.' And yet she knew that, [illegible] even half her inmost thoughts were read, could she bring any charge of doubtful love or allegiance against herself. Sutton's men had, she had often heard, begun to worship him when his exploits in the Mutiny had raised their enthusiasm to its height. Maud felt that she could understand the feeling; in fact, she did worship him with all her being. But then worship is not all that is wanted for a happy married life. Maud, at any rate, felt it delightful to be with Felicia once again.

CHAPTER XXIX.

THE HILL CAMP.

> And hope to joy is little less in joy
> Than hope enjoyed——

MAUD soon lost sight of her troubled spirits in Felicia's society. Her doubts about her happiness in married life were forgotten in the midst of pleasures which pleased Sutton no less than herself. Her devotion to Felicia was a sentiment which her husband thoroughly understood and cordially approved.

'I used to be finely jealous of her, Jem, I can tell you, in old days,' Maud would say to him, 'and to think you liked her twenty times better than some one else; and indeed I am not sure that I am not jealous now; only I am so much in love with her myself that I do not feel it.'

'Jealous!' Sutton would plead. 'Felicia is like a sister to me. It was she, I believe, who first hit out the brilliant idea of our being married.'

'Was it?' said Maud blushing. 'I [illegible] that

happy thought had been my own. Well, Jem, if you never flirt with any one but her I will forgive you, because in my opinion she is an angel.'

The pleasant visit ended. Sutton had to go off to his camp, a tiny hill station some three thousand feet above the sea, and therefore, as its enemies declared, combining all the drawbacks of hill and plain. Here they were to stay till June, when Sutton was to have his leave and to take his bride up to Elysium for the rest of the summer. Even this prospect had not enabled Maud to bear the parting from her friend with equanimity. 'I wish—I wish,' she had said, wistfully, with the tears in her eyes—'what do I wish? If only, dear Felicia, I could never go away from you!' Felicia bade her farewell with an aching heart, and some dark misgivings. They were not to meet at Elysium, for this year she had determined to establish her children in their little mountain abode at the 'Gully' and to divide her time between them and her husband till he could come up and join them. Then they had resolved to take a little march into the interior, where Felicia might get some new sketches and enlarge her stock of ferns; while Vernon might have a few days' shooting, unharassed by a pursuing train of official cares and correspondence.

The Hill Camp proved a fearful place; worse,

far worse, than anything on the march. It was only to be endured till June, happily, but still it looked terrific. The long lines of huts; the horrible little abodes which were honoured by the title of Officers' Quarters; the gaunt, hideous, treeless hills; the valleys blazing and withered, the dry, blistering scene uncheered by a single streamlet; the dusty plateau, where the soldiers were eternally marching, galloping, cannonading—all the outer world seemed dull, parched, repulsive. There was no other lady in the camp but one, the surgeon's wife, large and dark and hot, and, as Maud felt, horribly realising one's ideas of an ogress. This lady used to come and see her, and sit gossiping and questioning and telling long stories, and shaking a great bird of paradise feather in her head, till she made Maud's life a burthen to her. Then, after about three of these visitations, which Maud imagined that she had endured with angelic sweetness, the lady, for some inscrutable cause, took offence, and when next they met out of doors flung up her head, brandished the bird of paradise feather in the most menacing and defiant manner, and had evidently proclaimed a social war of an altogether implacable order.

'O Jem! what *have* I done?' said Maud with a shudder, as she passed.

'Something unforgivable evidently,' said Sutton;

'we must make peace at once, because Surgeon Crummins could poison us all, if he pleased, next time we happen to be poorly and to fall into his hands. Let us have them to dinner.'

So the irascible lady and the surgeon had to be asked to dinner; and dull and stiff and wearisome the dinner proved, and Maud's heart sank within her at the thought that these were to be her companions, and this the sort of life upon which she was embarked. She loved her husband, but what a price her love had cost her!

Flashes of brightness, however, break in upon the dreariest lot, and one cheering feature of this period was the arrival of a most interesting box from England, containing a highly important supplement to Maud's original *trousseau.* To take an array of pretty garments for a march of two months in the jungle had been out of the question; so that Felicia had determined that all Maud's dresses for the coming summer should not arrive till the time approached when they would be of use. In May, accordingly, there came two splendid cases, whose appearance announced the importance of their contents. Jem professed himself quite as excited as Maud and set to work at once with chisel and hammer to disinter the treasures. There is something very delightful in such unpackings—far from home—the very air within seems

English; the silver-paper has a charming familiar look; each package as it comes out and is revealed excites a pleasing pang of excitement. And then these boxes were mines of treasures. There were lovely ball-dresses, lying fresh, unruffled, ethereal as when they left the artist's hand; and a new habit, which made Maud feel how shabby hers had grown in her long tour; and a most charming morning dress, looped up into all sorts of fantastic costumes, which her prophetic soul told her would look very effective on the lawn at Government House; and there were hats and bonnets and flowers for the hair, culled surely by some fairy hand; and amongst the other treasures was a fine pearl necklace, which old Mrs. Sutton had guarded for many a year for this especial end, and had at last had reset, and now sent, with all sorts of fond wishes and blessings, to her dear son's bride.

Sutton insisted on Maud's trying everything on; and Maud, nothing loth, obeyed.

'Let us send across for Mrs. Crummins,' suggested her husband, 'if this will not appease her she is a fury.'

Accordingly Maud wrote a little note in great excitement:—'Dear Mrs. Crummins, *would* you like to see my new dresses, which have just arrived?' Mrs. Crummins *would* like it, of all things, and came across in about two minutes, under a big umbrella, bird of paradise and all, and was quite as much pleased as Maud, and plunged with her at once into mysteries of detail in which Sutton's male mind was incapable of sympathising. She heaved great sighs of wonder, delight, and satisfaction as each new treasure came to light, and ended by losing her heart and kissing Maud quite affectionately in her enthusiasm. 'Indeed they are very pretty, and so are you, my dear, and, as the surgeon says, quite a refreshing sight for weary eyes.'

So Maud, who was ever ready for a proclamation of amity, signed peace at once, and before the week was out she and her new friend were on terms of the utmost confidence, and had arranged the bird of paradise in the very latest fashion, as shown in Maud's own hats, so that it really looked lovely.

The result, however, of all this was, that Maud anticipated Elysium with greater glee than ever. A pearl necklace, a beautiful satin dress, a Paris fan with lovely Watteau ladies gliding all about it—well, it was something to go from day to day and look at these treasures, but the moment for fruition had not arrived. They would have been quite thrown away on Sutton's troopers and mule-men, amid the horses and the dust. Maud's grey habit, plaid dress and broad pith hat, was the only costume that would not have been ridiculous for the camp. No, the hour for real enjoyment had not arrived, and patience, as Maud had frequently occasion to observe, is a virtue easy to preach but hard to practise, when the present is dull and the expected future a blaze of pleasure.

Then other things had occurred to intensify her anticipation of enjoyment at Elysium and her wish to go there. Mrs. Vereker had written her a letter which set her heart beating. 'The Governor-General and I,' that excellent lady wrote, 'have both arrived, and so the Season may be said to have begun. Our friends of the Twentieth are here in force and are going to do wonders in the way of entertainment: everybody says it is to be *dazzling*. General Beau is here, as adoring as ever. The truth is, my rose bonnet is rather adorable, so, at least, *mes amis* inform me. By the way, that naughty Mr. Desvœux goes on as absurdly as ever about "some one," and declares quite seriously that he is broken-hearted.'

'Silly fellow!' said Maud, and yet it rather pleased her.

'Can you dance a minuet?' the letter went on. 'We are all having lessons. There is to be one at Government House. General Beau's shrugs and shakes over it are delicious. Everybody declares that I do it to perfection—but everybody won't say so when "somebody" arrives and carries all before her. So you see, my dear, I make hay while the sun shines, and am not a bit jealous; but come and eclipse me as soon as you please, for I, too, rather love you.'

Two hot, dusty, weary months had still to pass. Over that dull interval Maud's imagination travelled, each day with lighter steps, to a paradise of excitement and delight.

CHAPTER XXX.

TEMPTATION.

We fell out, my wife and I,
And kiss'd again with tears.

SUCH being the state of things at Elysium, and such the state of Maud's feelings at the camp, imagine her dismay when Sutton came into the room one morning, with a letter in his hand and a very vexed expression on his face, and said: 'Is not this a bore, Maud? Here is a letter from the Chief telling me to go and inspect and report on all the suspected villages at once and say what force we want. So we cannot go to Elysium after all.'

'Not go to Elysium!' cried Maud, flushing red and the tears gathering to her eyes before she had time to check them. It seemed to her, poor child, the very climax of disappointment.

Her husband kissed her kindly. 'I did not know, dear,' he said, 'that you would care about it so much. I am such an old salamander myself that I forget that other people don't enjoy being grilled as much as I do. But what can be done? These scoundrels—bad luck to them—must be reported on, and I must get the report finished before my autumn march begins.'

'It cannot be helped, I suppose,' said Maud, in a tone of despair, and retreating gloomily to her bedroom; for the tears kept coming fast, and the news seemed worse and worse each time she realised its import afresh. No Elysium! No holiday—no change—no charming balls—no beautiful dresses—no pleasant rides—none of the nice scenes on which her fancy had dwelt, the prospect of which had cheered her through the long, dull spring—no bright companions, full of mirth and flattery and devotion to herself! Alas! alas! Maud felt that her trouble was too great to bear.

Sutton followed her presently, in a great state of perturbation at her display of disappointment.

'Come, Maud,' he said kindly, 'cheer up. You shall go and see Felicia if you like.'

But, alas! Maud's tears had got the mastery of her. A long-pent-up stream of melancholy had burst and nothing could stop it. She was inconsolable; the disappointment, in itself a great one, had found her not too well prepared to bear it. She wept, and would not, or could not, be comforted.

Sutton was completely disconcerted: to see her

in trouble, and not be able to relieve it, wishing for anything that he could not give, grieving in this sort of hopeless fashion about what was to him scarcely more than an annoyance, was a new experience, and one which he was unprepared to meet. The fact was, though he did not know it, that Maud had got her head full of nonsense about Elysium. Distance lent enchantment to the view, especially when the view was taken from the dusty, stupid camp. Mrs. Vereker's foolish letter sounded bright and alluring: Desvœux's merry talk and romantic protestations, how full of amusement, interest, excitement it all seemed! How unbearably dull in contrast the life about her! Sutton often absent, often tired and silent; sometimes sad; never, Maud told herself, anything like amusing. Yes, it was too vexatious for all the heroism she could bring to bear upon it: her philosophy broke down.

'I know it is a hard life here,' said her husband, in vain attempts at consolation; 'it is hot and dull for you. I like it, but then I am used to it. But what can I do? If only Felicia were at Elysium you might go up to her.'

'There is Mrs. Vereker,' said Maud, suggestively.

'Mrs. Vereker!' exclaimed Sutton, in consternation; 'you surely'——

'She wrote very kindly the other day,' Maud said, cutting short her husband's protestation, 'and asked me to stay with her in her cottage.'

'But, Maud, you would not really like to go to her, would you?'

'I should not like to go,' Maud said, 'if you disapproved.'

'And I,' answered Sutton, suddenly nettled, 'would not have you stay unless you liked. How shall we decide?'

'You must decide,' said his wife, too much excited and too anxious to know well what she was about.

'Very well,' said Sutton, kindly, but with a sad tone that haunted Maud in aftertimes, 'I will decide. You shall go.'

Maud knew the tone in which he spoke as well as spoken words. She knew the look when he was hurt; she had watched it before. It told her now that she had never wounded him so deeply as to-day. Her heart smote her. He had hardly gone before she longed to repent and stay; and yet she could not make up her mind to the sacrifice which it would cost her. She had been reckoning so upon it that it seemed like the blotting out of all the brightness of her life. The prospect of the dreary, lonely summer, was too grievous. So her heart went swaying to and fro: she grew more and more unhappy. Sutton was doubly kind and tender to her, and his look smote her to the heart. At last her good angel carried the day. 'Jem,' she said, 'I want to change my mind, please. I was mad just now and do not know what possessed me. I do not want to go to Elysium or anywhere, if you cannot go with me. I am frightened at the idea of it, even at this distance. I am sure I should be wretched. You must forgive me, and forget my foolish tears.'

These two had perhaps never loved each other quite so much as at this moment, nor Maud been ever quite so lovable. She was in her sweetest mood; she wore a bright, serene air which spoke of an unworthy temptation overcome, a higher happiness attained, a victory over her weaker, baser self. Already, as happens in such cases, it seemed to her incredible that she could have wished for the lower pleasure which had so nearly won her. As for Sutton, the world was suddenly re-illumined to him; the gloomy, terrible, agonising eclipse had passed: all was sunshine and joy. His face showed what he was feeling. He drew Maud to him and kissed her with a serious, fervent air, as if it were an act of worship; he held her as if it were impossible to him ever to let her go. Maud knew that his iron frame was shaken with vehement emotion; she saw a kind of rapture in his eyes, and read in them that she was well-beloved.

'Dear Maud,' he said, 'I should be wretched, the most miserable wretch alive, if ever any shade of doubt or coldness came between us two. You hold my life, dear, in your hand: my heart is wholly yours and has no other life. If ever your love to me waned it would be death to me.'

And Maud, as she looked and listened, knew that it would.

'It can never wane, dear Jem,' she said, infected with her husband's mood and clinging to him, as was her wont, like a child that needs protection. 'Every day you bind me closer to you; only I fear—and ten times more after being such a goose as I was just now—that I am not half worthy of all you are to me.'

CHAPTER XXXI.

BOLDERO ON GUARD.

Oh ! never work
Like this was done for work's ignoble sake :
It must have finer aims to spur it on !

THUS Maud and her husband were more than reconciled. Maud packed up her dresses, with a few natural sighs that so much sweetness should waste itself unseen, and set about passing the summer with heroical cheerfulness. Things took a turn for the better. A few thunder-storms had come to cool the world, and the early rains were covering the barren mountains with verdure and bringing new life to Maud's garden. Mrs. Crummins was giving her lessons in water-colours, and altogether existence was less intolerable than she had believed it possible that it should be. Perhaps the momentary breach, followed so quickly by so thorough a reconciliation, had engendered an especial sweetness in her intercourse with her husband. Be that as it may, Maud had resigned

Elysium and settled down courageously to her home life, not, perhaps, without regret, but at any rate, without discontent.

Before, however, their reconciliation had time to take effect in any alteration of their plans, events occurred which gave their thoughts a wholly new direction and effectually settled for them what they were to do. Occasional cases of cholera, seeds sown by the scattered atoms of the great Fair the year before, had been occurring in various districts all through the winter, and at the first blush of spring the disease showed symptoms of breaking out in force. Week by week the 'Gazette' chronicled a marked diminution in other forms of sickness, an equally distinct increase in this. The doctors had a busy time in making preparations, and great were the cleansings, the whitewashings, the emptyings, the fillings-up in many an immund old town and ill-odoured village, where the kingdom of Dirt had prevailed in unbroken tranquillity for generations past.

Outside each city a cholera camp was formed, with a view to the isolation of the sufferers. The District officers were at work from morning to night. The natives took it all with that slightly wondering acquiescence which is the normal attitude of mind produced by the proceedings of the 'Sahib.' It was the order of God that cholera should come;

it was likewise the order of the 'Sirkar'* that houses should be whitewashed, cesspools cleared out, and chlorodyne administered gratis to all who liked it. Both visitations were inscrutable, and to be endured with philosophic calm. The English Doctor, however, was, so ran the orthodox belief, a dangerous fellow, and the old 'Hakim,' with his traditional nostrums, no doubt the proper person to be killed or cured by. The right thing therefore, if one became ill, was carefully to conceal the fact, have surreptitious interviews with the native physician, and, if die one must, be returned as having died of some disease which would not involve a visit from the 'Inspector Sahib,' a conflagration of bedsteads and clothes, a general effusion of whitewash and consequent topsy-turveying of all the household. English doctors and native doctors, however, were of much the same avail, for King Cholera has as yet defied science to read his deadly mystery and learn the secret of his rule. All that science can achieve is to narrow the limits of his ravages.

May had scarcely begun when two cases occurred in the Hill Camp, and Sutton, for the first time in his life, knew what it was to be afraid. He had given 'hostages to Fortune,' and death and danger for the first time looked really terrible when it was

* Government.

Maud who had to confront them. Fifty times Sutton cursed his folly and selfishness in not having sent her off earlier to the Hills, out of harm's way.

While he was harrassing himself with vain regrets and self-reproaches and puzzling his brains as to how the mistake might be even yet repaired, Maud herself added a new item to his perplexities by becoming decidedly unwell. She awoke unrefreshed and wretched; declined the great treat of the day, her morning ride; came shivering and appetiteless to breakfast and confessed to feeling completely miserable. Her husband, the moment that he felt her dry, burning hand, exclaimed that she had got fever, gave her a welcome prescription to go back at once to bed, and sent off for the Doctor.

The reader of these pages, who knows the Sandy Tracts, would think that I did them scarcely justice if I omitted from the picture all reference to a visitation which to many of them formed, too often, a main feature of Indian existence. There is a Fiend there, be it known, that comes, no one can tell whence—from earth or air, or marshy pool or frosty sky or blazing sunny morning. However, when he comes he speedily makes his arrival known to the guests whom he favours with a visit. He shakes them and racks them, and gets into their heads and beats a kettledrum there, and sets a tribe of imps to dance a sort of infernal ballet all about each quivering limb; he freezes them, so that the poor shivering wretches bury themselves under mountains of rags and blankets and go on shivering still; he parches them till they feel like Dives in torture; he turns their brains to mud, their thoughts to chaos, their high spirits to the very blackest gall. Most people, it is believed, when the demon first possesses them, signalise his accession by a hearty cry; and well they may, for among the other cheering thoughts which suggest themselves at the moment, one is that every time you have fever the likelier you are to have it yet again; and that your way to recovery lies through a remedy which for bitterness and bewilderment is only not as bad as the disease for which it is invoked—quinine. In the Sandy Tracts they serve it to you hot, out of a black bottle, stopped with a twisted coil of paper, and heated half to boiling by being carried through the sun. It is at such a moment that existence naturally wears a sombre look, and that the Indian exile curses the ambition or the ill-luck that bore him to such a fortune beneath an alien sky.

Maud, however, was so far fortunate that she had the best and tenderest nurses that could be wished. The surgeon, delighted with so interesting a patient, was assiduous, considerate and suggestive. Mrs. Crummins was more than a mother, and

Sutton suddenly discovered a perfect genius for the science of an invalid's room. When Maud, after a week or two, began to get strong again there was no doubt in the little conclave that she ought to go to the Hills. A great deal of illness was about—the cholera had become really serious—the fierce summer was coming quickly on—in another fortnight the journey would be almost impossible for all but the strongest. So it was settled for her to go; and Sutton became very impatient and uneasy till she was safely off.

Circumstances seemed to settle whither she should go. There had come the kindest letter from Mrs. Vereker, the moment she had heard of Maud's attack. Indian people are, it must be said for them, delightfully hospitable, and offer one bed and board for as long as one likes, as a matter of course. 'Let me know the day,' Mrs. Vereker had written, 'and I will send out my pony for the last stage in; and I shall take the children into my room, which they will think great fun, and turn the nursery into a bedroom for my pretty invalid. Come, dear Maud, and I will promise you back your blooming cheeks in a fortnight!'

Sutton was touched by the kindness of a person to whom he had never been in the least polite; and, in far too great a fright to be particular, or allow objections which would have suggested themselves at another time, he lost no time in writing to Boldero about the means of getting to Elysium (for, without a little pressure in the matter of bullocks and camels from the District officer, carriage in the Sandy Tracts is hard to find); and Boldero had written to say that happily he himself was going up on business, and would put his camp at Mrs. Sutton's disposal.

Accordingly Maud went up to the Hills in the utmost comfort, and with what would have struck European eyes as somewhat unnecessary pomp. The wild country in which they lived rendered an escort of cavalry an almost necessary feature of any but the shortest expedition, and she was quite accustomed to go out for her ride, in her husband's absence, attended by a couple of wild Sawars, whose rude attire, fierce aspect, drawn swords and screaming, prancing horses, rendered them somewhat incongrous companions for a young lady's morning canter. It seemed, therefore, in no way strange for their party to assume the aspect of a military expedition. Boldero, however, added all the civil splendour at his command and called into requisition all the resources of the District officer's establishment to make Maud's journey luxurious.

All along their route there were signs of due preparation for the 'Deputy Commissioner Sahib's' party. Whenever they came to a halting-place they found a little encampment of tents already pitched, surrounded by a host of willing ministrants; a meal awaiting them, the tea-kettle simmering or champagne cooling, and all the little comforts that Indian servants have so ready a knack of extemporising on a march. Maud, though still weak, had sufficiently recovered to enjoy it all extremely, and found her companion very much to her taste, yet not altogether as she would have him. He watched over her with as anxious and tender a care as Sutton himself could have done. Everything that could by any possibility contribute to her comfort had evidently been thought of with a sedulous attention. Their dinner each evening was a little banquet of a very different description from the rough-and-ready meal which sufficed for Boldero's simple tastes on ordinary occasions. Maud's every wish was watched. Twenty miles from home she had said casually that she had left her scent-bottle behind her, and thought no more of it till it made its appearance next morning at breakfast. Horsemen had been riding through the night in order that she might not lack her eau de Cologne. Sutton had insisted on sending with her his own especial body-servant, who had been with him ever since he was a lad, and was, Maud knew, essential to the comfort of his existence. He might, however, have spared himself the sacrifice, for Boldero proved himself a brilliant organiser and was full of resources. Maud simply rode from one pleasant drawing-room to another. The journey kept her in a glow of pleasure. 'How pretty it is!' she cried, as they alighted after the first morning's march and found the camp-fires alight, the relays of ponies picketed, and a banquet ready under a vast peepultree's shade; 'how pretty it is, and how good you are to me! I am beginning to feel like an Eastern queen on a royal progress.'

'Pray rule us as you will,' said Boldero gallantly; 'you will find us loyal subjects. Meanwhile let your Majesty's cup-bearer offer you some hock and Seltzer-water, the best of beverages after a thirsty ride.'

But, polite and kind and hospitable as Boldero was, he was yet not quite as Maud would have liked him to be. His mirth, formerly so ready and unconstrained, had departed. He made no approach to familiarity, scarcely to unconstraint. He was ready to talk, if she began the conversation; but he was equally well pleased to ride for miles without a word. His object seemed to be to make her journey pleasant, but he gave no symptom that it pleased himself. He never for a moment forgot that she was the Colonel's lady and he the District officer in attendance upon her. This reserve jarred somehow with Maud's idea of what was interesting, natural, romantic. Many nice men, most nice men, she thought, were eager in rushing into friendship with her and required a little putting down. It was provoking that Boldero showed no tendency to stand in need of this gentle repression. She had liked him especially last year and he had seemed quite alive and responsive to the fact; now it piqued her that, beyond the assiduous politeness required by his position as a host, he showed no symptom of being fascinated; in plain language he quite declined to flirt, and yet she gave him every opportunity. This was provoking, since Maud herself felt especially disposed to be gracious.

'Now,' she said, after luncheon, when Boldero showed symptoms of retreating, 'please do not go away to smoke; let us sit in this pleasant shade—you shall read me some poetry—no—if you like, you shall smoke and I will read to you. See, now, have my beloved Browning—I am so fond of this.' And Maud began to read, which she did very nicely:—

> Constance, I know not how it is with men:
> For women (I am a woman now like you)
> There is no good of life but love—but love!
> What else looks good is some shade flung from love;
> Love gilds it, gives it worth. Be warned by me,
> Never you cheat yourself one instant! Love,
> Give love, ask only love, and leave the rest!

'Will you have some more of this hock before it is packed up?' said Boldero, in the most determined manner.

'No, thank you,' said Maud, with a sigh of real annoyance, 'I will not have any more hock before it is packed up nor shall you have any more poetry. And why, kind Fates, is it that I have so prosaic a companion for my journey just when I happen to feel poetical?'

'It was because the prosy companion happened to be going at the right moment,' Boldero said; 'I am afraid this sounds very unromantic too, but I advise you to go into the tent and have a thorough rest before we start again. And, by the way, I shall be sending back to the camp: do you want to write a line to Sutton?'

'Of all things!' cried Maud. 'And I shall tell him how pleasant you have been about the poetry.'

Before their Elysian residence was ended Maud discovered that it was Boldero's particular function to recall her husband to her thoughts: sometimes at moments when oblivion would have been preferable.

CHAPTER XXXII.

A GRASS WIDOW.

Let's teach ourselves that honourable stop
Not to outsport discretion——

Maud found Mrs. Vereker's promises of hospitality and enjoyment fully verified. The change from the Camp was delightful; the extra four thousand feet of altitude made life a luxury. Energy, in a hundred different forms, returned to her: some new spring of life quickened her powers alike of mind and body. Mere existence once again became delightful; the pleasant consciousness of health and strength again put her in high spirits. The dull routine in which she had been living of late seemed in retrospect extremely dull. She missed her husband and wrote him enthusiastic letters to tell him so; but a hundred fresh pleasures and interests rushed in to fill the vacant space and to deaden the feeling of regret. And then it had been settled that as soon as the inspection was finished Sutton should get leave to come up and write his report at Elysium, so that their separation promised to be a very short one.

Mrs. Vereker's cottage was the scene of a great many quiet but enjoyable festivities. She had the most charming little luncheon parties, over which she presided with a modesty, liveliness, and grace which her guests found irresistible. There was not much to eat, but each one in his turn received a smile and a glance from the purple eyes and found his glass of sherry turning into nectar before him. These happy guests were mostly military; and he must have been a severe critic indeed who would have denied them the merit of faultless attire, good looks and chivalrous dispositions. The very atmosphere was infectious with flirtation. Mrs. Vereker kept a little court of gentlemen, each with his acknowledged position in the hierarchy of adorers. Nor did she appear to question that her guest would do the same. She took for granted that Maud would accept Desvœux's proffered politeness; she laughed a little gentle laugh at her girlish scruples, and turned her sweet eyes upon her in amused wonderment at such innocent prudery.

'My dear child,' she said, 'what are we poor wives to do? Sit, with our hands crossed, singing hymns and thinking of our *cari sposi* in the Plains? How would my good man be the better if I went out moping for rides all alone, instead of being attended by my cavalier? Besides, no one ever would believe that one was alone, and one would be gossiped about as much as ever. And then did not your old Othello wish that Boldero was here to look after you? No, no, I don't find "moping" among the other disagreeable things we vowed to do when matrimony marked us for its own. And then you must know that three is quite an impossible number at the Hills—the paths are too narrow, happily—and three is an odious number, which ought to be turned out of the arithmetic-books. So you must start a flirtation not to interfere with mine. Besides, Mr. Desvœux is too charming. I only wish that he would flirt with me!'

So Maud found herself taken possession of by Desvœux, and assigned to him as a matter of course in the set in which she was living. The worst of it was that she found it rather pleasant. It was, of course, convenient to have some one ready to fetch and carry, who was always on the look-out for one at parties and only too delighted at having any command to obey. It was all above-board and recognised as right. Every one knew that there was not the least harm in it. The only drawback was that Maud found it very difficult to describe the state of things to Jem, and her letters grew shorter than was right. Mrs. Vereker was too volatile, too frivolous, too much in love with herself and the world around her, to allow of her companion lapsing into a serious mood. She spent hours over a succession of toilettes, each of which was perfection; hours more in designing how such perfection should be achieved. High spirits and fun pervaded her every thought, but dress was the matter about which Mrs. Vereker was most nearly feeling serious. The two ladies had a long discussion over the attire which would do most justice to their charms at the Viceroy's Fancy Ball.

'I can't go as a Marquise,' said Mrs. Vereker, 'because powder does not set my eyes off well, and paint spoils my complexion. I mean to be Night—holy, peaceful Night—black tulle, you know, with a crescent moon glittering on my forehead, and little diamond stars twinkling, twinkling in both my ears, which you know are loves. See, now!' And Mrs. Vereker caught up a great piece of muslin which was lying on the sofa, threw it over her shoulders, turned her beautiful violet eyes to the ceiling, and went sliding across the room with a sweet, demure smile and graceful undulations.

'See, now!' she cried, 'don't you feel the moonlight and the nightingales and the tinkling folds, and how very sacred and peaceful it all is?

I shall be furious if at least sixteen men don't break their hearts about me. But, my dear, you shall be a *vivandière* and show your pretty ankles; or a Normandy flower-girl, with a high cap and crimson petticoat. Or why not be Morning, and dance in my quadrille; a Rising Sun, with rays?'

'Oh no, thank you,' Maud answered; 'I intend to have a quadrille of my own. I leave you the sun, moon, and stars to yourself. Mr. Desvœux is arranging one for me out of Sir Walter Scott—something historical and romantic.'

Then Desvœux would come (oftener than ever, since this Historical Quadrille gave a new excuse for frequent calls) and turn everything into ridicule. 'As usual,' he told them, 'Mrs. Fotheringham has been trying to drive a bargain. The two young ladies are to go as Mediæval Princesses; and poor Giroflont, who had come all the way from Calcutta to dress the ladies' hair for the Fancy Ball, stipulated for his accustomed five rupees a-head. Fotheringham *mère* stuck out for three. Giroflont rejected the suggestion with scorn. "Impossible, madame," he said, "ce sont des coiffures historiques!" So exit Mrs. Fotheringham in a fury.'

'And the poor girls will have to go as milkmaids,' said Mrs. Vereker. 'What a shame! And what a mother!'

'And what a father!' said Desvœux. 'He has just been to interview the Agent and has made us both extremely ill. Such vapid dulness!

He spoke of virtne—not the gods
More purely when they wish to charm
Pallas and Juno sitting by;
And with a sweeping of the arm,
And a lack-lustre dead-blue eye
Devolved his rounded periods.'

'What a comfort you must find it, Mr. Desvœux,' said Mrs. Vereker, 'to fly for refuge to eyes that are neither lack-lustre nor dead-blue! Now I come to think of it, though, I believe dead-blue is just the shade of mine.'

'Yours!' said Desvœux, in a tone of fervour which spoke volumes.

'These poor girls!' cried Maud, 'how shamefully they are dressed! Perfect Quakeresses!'

'Quakeresses!' answered Desvœux; 'but Quakeresses are too charming, dear little tender doves, in the softest silk and freshest muslin. I suffered agonies once upon a time on account of one.'

'Profane!' cried Mrs. Vereker; 'Quakers are really a sort of monks and nuns, only that they happen to have husbands and wives.'

'Yes,' said Desvœux, 'monasticism without its single recommendation!'

'Rude man!' Mrs. Vereker cried; 'let us send him away, Maud. I should like to know, sir, what would become of you without us married women?'

'What indeed?' cried Desvœux; 'but, you know, when the Pope offered Petrarch a dispensation to marry, he declined on the ground that he could not write poetry to his wife.'

'That reminds me,' said Mrs. Vereker, 'that I must write some prose to my husband, and Mrs. Sutton some to hers; and the post goes in half-an-hour. Mr. Desvœux, you must really go.'

'I obey,' said Desvœux, with a sigh; 'my exile from paradise is cheered by the thought that I am coming back at four to take Mrs. Sutton for a ride.'

CHAPTER XXXIII.

FACILIS DESCENSUS AVERNI.

Birds, yet in freedom, shun the net
Which love around your haunts hath set.

The pleasant weeks flew by, a round of enjoyments. Maud found herself in great request. She and Mrs. Vereker held quite a little levée every morning. Day after day a never-failing stream of visitors poured along the path to the modest but picturesque residence where these two beauties waited to charm mankind. The grass-plot in front was worn quite bare by a succession of ponies, who waited there while their owners were worshipping within.

No young officer who arrived for a holiday considered himself at all *en règle* till he had been to pay his respects to this adorable couple.

Mrs. Vereker was none the less attractive, as she knew very well, for being contrasted with another charming woman, whose charms were of a different order. 'Blest pair of syrens!' Desvœux used to say in his impudent fashion; 'it is too charming to have you both together—a dangerous conspiracy against the peace of mind of one-half of the species.'

'Ah!' Mrs. Vereker would answer, turning her violet eyes upon him, with a sweet reproachful smile, which would have melted any heart but Desvœux's; 'and when one of the syrens is young and lovely, and just arrived from the Plains. There *were* days, my dear Maud, when Mr. Desvœux used to want to ride with me and used to run my errands so nicely! Alas! alas! for masculine weathercocks! I am very jealous of you, my dear, I'd have you to know, and shall some day tear your pretty eyes out. You do too much execution by half. Meanwhile, here is my dear General Beau coming up the road.'

Maud shrugged her shoulders and arched her pretty brow, and both Desvœux and Mrs. Vereker burst out laughing to see the General portrayed.

'The General to the life!' cried Desvœux, '"like a poet or a peer

With his arched eyebrow and Parnassian sneer."'

'I protest against the poet,' cried Mrs. Vereker,

laughing; 'we always flirt in the very plainest prose. As for his eyebrows, they are adorable.'

Then the General arrived, as great a dandy as ever Poole turned out, and was in the drawing-room before Maud's gravity was at all re-established. 'And what was the laugh about?' he inquired.

'About a Parnassian sneer,' said Desvœux with great presence of mind; 'and where do you come from, General?'

'I have been calling at the Fotheringhams,' said the General; 'my intimacy with Mrs. Fotheringham does not incline me to wish to be one of her daughters.'

'Poor girls!' said Mrs. Vereker, 'we were commiserating them the other day, and saying how cruelly their mother treats them.'

'Ah!' said the General, 'she does indeed; actually makes the poor things do lessons all the morning. A certain gentleman, a friend of mine, I cannot tell you his name, went there the other day with the most serious intentions towards the little one, the one with yellow hair, and actually found them hard at work at Mill's "Logic."'

'Two women were grinding at the mill,' said Desvœux, 'and one was taken and the other left, I suppose?'

'I am afraid,' said Mrs. Vereker, 'that both were left. But fancy a woman who was also a logician! For my part, I consider it a great privilege to be as unreasonable as I choose.'

'The arguments of beauty,' said the General, 'are always irresistible; but I am quite for female education.'

'And I,' said Mrs. Vereker, 'am dead against it. We know quite as much as is good for us as it is. What do you say, Maud?'

'I have quite forgotten all I learnt at school already,' said Maud. 'General Beau, can you say your Duty to your Neighbour?'

'And your duty to your neighbour's wife?' put in Desvœux. 'But I object to all education as revolutionary—part of this horrid radical epoch in which we live.'

'Yes,' said Mrs. Vereker, 'one of the nice things about India is its being a military despotism. As for Europe, the mobs have it all their own way.'

'Horrid mobs!' said Desvœux, 'as if an unwashed rabble was Nature's last achievement.

Her 'prentice hand she tried on lords,
And then she made the masses O!'

'But you must teach them religion, you know,' said the General, 'the Catechism, and so forth.'

'Of course,' said Maud; their Duty to their Neighbour, for instance.'

'I don't know,' said Mrs. Vereker; 'they only learn it all by rote. When I was last in England our clergyman gave us this specimen of one of his parishioners, to whom he had been detailing the mysteries of faith:

'"*Clergyman.* And now, Sally, how do you expect to be saved?"

'"*Sally.* Dun'noa; please, sir, tell I."'

'Well,' said Desvœux, 'theology is a thing I never could understand myself. Now I must be off to my Agent.'

'When shall we see you again?' said Maud.

'Dun'noa,' said Desvœux; 'please, ma'am, tell I. What time shall I come and take you out this afternoon?'

But the ladies had visitors more distinguished even than the General. The Agent himself came in one Sunday after church and asked to be allowed to stay to lunch. Cards flowed in apace from Government House, for the Master of the Ceremonies there knew that no entertainment would be complete where Maud was not.

There were little dances got up expressly in her honour, for which her card of engagements was filled for days before: at every point homage, the sweetest that woman's ears can listen to, awaited her. A chorus of worshippers assured her she was beautiful; the incense was for ever burning on her shrine, till the very air became drugged with flattery. Yet Maud was not completely happy; her conscience was ill at ease. The scene around her was pleasant; but, tried by certain standards, she knew that it would fall short. She remembered, with a sigh, the sort of way in which her cousin Vernon would have turned up his nose at the people among whom she was living, and she knew that in many ways they deserved it. Felicia, she knew, thought Mrs. Vereker utterly frivolous, fast and slightly vulgar; and she felt that Felicia was right. Her husband, conscience reminded her, disapproved of and despised Desvœux: and was there not something to disapprove and dislike about him? Still Maud felt herself unable to resist the current that was hurrying her along. The consequence was that she had fallen out of harmony with those stricter judges whose tastes just now it was convenient to forget. It gave her no pleasure to think of them. She fancied Jem in a silently reproachful mood, Felicia daintily contemptuous, Vernon with an outspoken sneer. Her letters to her husband, though they never contained the hundred-thousandth part of one untruth, began to be less faithful and complete transcripts of her life than of old. Desvœux ought, in truth, to have occupied a more prominent place. She felt ashamed to tell her husband, toiling hard in solitude and heat, of the round of gaiety in which her life was passed. On the other hand, her husband's letters gave her no satisfaction. They were far from amusing; indeed, the life which he was leading was hardly susceptible, in livelier hands than his, of being rendered amusing or picturesque. He missed her, of course; but then he would be with her again in a few weeks, and Maud did not think it necessary to be sentimental about it. His pen was far from a ready one, and this Report, Maud knew, would be worse to him than a campaign. In his letters to her his one idea would have been to conceal from her anything that was disagreeable, and she might, if she had chosen, have augured ill from his reticence; but life just now was too bright and exciting for such inward monition to get a hearing. Her companions had infected her with a passion for pleasure, and duty had faded into indistinctness. Then, too, her new position as a married lady and as Sutton's bride was not without its charm. She was a much grander lady now than she had been the year before as Miss Vernon, and this access of dignity was pleasurable. It involved, however, being taken in to dinner by officials of an age, dignity, and disposition which she found anything but congenial to her own, though Desvœux protested that she was trying to establish a flirtation with the Agent. Once at Government House she had the honour of sitting next the Viceroy, an alarming but yet delightful eminence. How kind he seemed, how full of friendly talk, how eager to know about her husband and his doings!

'How is your *preux chevalier?*' he said. 'What would become of everything, I wonder, in that stormy corner that he keeps in such good order, but for him? He is one of the people whom I completely trust.'

Maud felt her cheek glowing with pleasure, yet the pleasure was not without a sting. Everybody conspired to speak of her husband as some one beyond the usual flight in goodness, chivalry, nobility of soul. Was she behaving as became the wife of such a man? Was she loving, honouring, and obeying in the full spirit of her vow? Was it honourable or right that half-a-dozen foolish lads should be competing for familiarity with her, and a man like Desvœux be her habitual companion? Ought her husband to hear such things of her? This was the little skeleton which Maud kept locked up, along with many lovely dresses, in her bedroom closet—this the little prick her conscience gave her—this the drop of bitter in the glittering, ambrosial draught of pleasure.

She drank it all the same and found it too sweet to put it from her lips.

CHAPTER XXXIV.

BAD TIMES IN THE PLAINS.

Where nature sickens, and each air is death.

WHILE the fortunate Elysians were thus bravely keeping up their own and one another's spirits by a round of gaieties, the people in the Plains were busy with a round of work of quite a different description. Cholera having broken out, all leave in the infected regiments had been cancelled, and many a luckless officer had come back to his cantonment, grumbling at a curtailed holiday and the stern mandate which recalled him just as he had reached the snow scenery of which he had dreamed for months, or established himself in some happy hunting-ground for a two months' campaign against ibex or bison. Back they all came, however, poor fellows, to take their equal chance with rank and file against an enemy of whom even the bravest men are not ashamed to be afraid.

The prevalence of illness and the precautions ordered to prevent its increase entailed a deal of extra labour, and kept all the officers busily employed. The hospitals required constant visiting, for the men were moody and disheartened, and stood in need of all the encouragement that their leaders could give them. Sutton, always thinking of every one but himself, had ordered two of his 'boys' away to an outpost forty miles off, nominally to look after a turbulent Zámindar, really to be out of harm's way. This threw all the more work on his hands, and it was work that he felt himself specially capable of doing with good effect. His visits at the hospital were, he knew, eagerly looked for, and a few kind words from the Colonel Sahib often inspired cheerfulness and hope at a moment when gloom and despondency were telling with mortal effect on men's minds and bodies. His regiment had already lost several men, and they had died happy in the thought that the well-loved leader was ever close at hand, and ever on the look-out for something to alleviate their suffering. Many a gaunt visage, with death already written in each ghastly feature, lighted up with sudden brightness as he came, and, when exhaustion had gone too far for speech, smiled him a heartfelt benediction of gratitude and love. The scene was, indeed, one full of pathos, even to a less interested looker-on than the Colonel. It was horrible to see these sturdy, joyous, much-enduring, dare-devil troopers lying so utterly prostrated, unnervéd and helpless. Death, it seemed, should have come to them in the form of steel or bullet, the thrust of lance, the crashing sword-cut or wild cavalry charge; not as a pestilence, creeping on them unawares and slaying them in their beds. Sutton, who had looked death in the face a hundred times with perfect indifference, began to understand why people feared it. After all some aspects of life are, he felt, too delightful to leave without a sigh. For the last few months he had been, for the first time in his life, completely happy. A new era had begun for him, new vistas of pleasure had opened up. All that had gone before had been duty, excitement, hard work; not, indeed, without its enjoyment, but, after all, something far from happiness in the sense in which Sutton had now begun to understand it. Fighting was all well enough, and the hazardous ambition of a soldier's career delightfully spirit-stirring; but it was not here that the real end of life was to be found. Sutton's real end of life was now the little being who was flirting away at the Hills, in happy forgetfulness of all but the present moment. Sutton, however, thought of her only as he had seen her, tender, affectionate, devoted to himself. Since the half-quarrel about her departure for the Hills and the reconciliation which followed it, his life with her had been one of perfect happiness. Maud had been raised by her conquest over herself into a sweeter, nobler mood, and was more than ever mistress of her husband's heart. Her departure, peremptorily insisted on by her husband, had none the less cost them both a bitter pang; though Sutton promised that it should be for a few weeks at the utmost, a promise which cheered Maud more than it did himself, as she knew not, as he did, how easily its fulfilment might be rendered impossible. So Sutton went about his work in his own determined, loyal fashion, but with his heart no longer in it. His treasure was elsewhere and his heart with it. The collection of materials for his Report gave him a deal of trouble and involved many weary rides. He had to see District officers, Zámindars, police inspectors, heads of villages, spies, and then to determine what the real necessities of the case were and where the posts should be fixed. Everything depended on his work being well, wisely, and thoroughly done. The responsibility weighed on him: the peace, safety, prosperity of a whole District was hanging on his judgment. This is the kind of work which tries conscientious and loyal men far more than physical exertion. Then the cholera, which had shown symptoms of abatement, broke out all of a sudden with more violence than ever, and it became apparent that Sutton's regiment was thoroughly infected. Then all real hopes of his getting up to the Hills for the present, at any rate, had to be abandoned; but of this he said nothing to his wife. It was of no use to distress her beforehand with bad news, which she would be certain to learn quite soon enough.

One evening, when Sutton had returned, thoroughly tired with a long, hot expedition, the orderly, whose task it was to bring him the returns of the sick for the day, told him that in the list of seizures for that afternoon was a Pathan boy, who had been picked up years before by some of the troopers in a suddenly deserted village, and who had lived as a pet child of the regiment ever since. Sutton had been kind to the lad, had defrayed such small charges as his maintenance in the lines involved, and had secured him the beginning of an education in the regimental school. Sutton on hearing the news went off at once to the hospital. Already the disease had made fearful progress, and he saw in a moment that the boy was in the most critical condition. He bent over the exhausted, helpless form, and said a few kind words of hopefulness and sympathy. The boy listened with glistening eyes and lips quivering with agitation;

and as Sutton turned to go he sprang up in bed, forgetful of everything but the master-feeling which overpowered him, and clasped his protector round the neck with a single outburst of affection: 'Ma-Bap,' 'My father and mother!'

Two hours later they came to say that the boy was dead, and before the next morning Sutton began to be aware that that last embrace had been a deadly one, and that the dread malady had laid its hand upon himself.

CHAPTER XXXV.

AN ELYSIAN PICNIC.

Nay, the world—the world,
All ear and eye, with such a stupid heart
To interpret ear and eye, and such a tongue
To blaze its own interpretation!

THREE gallant officers, who had been enjoying the hospitality of Elysium for many weeks, were fired one day with a noble resolve to show their gratitude to the gentlemen and their devotion to the ladies by whom they had been so pleasantly entertained. It was an inspiration, everybody felt at once, and all Elysium thrilled with conscious responsiveness at the happy thought. There is a little valley near Elysium, a mile or two from the mountain's summit, where a green, smooth sward invites the weary climber to repose; where venerable deodars, towering on the steep hill-side, stretch their limbs to ward off the fierce afternoon sun; where a headlong stream comes bubbling down among the thick-grown ferns and falls in a feathery cascade and disappears in the gorge below; where the Genius of the Mountains has, in fact, its chosen haunt. There you may sit and watch the rose-tipped snowy range warming into fresh life and beauty as the sun goes down, and fading into cold gloom as he disappears. Here, in a hundred suggestive nooks, Nature has hinted at a sylvan *tête-à-tête*, or spread a verdant curtain of wild growth to festoon an *al fresco* banquet; and here it was that the three inspired officers resolved to give an entertainment that should at once do justice to the warmth of their feelings, the correctness of their tastes, and the profuseness of their liberality.

It was to be a picnic—the picnic of the season—the picnic of the world; and if enchanting scenery, a cloudless sky, enthusiastic hosts, a crowd of pretty women, an army of devoted men, a community not too blasé to be easily amused, nor yet so unused to pleasure as not to know how to take it—if all these ingredients, backed with the music of a lovely band crashing out among the rocks, cookery over which, by gracious permission, the Viceroy's own chef presided, and champagne, iced to perfection in Himalayan snows, could make a success, then it would, as Maud expected, be indeed an era in the lives of all concerned.

Mrs. Vereker, though perhaps less sanguine than her more youthful companion, determined to have a new dress for the occasion; and a committee of adorers discussed the rival merits of half-a-dozen projected costumes. Mrs. Vereker, however, treated all their suggestions with contempt, and determined in the depths of her own consciousness on something that should be a sweet surprise.

Maud, happily, had one of her English treasures which was still unknown to the admiring public, and which she felt at once would be the very thing.

For some days nothing but the picnic could be talked of in Elysium; what to wear at it, how to get to it, how to return, were topics of the liveliest interest to all. A hundred pleasant plans in connection with it shaped themselves into being. General Beau, who liked being beforehand with the world, secured for himself the honour of escorting Mrs. Vereker; and Desvœux, as a matter of course, established his claim to act as Maud's gentleman-in-waiting on the occasion. By this time her spirits were very high and impatient of all that seemed to check their flow. She was flirting with Desvœux, she knew, in the most open manner, yet she resented any notice being taken of it. Boldero had met her at a croquet party and been very disagreeable. He confessed to having been two days in Elysium, and could or would give no account of why he had not been to call. 'How unkind and unlike the old Mr Boldero whom we all liked so much! How you are changed!'

'Yes,' Boldero said, flushing up quite red, so that Maud knew that he meant more than met the ear, 'and some one else is changed too and might not care about her former friends.'

'What do you mean?' Maud said, disturbed at Boldero's serious air; 'how can I care about you, if you won't come and see me? Come now, and take me across the lawn for an ice, and tell me what it is that is the matter.'

'I do not think I can tell you,' said Boldero, greatly alarmed at finding himself committed to a lecture; 'you will not like it; you want a scolding.'

'Well,' said Maud, 'I like scoldings from my friends, and I often deserve them, and often get them, goodness knows. Give me one now; only you must be quick, please, because there is Mr. Desvœux signalling me, and I have promised to go for a ride with him.'

'Don't,' said Boldero, with great alacrity; 'stay and hear my lecture. Let me go and say you would rather not.'

'Not for the world!' cried Maud; 'I am looking forward to it immensely; he would be broken-hearted if I disappointed him, poor fellow. How would you like it yourself?'

'Broken-hearted!' said Boldero, with that peculiar turn of contempt in his voice with which her husband and his friends always vexed Maud by speaking of Desvœux.

'How disagreeable you are!' said Maud. 'Don't you know he is my particular friend?

'Friend!' said Boldero; 'he is the very worst enemy you have, believe me. Forgive me, as your husband's old friend, if I tell you the truth when, it seems, no one else will. He is making you talked of; and if you could only know how people talk! He knows it, and he likes it, and it is what he is always doing.'

'And what you are always doing,' said Maud in a passion, 'is coming and saying the most horrid things in the most disagreeable way and joining the horrid people who gossip about one. Do they talk of me? Then why don't you make them eat their words—you, who used to be my friend?'

'I am your friend,' said the other with a grave persistence, 'and Sutton's too. It is because I am that I risk your displeasure by telling you that you are doing wrong.'

'Doing wrong?' cried Maud, by this time quite flushed with excitement and hardly mistress of her words; 'how dare you say so? You know it is false. I am alone, or you would not venture to insult me.'

'Come,' said Boldero, unmoved by the taunt, of

which Maud herself felt the outrageous injustice, 'be sensible, and let me take care of you this evening: do me a kind act for once.'

'Thank you,' said Maud, the tears gleaming in her eyes, 'and hear such things as you have been saying over again? Take care of me, indeed! Please never speak to me again!'

She was gone, leaving her companion discomfited. In another instant Desvœux was at her side, and, as he lifted her to her pony, said something which made her laugh and blush. Boldero would have liked to throttle him.

Maud's conscience, however, prevented her full enjoyment of the ride. She knew as well as possible that Boldero was telling her truth: she *was* doing wrong, she felt only too distinctly. Boldero would have cut his fingers off to please her, and she had chosen to misunderstand him. Still it was too provoking to be lectured. When she got home there was a letter from Dustypore, which told her that Felicia too had heard of her proceedings and was wanting to warn her. 'You must not forget, dear Maud,' the letter said, 'what a home of gossip Elysium is, and how all that is young and pretty and interesting is what gossip busies itself most about. Some men, like Mr. Desvœux, for instance, have only to look at one for the gossipers to begin; but I know you will be very judicious, even at the expense of being somewhat too particular. How I wish I were with you!'

'They all want to tease me with their horrid advice and hints,' Maud thought, in vexation of heart; 'as for Mr. Boldero, he was too odious: I can never, never forgive him.'

Then, as if all the world were in a conspiracy, Mrs. Fotheringham, whom Maud met at a dinner-party that night, pounced upon her as the ladies were filing into the drawing-room and made her come and sit down on a remote sofa.

Maud always believed, probably not without justice, that Mrs. Fotheringham bore her a grudge for being married before the two Miss Fotheringhams. She was, accordingly, quite indisposed to be lectured.

'My dear,' Mrs. Fotheringham said, 'an old woman may sometimes give a young one a friendly hint. You don't know the world as I do, with my twenty years of India. Now, don't be angry with me if I give you a bit of advice. Take care! Young wives whose husbands are in the Plains cannot take too much.'

This seemed the last drop in the overflowing cup of annoyance and humiliation. Maud felt excessively indignant. It was an impertinence surely for Mrs. Fotheringham to venture to speak so.

'And what am I to take care of?' she said;

and what right have you to speak to me in this way?'

'Take care of your companions, my dear. You have chosen the most dangerous, the worst you could find—Mr. Desvœux.'

'Stop, stop!' cried Maud, jumping up in a fury; 'he is my friend, my kind friend. I will not hear him abused.'

'You must be on your guard,' continued the other, with exasperating pertinacity; 'he is very unprincipled.'

'I know he is very agreeable,' cried Maud; 'unprincipled! what do you mean by that?'

'I mean—I mean,' said the other, 'that he is dangerous—just the sort of man to try to kiss you, if you gave him the chance.'

'Indeed?' cried Maud, by this time in far too great a passion to be either courteous or discreet, 'I should think none the worse of him for that. *I believe they all would!*' Having delivered this parting shot, Maud hurried away in a great state of agitation, and Mrs. Fotheringham shrugged her shoulders in despair at so unseemly an outburst of temper, so awful a view of human nature.

When they got home that night Maud told Mrs. Vereker her troubles, and was relieved to find what slight importance she attached to them. She burst out laughing, and clapped her hands in delight at

Maud's account of the encounter with Mrs. Fotheringham. 'But, my dear child, what induced you to make such a foolish speech? And as for Mr. Boldero, he wanted you himself, don't you understand? Flirt a little with *him* to-morrow and see how much he will want to lecture you then.'

'But he won't flirt with me,' said Maud; 'it is very odd. Besides, I was in a passion, and told him never to speak to me again. Poor fellow!'

'You dear little goose!' Mrs. Vereker said, kissing her, 'sit down this instant and write and tell him you are broken-hearted for being so rude, and that he is to come to lunch and finish his lecture to-morrow. You must not quarrel with all the world at once.'

Of Felicia's letter Mrs. Vereker equally made light. 'She means nothing, my dear, except what I preach to you and practise myself, discretion and moderation. So many dances in the evening, so many rides in the week, so many lunches, so many looks, so many smiles, and so forth. Besides, you know, Mrs. Vernon is a prude, a born prude; she breathes a congenial atmosphere of proprieties where I should be suffocated. She likes men to be polite, and only polite; I take them up where politeness ends and something else begins. She likes small-beer; I happen to prefer champagne, bright, sparkling and intoxicatingly delicious!

Besides,' rattled on Mrs. Vereker, quite at ease with a familiar topic, 'Mrs. Vernon is a flirt too, in her prudish way. She flirts, she used to flirt with your husband scandalously, I hope he behaves better now. Mine is a monster, and makes me cry my eyes out. But, I tell you what, my dear Maud, there is great safety in numbers. Don't speak to that saucy Desvœux for a fortnight, and turn your pretty eyes on some one else, the first you fancy. Would you like my General? or Parson Boldero? Take him in hand, my dear, and in a week we will make the horrid fellow flirt just as much as his neighbours.'

'He's a very bad hand at it at present,' said Maud, with a laugh.

However, the result of the conference was that Maud sat down and wrote a pretty little repentant note: and the next day Boldero came with a beating heart and took the little scapegrace for a ride, and scolded her very affectionately, much to his own satisfaction, through a whole pleasant summer afternoon.

CHAPTER XXXVI.

A KISS.

As she sped fast through sun and shade
The happy winds upon her played,
Blowing the ringlets from the braid;
She looked so lovely as she swayed
The rein with dainty finger-tips.

A man had given all other bliss
And all his worldly worth for this:
To waste his whole heart in one kiss
Upon her perfect lips.

When Mrs. Vereker suggested Desvœux's temporary deposition, she overlooked two obstacles which proved fatal to the scheme's success: in the first place, Maud did not quite wish to depose him; in the next, Desvœux had not the slightest intention of being deposed. Despite all hints to stay away, he presented himself with provoking regularity at Mrs. Vereker's cottage-porch, outstayed later callers without the least compunction, and evidently felt himself quite master of the situation.

At Maud's first symptom of neglect he was more devoted, more assiduous, more amusing than ever.

Both ladies were constrained in their hearts to admit that his presence was a great enlivenment. Maud, though she would not have admitted it to herself, felt sometimes impatient for his arrival. She had given Desvœux to understand that his attentions were unwelcome, but she had not the least wish that he should become inattentive. As the French song says—

> Lorsque l'on dit, 'Ne m'aimez plus jamais,'
> On prétend bien qu'on obéira, mais
> On compte un peu sur des révoltes.

So Maud, when she tried to keep Desvœux at a distance, probably only made it apparent how much she liked him to be near; at any rate, the attempt at a little quarrel had only the result of making them better friends than before. Then there was a sort of familiarity about him which Maud was conscious of only half-disliking. Mrs. Vereker declared she had not breathed a word; but something in his look, when he spoke of Mrs. Fotheringham, convinced Maud that he had heard of her unlucky speech to that lady. When she rode with some one else she was sure to meet him, looking the picture of dulness. She knew that if they had been together they would be both having the greatest fun. And then how flat and what a bore her own companion seemed! One day she did actually go for a ride with General Beau. Mrs.

Vereker asked him afterwards how they had got on, and the General arched his brow and said, 'Ah!' in a manner which suggested that he had not altogether liked it. Then, one day, in a pet, Maud went out alone, saying, 'No one can find fault with me for *this*.' Alas! alas! she was sauntering along in the most disconsolate manner, when, round a corner of the hill, who should come sauntering along but Desvœux, also alone and disconsolate and in the direst need of a companion! Of course under such circumstances there was nothing to be done but for Desvœux to turn his pony round and accompany her for the rest of the expedition; and then, no sooner had they done this, than, as bad luck would have it, they came upon all the people whom they particularly did not wish to meet—first the Fotheringhams, the mamma and two young ladies in palanquins, a nice young civilian escorting each; Fotheringham *père* on his pony, bringing up the rear—in order, as Desvœux said scornfully, to cut off retreat if the young men's hearts failed them.

'If that is courtship *à la mode*,' he said, 'Heaven preserve us! Fancy four parental eyes glaring at every act! My love is a sensitive plant and would shrink up at every look.'

Maud, however, felt that it was no joke, and was very much provoked with Desvœux. She was in the act of turning back to join the Fotheringhams.

'Don't, pray don't,' said Desvœux; '*qui s'excuse s'accuse.* Why don't the two young gentlemen come and ask to be allowed to walk with us and be taken care of? If only we could *afficher*

"MET BY ACCIDENT,
UPON OUR HONOUR"

on our backs, and let all the world know how innocent we really are!'

And next, before Maud had at all recovered her equanimity, a turn in the road brought them face to face with all the Government House party—ladies and ponies and aides-de-camp in attendance, and, last of all, the Viceroy himself, with a big stick and wide-awake hat. 'Ah! how d'ye do, Mrs Sutton?' he said, looking, Maud fancied, not near so good-humoured as of old and taking no notice of Desvœux; 'I hope you have good accounts of your husband?'

'Yes, very good, thank you, Lord Clare,' Maud said, blushing at a question which seemed to convey a reproach to her guilty conscience, and at the thought of how little her husband had been present to her mind of late. Altogether, Maud's attempt at a solitary ride turned out a thorough failure.

Then came the picnic, and Maud, it must be confessed, behaved like a little idiot.

'The best way to treat gossip,' Desvœux suggested, 'is to ignore it and show the world that you have nothing to be ashamed of.' By way of enforcing his doctrine he proceeded to monopolise her in the most outrageous manner; nor did she refuse to be monopolised. When other people came and tried to talk to her Desvœux stood by and contrived to make them feel themselves *de trop*. He put poor Boldero, who flattered himself that his afternoon's sermon was to bear good fruit, utterly to the rout; insulted General Beau by some absurd question about the Carraway Islands; put all the aides-de-camp to flight; and, even when the Viceroy came by and stopped to speak to Maud, seemed to consider it a very great intrusion.

'Really, Mr. Desvœux,' Maud said, with a laugh, 'you give yourself all the airs of a jealous husband.'

'I only wish,' said her companion, 'you had ever given me the chance of being one. But don't these people bore one? I don't feel a bit inclined to-day to be bored.'

'No more do I,' said Maud, 'but I feel very cross with you all the same. Let us go and sit by the Fotheringhams.'

'Please do not,' said Desvœux; 'here is a delightful nook, with a smooth stone for your table, and the stream making too much noise for any one to overhear us. It was evidently intended for you and me.'

So all the world had the opportunity, at lunch, of witnessing Desvœux in the act of adoration; and Desvœux, if he would let no one else have a chance of talking, had, Maud felt, plenty to say himself, It was indiscreet, but very pleasant. Even Mrs. Vereker grew alarmed, and making an excuse to pass close by them, came and whispered in Maud's ear a solemn 'Don't!'

'Don't what?' said Maud in ill-affected wonderment.

'Don't be a goose,' said her companion; 'Mr. Desvœux, would you be good-natured and go and fetch me some ice-pudding, while I sit and talk to Mrs. Sutton?'

'With pleasure,' said Desvœux, smothering his resentment as best he could; 'but where am I to sit when I come back?'

'You need not come back for half-an-hour,' said Mrs. Vereker quietly; 'go and talk with some one else. I see I must keep you young people both in order.'

Desvœux went off in dudgeon, and Mrs. Vereker lost no time in supplying his place. 'Ah, Mr. Boldero!' she said, 'come and be amusing, please, and give us the latest news from Dustypore.'

For once in his life Boldero thought Mrs. Vereker very nice.

'Be amusing!' thought Maud; 'why does not she ask him to fly to the moon at once? Only Mr. Desvœux can be that.'

And so it proved. Even Mrs. Vereker could not make conversation go. Boldero was stiff, uncordial and ill at ease. Maud was vexed, and did not care to conceal it. It was a relief when General Beau appeared, and Maud, in a pet, asked him to take her to the waterfall.

The General, who had been intending to perform the pilgrimage with Mrs. Vereker, did not betray that he was disconcerted, and professed his delight at the suggestion.

'But,' said Maud, 'can we trust those two naughty people together? My dear Mrs. Vereker, "Don't!"'

'Is not she growing saucy?' Mrs. Vereker said to Boldero; 'it is all your fault; all you gentlemen conspire to spoil her.'

'No,' said Boldero, 'begging your pardon, it is all your fault. You let one of us have it all his own way. You encourage him to flirt, and encourage her to encourage him. It is a shame, Mrs. Vereker; in another fortnight her reputation will be gone.'

'Fiddlededee!' cried Mrs. Vereker. 'See what jealousy will do! You might as well accuse me of flirting with you, and every one knows that I am a saint.'

'A very pretty one and in a very pretty dress,' said Boldero, whom Mrs. Vereker's violent eyes always threw off his balance in about two minutes.

'No, thank you,' she said, tossing her shapely head in pretty scorn, 'I don't want any flattery; we are too old friends. My dress is lovely, I am well aware, and it has pleased God to make me not quite a fright. But about Maud, now: don't you know that all the gossip is simple envy; some horrid unkind old woman like Mrs. Fotheringham, with about as much heart as one of these rocks, and her two hoydens of girls? But here comes Major Fenton, who has, I consider, quite neglected me to-day.'

Major Fenton was one of the hosts, and the most eligible of the trio.

'Impossible!' he said, melting under the sweet smile from a stern, languid air which he wore to all the world; 'the duties of my day performed, its pleasures are now, I hope, about to begin. Will you come with me to the waterfall?'

Mrs. Vereker bent two soft orbs on Boldero with a reproachful look, as if to say, 'Why did you not ask me sooner?' and went off in glee with the Major;

and Boldero, left in solitude to his own meditations, mentally voted this the dullest, flattest, and most unsuccessful picnic at which it had ever been his ill-luck to be a guest.

When Maud and General Beau arrived at the waterfall, there, of course, was Desvœux, trying to encourage the Miss Fotheringhams to cross the stream and so ascend to the finest point of view. This was a little more than the Miss Fotheringhams' nerves were equal to: the stream was full and foamed and tossed itself into an angry crest; the water looked black and swift and treacherous. You had to jump on to one boulder, then balance yourself on three stepping-stones through the shallows, then make one good spring to the rock opposite, and the feat was done! This, however, was just too much for the Miss Fotheringhams, who had not been trained in athletics and were not naturally what the Irishmen call 'leppers.' As they were hesitating and refusing, Maud and the General came up, looking very much bored. Maud had been finding her companion almost intolerable, and would have jumped *anywhere* to be free of him. There was nothing in it: Desvœux had been skipping across half-a-dozen times. 'Look,' he said, 'a skip, two hops and a jump, and there you are! Do try. Don't you see?'

'I see, exactly,' said Maud, gathering up her petticoats and giving her parasol to General Beau.

'Stop! it is not safe,' he cried; 'stop, I implore; the rocks are slippery, the water is deep. I implore, I beseech, I command!'

But the General might as well have commanded the stream to stop, for Maud was gone, and in about two seconds was standing, flushed, beautiful and triumphant, on the opposite side.

'If you will not come with us,' said Desvœux, calling to the people on the other side, 'we must go up to the Point without you. General Beau will, I am sure, take care of the Miss Fotheringhams.'

'A most wilful girl,' thought the General, 'and dull, but a fine jumper, and feet and ankles quite perfection.'

Maud, when she got across the stream, had passed a moral Rubicon; she left propriety, prudence, and prudishness on the other side with the General and the Miss Fotheringhams.

Desvœux was in the greatest glee at the result which had come about. 'I wish the General had tried and tumbled in,' he said, 'and got a ducking.'

'Oh,' cried Maud, 'what a dreadful man he is, with his shrugs and his "Ahs!" How lucky that you came to save me!'

'And you to save me,' said her companion; 'I was having a sad time of it with the Fotheringham girls. What a thing it is to have a deliverer!'

'But,' said Maud, 'I think the younger one is

looking very pretty. You know you used to love her. What lovely hair!'

'Yes,' said the other. 'Hair

> So young and yellow, crowning sanctity,
> And claiming solitude: can hair be false?'

'It can,' exclaimed Maud; 'Mrs. Blunt showed me two large coils, which had arrived from Douglas' in her last box from Europe. When one has a diamond tiara I suppose one must have hair to put it in, *coûte qui coûte*.'

'Mrs Blunt and her eternal tiara!' cried Desvœux; 'like the toad and adversity, ugly and venemous, she wears a precious jewel in her head. But is not this lovely? Look at the rainbow in the foam and the deep green of the ferns beside it. Was it not worth a jump?'

'Was not *what* worth a jump?' said Maud, with one of her pretty blushes.

'If only,' cried Desvœux, 'there was somewhere we could jump to, where I could have you all for my very own! But see, here is the Speaking Rock; call out something now and see how it will answer you.'

'Hoop!' cried Maud, and 'Hoop!' answered the steep crag opposite, and Maud, in a mood to be pleased with everything, was quite delighted. 'Hoop, hie!' she cried again, and all the hillside seemed to echo to her joyful tones.

'See,' cried Desvœux, 'you have waked the Genius of the Mountain. If you called long enough the nymphs would come and dance and crown you for a rural queen, the fairest that Arcadia ever saw!'

'Now,' said Maud, quite breathless with her calls, 'shout out something, Mr. Desvœux, and see what the mountain nymphs will have to say to you.'

'No,' Desvœux said sentimentally, 'the nymphs would answer nothing: my voice is too rough to please them. Besides I know by experience it is my fate to call and call, and rocks and other things just as hard will give me no response.'

'Indeed,' said Maud, 'I think they answer quite as much as is good for you.'

'Our echoes,' cried Desvœux, turning suddenly upon her and speaking with a vehemence that was only half in play—

> 'Our echoes roll from soul to soul,
> And grow for ever and for ever——'

'And ever and ever,' laughed Maud. 'Well, now, it is high time that they stopped growing for the present. Come, Mr. Desvœux, let us get back before our dear friends have torn us quite to pieces.'

Maud came back in great spirits and made a

public laugh at General Beau for his desertion of her.

'"The rocks are slippery, the water is deep!"' she cried, taking him off to his face with great success, '"I implore, I entreat, I command"; but I don't jump! O faithless, faithless General Beau!'

The General was not in the least disconcerted. 'Ah!' he said, in his usual mysterious way; and everybody felt that he could have jumped if he had chosen, but that he had some particular reason for not choosing to do so.

Then the party reassembled for tea and they played at games. Some one proposed 'What is my thought like?'

'Delightful!' cried Maud. 'General Beau, what is my thought like, pray?'

'Like?' said the General, quite unprepared for such sudden demands on his conversational powers, 'it is like yourself, no doubt.'

'Enough, enough!' cried Maud. 'Now, then, please say how wit, which is my word, and I are like each other?'

'Ah!' said the General, as if to imply that he mentally perceived the resemblance; 'because, because'——

'Because,' said Mrs Vereker, 'you are both to "madness near allied."'

'Or because,' said Desvœux, cutting in with great promptitude, '"true wit is nature to advantage dressed;" and so, I am sure, is Mrs. Sutton.'

'Very nice!' cried Maud, glowing with pleasure; 'now, General Beau, you must pay forfeit, you know. I will give you a bad one for deserting me so cruelly.'

'Forfeits!' said Desvœux, 'spare us, spare us—they are too fatiguing.'

'Not a bit,' said Maud, 'you bow to what is wisest, and kneel to what is prettiest, and kiss what you love best.'

'Well, then,' said Desvœux, kissing his hand sentimentally and blowing it into the air, 'there is a kiss for what I love best, wherever it may be.'

'Dear me,' said Mrs. Vereker, 'what a touching idea! There goes my kiss.'

'And,' cried Maud, laughing and kissing the tips of her pretty fingers, 'there goes mine! What a state the air will be in! But here comes Major Fenton with a plate of plumcake, which is what I love best; so my kiss is for that!'

'Happy plumcake!' said the Major, gallantly, 'to be loved, eaten and kissed by a mouth so fair.'

'Give me a bit too, Fenton,' said Desvœux; 'I must eat some for sympathy, though it is not what I love best.'

Then the quiet valley shadows crept about them,

and it grew sad and sombre; and while they sat and talked and laughed, the day was done and all steps were turned towards home.

So Maud and Desvœux found themselves travelling home together in the moonlight and falling behind the crowd of riders, to enjoy, undisturbed, the pleasure of a *tête-à-tête*. One of the great dangers of the Hills is that the paths admit only of two people riding abreast; the *terzo incommodo* must ride behind, and might, so far as prudence is concerned, just as well not be there at all. No such inconvenient intruder, however, threatened Desvœux's enjoyment of the present occasion or aided the faltering monitions which Maud's half-silenced conscience whispered to her. Her nerves were overstrung, and the excessive loveliness of the scene seemed only to add to her excitement. Along the winding path which crept up the mountain-side, and through the dark green forest-trees towering sublimely over them and all ablaze in moonlit patches with silver floods of light, their journey took them. Far away, miles below, a hundred tiny sparks showed where the villagers were cooking the evening meal; across the valley, on the opposite side, a great streak of woodland was blazing, scarcely seen by day, but now a ruddy lurid glow in the white light that lit up all the scene around. In the horizon was the great, cold, snowy range, standing out hard and clear in the moonlight—still, majestic, awful. How sweet, how bright, how exhilarating to a heart so prompt for enjoyment, senses so quickly impressible, nerves so alive to every surrounding influence as Maud's! Again and again she burst into exclamations of pleasure as each turn in the road brought them to some new scene of enchantment.

'Let us stop,' she cried, 'I must get off and sit down here and enjoy this in peace.'

'Let us walk a little,' said Desvœux, 'and send our ponies on to await us at the half-way point. Are you too tired?'

'I am not a bit tired,' Maud said, glowing with pleasure; 'it is too lovely to think of it. This is the best of all the day's pleasures.'

'It is lovely,' said her companion, 'but to me its greatest charm is that I have you to myself.'

'Well,' said Maud, who was accustomed to pulling up Desvœux when he became inconveniently sentimental, 'we have had a delightful day and great fun. I wish we had had the forfeits all the same and made General Beau do something nice. You stopped it all, Mr. Desvœux, by being so idle. Why did you blow your kiss into the air?'

'It was the only thing I could do with it,' said Desvœux, 'and see—it has alighted on your cheek!'

'And *that* on your arm,' cried Maud, wielding her whip with a sudden vehemence which made Desvœux feel that his kiss had been, at any rate, well paid for; 'when I want to be kissed I will tell you; but no robberies!'

'You little spitfire!' said Desvœux, rubbing his shoulder with a comic air.

'Well,' said Maud, suddenly repentant, and trying her whip across her knee, 'it *does* hurt, I confess. I beg your pardon. You deserved it, however, and I was in a passion at the moment. Do you forgive me?'

She gave him her hand—that little, delicate, exquisitely-fashioned piece of Nature's workmanship, which Desvœux had often vowed was the most beautiful thing in India. Its very touch electrified him.

'Forgive you?' he said, with a sudden sadness in his voice; 'you hurt me once in good earnest, and I forgave you that, and do forgive it, but it hurts me still.'

Desvœux's voice trembled with feeling. Something in his look struck Maud with a sudden pang of pity, sympathy, remorse. Was Desvœux then really suffering, and his life darkened on account of her? A sudden rush of sentiment streamed across her soul, carrying everything before it. A passionate, irresistible impulse possessed her. She stooped towards him, bent her cheek, flushed with excitement, to his, pressed to his the lips on which Desvœux's thoughts had dwelt a hundred times in impassioned reverie, and kissed him with a long, sweet, earnest caress, the sudden outburst of gratitude, tenderness, regret.

Desvœux said not a word, but he still kept possession of her hand, and the two stood looking silently across the misty valley and the precipice that fell away at their feet into solemn gloom below. The tramp of a horse's feet was heard behind them and Boldero came trotting innocently up the path.

'We are walking home,' Maud said, 'the night is so delicious. You may get off and come with us, if you please.'

Boldero, who would have jumped over the mountain-side if Maud had bidden him, at once dismounted. Desvœux fell behind, and said not one word during the rest of the homeward journey.

CHAPTER XXXVII.

ILL NEWS FLY APACE.

Never any more, while I live,
Need I hope to see his face as before.

MAUD reached her house over-tired, over-wrought, and somewhat sad at heart. She had gone much further than she meant, much further than her real feelings prompted. Even as she yielded to the sudden impulse she had repented, and while still doing it begun to wish the deed undone. She had been vexed and teased and excited till she scarce knew what her actions meant. The man to whom she had committed herself by so compromising an indiscretion had no sooner reached the dangerous eminence in her regard than he began to fall away and make her doubly remorseful for the act. She resented his ascendency over her, the force of the liking with which he inspired her and the degree to which he led her where he would. His language, when he was not there to carry it off with fun and daring, seemed unreal, exaggerated, absurd. Even before they got home her taste had begun to turn against him. Boldero's almost reverential care of her set her upon disparaging the other's lawless, inconsiderate homage. The very way in which he stayed behind was, she knew, intended as a sulky protest against Boldero's intrusion. A man who really cared about her would, Maud felt, have acquiesced in what she chose, what it was obviously right for her to choose, without any such display of temper. Then there had been something in Desvœux's manner, when he wished her good-night, which implied a private understanding and set her heart beating with indignation. A really fine nature would have been doubly deferential, doubly courteous, doubly watchful against seeming to take a liberty. Desvœux's tone had something in it to Maud's ear, which was familiar, easy, only just not disrespectful. She had been defying public opinion for him all day; she had at last, in a sudden impulse of pity, put herself at his mercy: already she began to doubt whether he was a man who would use his advantage generously. Perhaps after all Felicia had been right about him.

Then, when she got home, everything conspired to try her nerves. In the first place, no letter had come from her husband; there had been no letter for two days before, and this was a longer interval than had ever yet occurred. She tried in vain not to be frightened at the unaccustomed silence. Mrs. Vereker laughed her anxieties to scorn, but Maud knew better what such a long cessation implied. Her conscience was too ill at ease not to be apprehensive at the first occasion, however trivial, for alarm. Either something had happened or, dreadful possibility, her husband was displeased, and too displeased to write. While she was taking off her things and harassing herself with all sorts of fancied troubles, Mrs. Vereker came in and completed her discomfiture.

'Maud,' she said, and Maud thought her tones sounded harsh and unsympathetic (how different from Felicia's gentle lectures! which always thawed her heart at once), 'I have been commissioned to give you a scolding and by whom, do you suppose?'

'I really don't know, and don't care,' said Maud, in a pet, 'I have had enough the last few days to last me for some time. Will it not keep till to-morrow or the day after?'

'No, it will not,' said Mrs. Vereker, who was herself sincerely provoked at the notoriety which Maud's indiscretion had attained; 'it is from the Viceroy. I have something to say to you from him. Now do you wish to hear?'

'No,' said Maud, 'unless it is an appointment for my husband.'

'No, but it is about your husband, or about things your husband would not like. He told me to scold you thoroughly.'

'Then,' said Maud, her heart beating so that she could scarcely speak, 'he took a great liberty. I know, however, that he did not.'

'Guilty conscience!' cried the other; 'how white you look! Well, it is not exactly the truth, but it is not far off it. He gave me a hint.'

'He gave you a fiddlestick!' cried Maud in a passion; 'he meant to tell you not to flirt yourself.'

'Oh no! Lord Clare and I understand each other far too well for that. He said quite seriously, "When is Colonel Sutton coming up? Why don't he come? He ought to come; write to him and say so; say so from me." Now, what do you think that meant?'

Maud felt her colour gone and her heart beating violently, and could venture on no reply.

'You see,' said her monitress pitilessly, 'you will be injudicious. I am always telling you. You can't be content with fluttering round the candle, but must needs go into the flame and singe your wings, and then of course it hurts you. People should know when to stop.'

'And,' cried Maud, in a thorough passion,

'people should not throw stones who live in glass houses. Why, Mrs. Vereker, if I am a flirt, I should like to know who taught me?'

'Now you are rude and cross. You should never throw stones, whether you live in a glass house or not. The best thing I can do is to leave you to recover your temper.'

Mrs. Vereker was gone and Maud's last friend seemed lost to her. She had offended every one; or rather every one had done something to offend her. She disliked them all. She flung herself upon her bed and wept in very bitterness of heart. She longed for a really friendly, loving hand to take her and set her right; she longed for her old mistress to confess to; she thought of Felicia, considerate, tender, sympathetic, and she seemed like an angel compared with those amongst whom she was living. If she could but have crept to her embrace and breathed her troubles in her ear! She thought of her husband—the pure and faithful heart beating with no thought but for her, where nothing coarse or unchivalrous could ever find a place; where she knew that she alone was enshrined; of his perfect trust in her, his spotless faith, his transparent honour. She looked at his photograph standing on the table: how grave and sad it looked! She flung herself on the bed; the bitter tears of remorse and repentance began to flow, and while they flowed—for Maud was far more exhausted than she knew—she slept; and in her sleep of a few minutes passed into dreamland; not the happy, silly, aimless dreamland of easy minds and tired frames, where Maud's nights were chiefly spent; but into a sad weird region, where everything seemed horribly real and connected and designed and to bear some frightful relation to actual life that makes it part of our being and haunts one's after-thoughts. She was with her husband once again, and yet it was not quite himself; an undefined something separated him from her and all the past. She was riding by him. How grieved and reproachful a mien he wore, as of a man with a hidden sorrow cankering his heart! And then he fell, and Maud saw him crushed and wounded and helpless as once before, and agonised in some frightful entanglement with his horse. She meanwhile was trying in vain to help or to approach him, for a hidden hand restrained her, and Sutton himself, sad and stern, was waving her away. And then came a fierce struggle and blows and cries, and Maud found herself waking with a scream and her servant standing by her bed and saying that a 'Sahib' had come and wanted to see her directly.

She knew what it meant and went with a beating heart into the drawing-room, as fresh from the land of sorrow and ready for news of disaster.

She found Boldero in the drawing-room, looking ominously grave.

'Well, Mr. Boldero,' Maud said, with an unsuccessful attempt at gaiety and a dread of the answer which she would receive, 'why have you come back? Do you want me to give you some tea or to receive some advice?'

'Have you heard from Sutton to-day?' said the other, not heeding her inquiry.

'No,' said Maud, turning sick at heart and deadly white; 'why do you ask? Quick, quick!'

'Because I have bad accounts of him from Dustypore. You must not be alarmed.'

'But I *am* alarmed,' cried Maud, by this time in thorough terror; 'don't you see that standing there and giving hints is just the way to frighten one? I know quite well you have brought me some bad news.'

'Yes,' said Boldero, 'I am sorry to say I have. Your husband is ill.'

Maud started up and looked him straight in the face, with a serious, eager look, that made Boldero, even at that moment, think how lovely she was.

'Now,' she cried, 'tell me the truth. Have you told me all?'

'No, I have not. I can hardly bear to tell you;

but you have sense and courage, and would rather hear the truth. *He is down with cholera.*'

The words went like a sword through Maud's heart. A blank horror seized her. This, then, had been the meaning of her dream. The blow came crashing down upon her, and body and soul seemed to reel before it. She sank like a crushed, terrified child on the sofa, and, covering her face in her hands, hid herself, speechless, motionless, as from an ill that was too great to bear.

'Let me send for Mrs. Vereker,' said Boldero.

'No!' cried Maud, starting up, 'pray do not. Leave me for a minute or two. I shall be better directly. Will you come back in a quarter of an hour?'

'I will do anything you bid me,' said Boldero frightened at the task he had in hand and its probable results, and thinking that perhaps the best thing he could do was to leave Maud to deal with her sorrow alone.

So Boldero went out into the moonlight, and strolled about the pathway, now so silent, where so many joyous footsteps used to press, and Maud was left to herself with her first great trouble.

It was significant of the real nature of her relations to Mrs. Vereker that she shrank especially from seeking her now, in her time of sorrow, or following her counsel. Mrs. Vereker was essentially a fine-weather friend. The task which Maud had now in hand was something deeper and graver than anything that the other's feelings reached. What lay before her now to do, or to endure, was something between her husband and herself, and it would be profanity for a stranger to come into that sacred region. Mrs. Vereker's advice would, Maud knew instinctively, be all wrong. She herself felt already what she ought to do. She knelt weeping on the sofa, and the thoughts of sorrow, humiliation, remorse, came pouring thick upon her troubled mind. To what a precipice's edge had not her folly and madness brought her! her fair fame darkened, her husband's name dishonoured, her vows of love and honour how badly kept! Oh, how unutterably weak, faithless, heartless she had been! How ghastly all the afternoon's adventures, the evening's folly, seemed! how wicked, how base, how altogether bad! She had felt the thought stinging all the while, but other, stronger feelings had helped her to ignore it and forget. Now there was no other feeling, and it was overwhelming.

There was only one thing left to do, one good, one hope left—to fly to her husband's side, to pour out the pent-up stream of confession, repentance, and love, and, if only God would spare him, never, never leave him again!

When Boldero came in again Maud was herself

again. 'I am better and stronger now,' she said; 'the news came upon me too suddenly, but now I am calm. I have settled what I ought to do, and you must help me. I shall go down to him at once.'

'Indeed, you cannot do that,' Boldero said, decisively; 'it would be excessively wrong.'

'Indeed, indeed I will!' cried Maud; 'I feel that I ought and must. What is there to stop me?'

'It is out of the question,' said the other; 'you will be running into a great deal of danger unnecessarily.'

'I have no strength to talk about it,' said Maud, 'but I must go or I shall die, and you must help me. Do you mean me to stay quietly here, and Jem dying by himself? My God, my God! why did I ever leave him?'

Here Maud threw herself on the sofa, and cried a longer, sadder, more heartfelt cry than ever in her life before. Boldero went again into the garden in despair, for it was in vain, he saw, to try to soothe her.

It ended, of course, in Boldero telegraphing for two relays of horses to be sent out from the Camp, and sending out two more as fast as possible, to get as far as might be on the way for the forced march of fifty miles which Maud and he were, it was settled, at once to undertake. She was to rest for a few hours, start at three o'clock, get on as far as they could in the cool, rest through the day, and complete the remainder of the journey the following night. They would be at the Camp, Boldero reckoned, by the morning of the day after to-morrow.

It required all his official resources to organise such a journey, but a Collector on his march can do anything; and Boldero, with whom Maud was by a sudden reaction of sentiment rapidly being promoted from heroine to saint, was determined that her journey, so far as in him lay, should be as comfortable as money and care could make it.

CHAPTER XXXVIII.

FLIGHT.

In old days there were angels who came and took men by the hand, and led them away from the City of Destruction. We see no white winged angels now; but yet men are led away from threatening destruction: a hand is put into theirs, which leads them gently towards a calm and bright land, so that they look no more backward.

MAUD effected a speedy reconciliation with Mrs. Vereker, who had entrenched herself in her bedroom with a French novel till such time as Maud should have recovered her equanimity. Mrs. Vereker at once forgot her grievance, listened with real concern to Maud's alarming tidings, and lent herself with great alacrity to assist in the preparations for a hasty departure. Boldero had gone off and was to get coolies * together as speedily as possible, so as to be well on the way during the cool hours of the early morning, before the heat of the day would render travelling a work of distress.

By three o'clock, accordingly, a little army was collected in front of Mrs. Vereker's door. The urgent demands of the Collector and the subsequent

* Native porters.

zeal of his subordinates had done wonders, and some forty men had been assembled at an hour's notice for the task of carrying down Maud, her servant and her various belongings.

The moon had sunk and the torches glared fitfully with dreadful smell and smoke. The figures looked weird and strange and, to Maud's eye, horribly numerous. The arrangement of each box involved enormous discussion as to how the burden of carrying it could best be shared. At last all was ready; Maud was established in a palanquin; the carriers kept time to the cadence of a wild refrain; the torch-bearers shuffled along in front, relays of coolies came behind; close at her side rode the faithful Boldero, marshalling the little force, and ever on the watch to shield her from any possible annoyance. Maud appreciated his fidelity, and felt that she had never liked him half well enough before. Her conscience smote her for all her rude speeches, slighting acts and unkind looks; she determined henceforth to be very kind indeed. Boldero, accordingly, though in a great state of agitation and distress about his friend's condition, found the journey not quite without its charm. He had telegraphed to the Camp for Sutton's two horses to be sent out, and both of them were well accustomed to carry Maud when occasion offered. A messenger was to be sent up to each halting-place, so that Maud had not an hour longer to wait for news than was absolutely necessary. It was a relief, hour by hour, to find the distance growing less and the messages more recent; still the tidings were very grievous. Sutton, it was clear, was very ill. He had been thoroughly knocked up beforehand, and agitated and distressed about something, the doctors thought, and this no doubt had helped the evil. This was a cruel stab for Maud. For a few days, said the letter, it would be rash to say what turn the case might take; still there was reason to be hopeful: he was a very strong man, and very temperate, and these points, of course, were greatly in his favour. The mortality, however, had been terrible at the Camp, and the men were greatly disheartened. They were now marching every day, in hopes of keeping clear of their own infection.

An hour or two later the two travellers came to a halt. Maud found some early tea awaiting her, and joyfully exchanged the tiring captivity of the palanquin for the horse which had been hurried on for her use for this stage of the journey.

'I have been fast asleep,' she said, as Boldero and she rode down the hillside together and watched the faint glow in the east warming gradually into day, 'and this is very refreshing. The darkness, the crowd, the blazing torches, the confusion, the babel of tongues we had last night seem like a horrid dream. I was never more thankful for the light. I feel as if I were escaping; and, Mr. Boldero, you are my deliverer. I shall be grateful to you all my life. You must have had so much trouble and have done it all so kindly and like yourself.'

'Do not talk of that,' said the other; 'what are friends for but to serve us when we need them?'

'And to forgive us when we wrong them?' said Maud, whose conscience was goading her to confession; 'I know I have behaved ill to you—to you and to everybody. Now I am going to try to do better, if only I can get the chance—if only God in His goodness will grant me that.'

'I am hopeful,' said Boldero, 'for both of you. Sutton, I feel, has something greater yet to do. We have often laughed and said that nothing can kill him. You know in cholera it is as much mind as body: courage, calmness, and determination are half the battle.'

'Then,' said Maud, with enthusiasm, faith, and hopefulness glowing in her face, 'I am sure he will do well. His body is his soul's servant, you cannot fancy how completely; it does its bidding as a matter of course. I do not think it would even die without his leave. Have you telegraphed to say that I am coming?'

'Yes, but leaving it to the doctors to tell him

when they think best; or not at all, if they fear the intelligence will excite him. Very likely they will be afraid to do so.'

'They will do wrong,' said Maud, who knew her husband's temperament better even than Boldero; it will not agitate him, and it will make him resolve to live. He *will* live, I believe, if it is only in order to forgive me.'

'Do not say "to forgive,"' said the other, who, in a generously enthusiastic mood, began to think that Maud was pressing with undue severity against herself; 'to tell you all that you have been to him and all the sunshine you have brought into his life.'

'All I have been!' cried Maud, with a vehement remorse; 'I could tell him that best. You could tell him. I mean to tell him the first moment I can—and I am in an agony till I can do so. I have been mad, Mr. Boldero, or in a dream, I think, and you tried in vain to wake me. Now I am awake, and know the truth. All the things and people we have left behind are merely shadows, and I mistook them for realities; only one thing in the world is real for me: my love for my husband. Other people flatter and excite and amuse one, and one is carried away with all sorts of follies; but my heart never moves and never can. It is his and his only, and I never knew it fully till last night. My life, I find, is centred in his.'

'I pray God,' said Boldero devoutly, 'we may find him better; and somehow I believe we shall.'

A level stretch of valley lay before them, and allowed them to push sharply over the next five or six miles. By ten o'clock they arrived at their halting-place, where Boldero proposed that they should wait till the afternoon. Maud, however, was too restless to halt.

'Suppose,' she said, 'we push on another stage? The sun is not so very dreadful, after all.'

'The next two stages are bad ones,' said Boldero. 'Don't you remember that long, troublesome valley with the rocks on either side?—by twelve o'clock they will be all red-hot.'

'Well,' said Maud, 'we will tie a wet towel over my head. Will it do you any harm? or the horses?'

'Me!' cried Boldero, in a tone which at once reassured his companion that no danger need be apprehended so far as he was concerned; 'as for my horses, they can, of course, go as many stages as you like.'

So they dressed and breakfasted and Maud declared herself quite ready for an immediate start. Boldero brought in a great plantain-leaf from the garden of the little inn, and they tied this under her wide pith hat; then Maud armed herself with an enormous umbrella, and 'Now,' she said, 'I am prepared for anything.'

By the end of the stage, however, her strength was spent: she sank into the first chair that offered itself, and acquiesced thankfully, like a tired child, in Boldero's decision that they should not move again till the day's fierce glare was past. There was no need to hurry, for she was now within a night's march of her husband, and by the morrow's morning would have known and seen the worst.

CHAPTER XXXIX.

THE PRODIGAL'S RETURN.

Thus 'twas granted me
To know he loved me to the depth and height
Of such large natures, ever competent
With grand horizons, by the land or sea,
To love's grand sunrise. Small spheres hold small fires,
But he loved largely.

MAUD was inexpressibly shocked at her husband's appearance. Neither the telegrams nor the doctors' notes nor Boldero's description had in the faintest degree prepared her for what she saw. She had heard of death, and even seen it, but in its gentle, peaceful, unagonised aspect; she had seen illness, but in its milder mood, as it visits the European household: not the savage, destroying, desolating demon-angel that waves a sword across the cholera-stricken plain or city in the East. A sickness of a few days, a few hours, shatters the sufferer's frame, blurs out the familiar features, leaves the stalwart man a quivering skeleton, deadens the sense and clouds the strong mind with a deep, dreadful shadow of oblivion.

And to this stage Sutton had come. Maud, despite all entreaties and warnings, went straight to her husband's side and let the full horror of the scene take possession of her soul. It wrung her very heart to see him—the man whom, after all, she loved with a passion which, if sometimes forgotten, was never extinct for an instant. She had loved him at first; she loved him now ten times more than ever. She had wronged him, neglected him, dishonoured him—alas, how grievously!—her one hope lay in confession, reconciliation, forgiveness: and he lay there, more dead than alive—speechless, motionless, except when some spasm of suffering shook him—and, so far as outward sign showed, unconscious of her presence. Maud thanked Heaven that she was on the spot to know and see the worst, and yet it was almost more than she could bear. Her load of anguish seemed too much for one till now a stranger to sorrow. Again and again some old trait in the haggard, suffering face, a moan of pain, a gesture too slight from weakness to be intelligible to any eye but hers, touched a fresh chord in her heart, broke down her wavering fortitude, and sent her rushing to her room to shed in solitude the tears of sorrow and remorse. Again and again she washed away the useless tears, nerved herself once more to maintain a courageous exterior, and returned, with a fortitude which she felt gather strength within her, to the sad task of watching and waiting for the crisis which a few hours more must bring.

Let us leave that terrible passage of Maud's life, with its trembling, agonising suspense, its heartfelt vows and prayers, its remorseful tears, its thrilling hopes, its mysterious communings with another world. Let us drop a curtain over that solemn season. Maud will emerge from it, we may be sure, with a new-born fortitude, patience, loftiness of soul; courage, the child of suffering; calmness, the attribute of those who have been close upon despair.

A fortnight later Sutton was lying in the drawing-room, with no other malady than excessive weakness, and with no other occupation than to recruit his shattered powers. Maud was busied with the composition of some appetising beverage, which was, the doctor said, the only kind of medicine of which he now stood in need, and which could, in Maud's and her husband's opinion, be properly concocted and administered by no hand but hers. Then the invalid's pillows needed skilful arrangement, for he was still at the stage when mere lying still is an exertion which seems to tax every limb and muscle in the aching frame. Maud found an indescribable relief and pleasure in waiting on her husband, and proved herself a nature-taught adept in the kindly art of nursing. Every act, though her husband knew it not, had, to Maud's aching conscience, a sort of penitential devotion about it, and said a hundred things of love and sorrow which as yet found no utterance in spoken words.

'What a model wife!' said Sutton, as he lay watching her movements, in grateful admiration at her skill and care on his behalf.

'Ah! but,' said Maud, thankful for the opportunity of the confession she was longing to make, 'I am not a model wife at all, but just everything that a model ought not to be.'

'Then,' said Jem gallantly, 'I am for you, and not for the model, whoever drew it.'

'Jem,' she said, with sudden seriousness, 'I want to tell you something, and be forgiven. I meant to do so before, but you have been too poorly. I am afraid it will hurt you. I have been going on very stupidly at Elysium, and very wrongly, and doing everything that you would most have disliked, and that I dislike now—oh! how bitterly!'

Sutton, to Maud's great relief, did not seem in the least surprised or inclined to be serious about the matter. He took her hand and held it with the kindest caressing manner.

'I have no doubt,' he said, 'that Mrs. Vereker

did all she could to get you into a scrape. It was a shame of me to let you go to her.'

'No,' said Maud, 'it was not her fault at all. The truth is, I have been flirting with—some one.'

'Some one,' said Sutton, 'has been trying to flirt with you, you mean, and no wonder. Some one showed his good taste at any rate.'

'Yes, but,' said the penitent, 'I flirted with him. I think I must have been crazy.'

'You risked your life, dear, to come and be with me. Why look further back than that? I cannot.'

'But,' said Maud, her cheeks burning scarlet at the awful confession which conscience compelled her to make, 'that is not all: *I gave him a kiss.*'

'Then,' said her husband, 'you gave him a great deal more than he deserved, whoever he was. Well, now, give me one, and let us say no more about it.'

The blinding tears fell fast and hot as Maud bent over her husband's haggard face and exchanged the sweet pledge of reconciliation, confidence, and love. There was something so generous, sparing and delicately magnanimous in her husband's ready, uninquiring forgiveness, and his refusal to know more of a matter which it grieved and shamed her to narrate. Maud knew that his was a temperament which jealousy would torture like any Othello's, and that his passion against an offender, had it once forced its way to light, would have been a sort of fury. She could perfectly realise to herself her husband doing anything—the worst—to a man who, he thought, had in the slightest degree wronged him. He was accustomed to stern deeds and stern sights, and, as any man does who has a hundred times seen death face to face and found nothing to dread in it, held life the cheapest of all his treasures. Maud had felt an awful misgiving lest he should utter some dreadful, quiet threat at the wrong-doer. As it was, her husband would not even know his name and treated the whole thing as a mere childish misadventure. It was indeed an heroic kindness. Her whole nature went out to him in thankfulness and love; she bent her head beside him and hid her face and wept in the fulness of her heart. No wonder his soldiers had learnt to worship him. No word more was spoken, but Sutton had good cause to know that the last touch of waywardness, the last fickle mood, the forgetful moment, the girlish caprice, were gone for ever—the last spot in her heart that had not been wholly his was carried at last. 'I am thankful,' the surgeon said, 'that he is better: the poor child is ten times more in love with him than ever.'

Then the three friends had a very happy time. It is so pleasant to be getting well; and nursing, too, is a pleasant labour when the invalid is interesting and considerate and well-beloved. Happy the patient whose lot it is to pass from the dreary land of sickness with such sweet companionship! Boldero, though the gravity of his loss kept pace in his thoughts with each new-discovered charm in Maud, got himself into an heroic mood, and derived a satisfaction, less blackened with melancholy than he would have conceived possible, from the sight of his friend's felicity. At any rate he made himself very pleasant—was always available for whatever was wanted of him—submitted, it is probable, to a little delightful tyranny from the woman he adored, and went away at last leaving almost a little blank behind him.

'How kind and useful he has been!' Maud said, as they watched his cavalcade winding along the valley; 'and how clever about your barley-water! Yes—I certainly like him.'

'Like him!' said Sutton. 'I should think so. He is the best fellow in the world.'

'Yes,' said his wife, 'all the same there is something pleasant in a *tête-à-tête;* and I don't like anybody taking care of you but me.'

L'ENVOI.

> Joy, gentle friends, joy and fresh days of love
> Accompany your hearts !

HOPE, which catches up the brush as it falls from the narrator's hand, adds yet another scene, in the faint, hazy, indistinct hues of a distant horizon, to the picture at which we have been looking for awhile.

We are on Aldershot Heath. Troops are marching up from different directions ; orderlies are galloping wildly on their behests ; words of command ring noisily through the air ; great masses of red come looming out of the dust as each regiment tramps solidly along ; there is the roar of cannon from the neighbouring hill ; the horse artillery goes rattling by like a hurricane of horses and iron ; in front is a long array of spectators, and in the midst a blaze of uniforms and the carriage where a gracious Sovereign sits to inspect and compliment the heroes of the day—the men who had served their country well ; for there has been a successful expedition, led by an Indian General ; and the victorious army, with its leader, bearing his honours thick upon him, at its head, is marching past amidst the shouts of a joyful and sympathetic crowd. When Sutton, for it is he, has passed the Royal carriage and made his salute, he turns his horse and joins the staff who glitter round their Sovereign. Kind words are spoken and a Royal hand adds one more to his long list of decorations. Presently he makes his way to a group of ladies in a carriage near at hand. There is Felicia, with a sweet, matronly air, her beautiful features none the less fair for the lines that sorrow had left upon them and some silvery threads among the waving gold; she sits serene and joyous in the presence of two lovely girls, Sutton's playfellows of old; now, as he tells them, when he wants to be very polite, the very repetition of their mother. Vernon is in England, at home for his last furlough, and beyond lies, near enough now to be a source of pleasure, not of pain, the prospect of a final settlement at home. Beside Felicia sits Maud, blushing under her husband's honours, but rejoicing that all the world should recognise his claim to homage. As he comes up the smile that she gives him tells us that all is more than well between them. Suddenly she jumps up with an exclamation, for she has recognised a familiar face—it is Boldero, who is making his way to them through the crowd. He brings a blushing lady on his arm, and he is blushing too, and there are introductions and greetings which sound as if his old love-wound had been healed by the only effectual remedy.

Meanwhile the long armed array is flowing steadily past. Maud, who is quite the soldier's wife, criticises and approves. At length the last regiment has come and gone, the last band has crashed out its music, the Royal carriage makes a move, the staff gallops away, the crowd is pushing and hurrahing and scattering itself over the wide plain; the shades of evening are gathering over it; the Indian friends drive off merrily for home; the scene fades—fades and dies away.

Let us leave this party of happy people to themselves—we must be their companions no longer.

THE END.

PRINTED BY BALLANTYNE, HANSON AND CO.
EDINBURGH AND LONDON

Lightning Source UK Ltd.
Milton Keynes UK
UKOW021434150113

204895UK00004B/64/P